NEW MODULAR S

for GCSE

MODULE *Electricity*

Spread

Cover photograph *Turbines at a windfarm between Hebden Bridge and Halifax, Yorkshire*

1 So what is electricity?

You can't touch, taste, see, smell or hear electricity directly – but you can often see what it does. What could be going on to cause all these different effects?

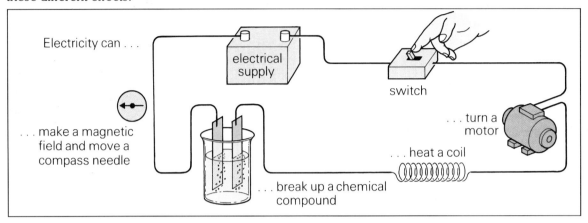

Electricity can . . .

electrical supply

switch

. . . make a magnetic field and move a compass needle

. . . turn a motor

. . . heat a coil

. . . break up a chemical compound

Static and spark

To get an idea about what might be happening, let's think about a different kind of electricity. Have you ever had a small electric shock as you've reached for a door-handle after walking over a nylon carpet? Or heard a crackling sound and seen flashes of light as you've pulled off a nylon jumper? (And you certainly will have seen lightning, which is just a bigger version of the same thing!) You've probably been told: 'That's static electricity!' But what does that mean?

crackle   crackle   BOOM!

Electrical charges

All substances contain electrical **charges**. These come in two opposite kinds – we call them **positive** (+) and **negative** (–). These charges are normally present in equal numbers and so cancel each other out. But if you rub two different materials together – such as shoe leather and nylon – it is possible to knock some charges from one to the other and so upset this balance.

All these opposite charges attract each other – they try to get back together. If enough of them have collected, they will have enough energy to 'jump' a small gap as a spark.

unbalanced charges spread over the body surface

charges jump back together

charges are knocked from shoe to carpet

Static can be useful . . .

Have you ever noticed how dusty TV screens get? The dust is attracted to them by the static charge that builds up there.

This static attraction is put to good use in coal-fired power stations, which use it in their chimneys to trap dirt and dust particles. Here electrostatic precipitators trap tonnes of material every day that otherwise would have poured out and polluted the environment.

Another good use is in photocopying machines. Light falling onto a special material gives a negative image in static charge! This is then transferred to a drum and powdered ink is made to stick to it, which is then rolled onto paper.

This fine powder forms an image by static.

. . . or very dangerous

Static charges can form wherever different materials move against one another – even where liquids flow through pipes. And where charges build up, sparking can occur.

When aircraft are refuelled, thousands of gallons of aviation fuel are pumped at high speed through fuelpipes. Any charge building up here could spark to the metal of the aircraft with catastrophic results. To stop this happening, the pumps, pipes and aircraft are first linked together by a metal cable, which is then '**earthed**' (as will be explained later). Any charge formed now can be led away safely through the metal, and so dangerous sparking will not occur.

. . . even for computers

The large static charges in lightning can play havoc with electronic equipment. Burglar alarms may be set off, computers may 'crash' and the microchips within them may be damaged permanently.

On a smaller scale, microelectronic devices must always be protected from electrostatic sparking. It has been known for office computers to blow up because of the disruption caused by static produced from their operator's nylon underwear!

Static charges could build up in aircraft fuelpipes, but the earth lead clamped to the front wheel prevents any build up.

1 What are the different effects that can be caused by an electric current?

2 How can we charge things up with static electricity? Explain what is happening.

3 What good uses can be made of electrostatic attraction?

4 Why do static charges sometimes lead to sparking? Why can this be dangerous?

5 How can electrostatic charges be discharged safely?

2 *What else is involved?*

Conductors and insulators

Static charges build up on some materials, such as plastics or rubber, because any charges 'knocked' onto them get stuck on the surface and are not free to move. We call these materials **insulators**.

Other materials, such as metals or carbon, however, allow the much smaller negative charges to move around within them. We call these materials **conductors**.

It is when negative charges move through a conductor that we say a **current** of electricity is flowing. We call these small, negative charges **electrons**.

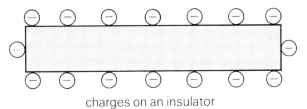

charges on an insulator

charges moving within a conductor
(not to scale)

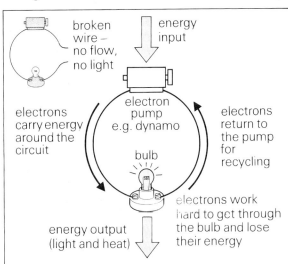

broken wire – no flow, no light

energy input

electron pump e.g. dynamo

electrons carry energy around the circuit

electrons return to the pump for recycling

bulb

electrons work hard to get through the bulb and lose their energy

energy output (light and heat)

Pumping charge – current electricity

The flow of electrons through a metal wire is often likened to the flow of water along a pipe. A hose full of water does not become 'useful' until the water is made to move. To make the water move, you need a pump, and that means energy is needed to work the pump.

Similarly, a disconnected wire is full of electrons, but some kind of 'pump' is needed to make an electric current flow, and an energy source is needed to drive it. You probably use many things powered by **batteries**. These use chemical reactions to produce the energy to pump the charges through your radio, Walkman and so on.

Recycling electrons

To use current electricity, there has to be a continuous connection from one terminal of the 'electron pump', through conducting wires to whatever is being worked by the electricity – a bulb, for example – and back through wires to the other terminal of the 'pump'. This is called a **circuit** and, as the name suggests, electrons flow around it. Break it at any point, and the flow stops – that's how **switches** work.

In this way, electrons are recycled – used over and over again – and are given a new 'kick' of energy each time they pass through the 'pump'. It is this energy which is given up to the bulb and turned into heat and light.

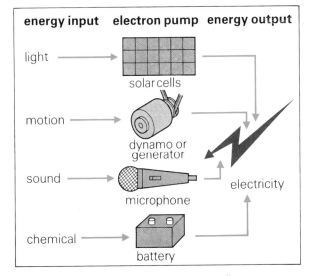

energy input   electron pump   energy output

light — solar cells

motion — dynamo or generator

sound — microphone

chemical — battery

electricity

Why do heating coils and bulbs get hot?

Many materials conduct electricity to some extent, but do not allow it to pass freely. They are said to 'resist' the flow and so are called **resistors**. The coils of wire in bulbs and heaters are made from special resistance wire like this.

In 'water model' terms, it's like 'shooting the rapids' – the electrons crash into the particles in the wire, giving up some of their energy as heat before moving on. This makes the wire heat up. The wires in light bulbs are designed to get 'white hot', and give off white light!

Resistance and control

If a second bulb is added to a simple circuit, both bulbs now glow more dimly than before. This is because the extra bulb *increases* the overall resistance in the circuit, so the 'pump' is unable to push as much current around, and less heat is generated. Any extra resistance added into the circuit will have a similar effect, and this can be used to control the brightness of lamps.

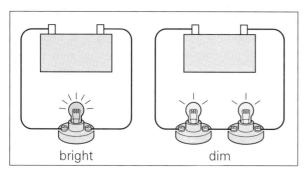

bright   dim

Cells and batteries

Just how big a 'kick' of energy the electrons are given as they are sent around the circuit depends on the **potential difference (p.d.)** provided by the pump. This is measured in **volts** – the higher the voltage the bigger the 'kick'.

An individual electric cell gives a potential difference of about 1.5 volts (1.5 V). But if you 'stack' these cells in a circuit, you can stack up the voltage. This drives a bigger current through the circuit, and provides more energy to make a bulb glow brighter, for example.

The 4.5, 6, 9 or 12 volt batteries you can buy are made by stacking individual cells like this in one package.

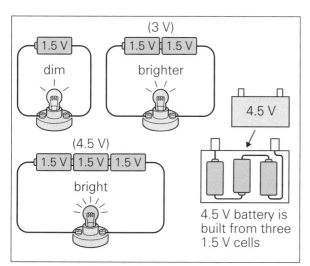

4.5 V battery is built from three 1.5 V cells

1. What are the differences between conductors and insulators?

2. Why is it only the negative charges that move through a conductor?

3. What is an 'electron pump'? Give some examples.

4. How do resistors differ from simple conductors and insulators?

5. What happens to the flow of current in a circuit:
   a if the circuit breaks
   b if extra resistance is added?

6. Why does a heating element get hot when current flows?

7. How many 1.5 V cells must there be in a 9 V battery?

3 Circuit shorthand

A tip from the tube

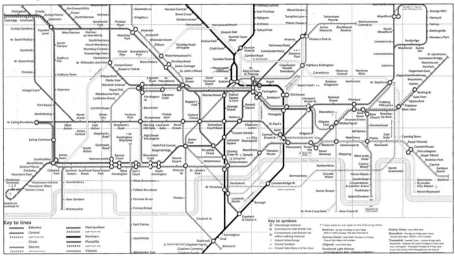

London regional Transport User Number 96/2385

If you wanted to find out how to get from New Cross to Leicester Square on the London Underground, you could look at an accurate street map and try to follow the lines and stations as they snake around and cross. Or you could just look at the Underground map – even though this is not actually accurate in terms of station and line positions and distances! But it does show very clearly which stations are on the same line, and where you can change trains – which is all that you actually need to know. It also uses standard symbols for stations, British Rail links, time restrictions, and so on, which make it easier to find the information you need.

Electricians face a similar problem. The wires connecting pieces of electrical apparatus can get very messy – 'benchtop spaghetti' is a common description!

So electricians, too, resort to an agreed, *stylised* way of representing the information that really counts – showing which parts are electrically connected to which. They also use standard symbols to represent pieces of equipment.

'Spaghetti' versus style

The **circuit diagrams** produced in this standard style are much easier to follow than more realistic versions – once you get used to using them! The trick is to practise. Try drawing circuit diagrams from 'benchtop spaghetti' and setting up circuits from circuit diagrams as often as possible, then you will soon be totally familiar with them.

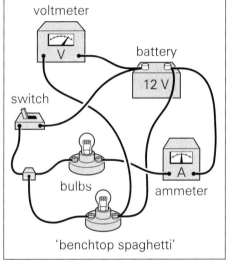

'benchtop spaghetti'

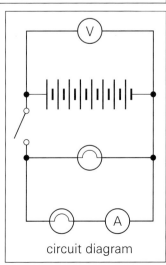

circuit diagram

Lighting up

It is possible to set up a simple **series** circuit with two dry cells, a bulb, a switch and some connecting wire. This may look very different but, electrically, it is exactly the same as a standard torch circuit, so they have the same circuit diagram. (See right.)

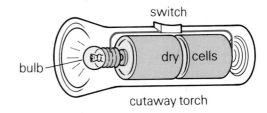

cutaway torch

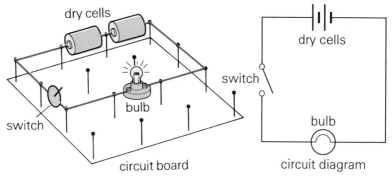

circuit board

circuit diagram

power supply terminals	
connecting conductor	
joined wires (conductor)	
wires crossing with no connection	
switch (open)	
cell	
battery of cells	
ammeter	
voltmeter	
bulb/lamp	
fuse	
diode	
motor	
resistor	
variable resistor	

Some standard symbols.

The circuit board shown on the right has three dry cells driving two bulbs in **parallel**, with switches in each of the branches and another in the main loop. This could be used as a mock-up for the lighting in a dolls' house, where lights in two rooms could be controlled independently, driven by a 4.5 volt battery with its own master switch. Again, they are electrically the same and so have the same circuit diagram.

Note carefully here why it is that the switch in the main branch is the 'master' controlling both lamps, but the other switches control the individual lamps.

(For more information on series and parallel circuits, see page 23 later in this module.)

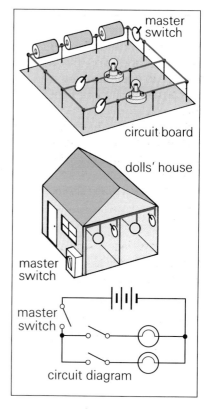

circuit board

dolls' house

circuit diagram

1 Describe how you could get from New Cross to Leicester Square on the London Underground.

2 Draw circuit diagrams for:
a a dry cell, two bulbs, a switch and an ammeter in a series circuit;
b a dynamo working three lamps in parallel.

3 Design a circuit diagram that could work a model set of traffic lights, with separate switches for red, amber and green.

4 Mains electricity

a.c./d.c. – the difference is easy

So far we have talked about current flowing around a circuit. In the case of **batteries**, this is exactly what happens. Electrons leave the *negative* terminal and flow round to the *positive*. This simple flow of charge is called the **direct current** (d.c.).

However, with '**mains**' electricity the electrons move *backwards and forwards* around the circuit. This happens because the driving **voltage** (see page 22) goes through 50 cycles of change every second. This is called an **alternating current** (a.c.). It may seem odd, but for most household uses, it does not matter which way the electrons are moving. As long as they *are* moving, they have enough energy for heating, lighting and driving motors.

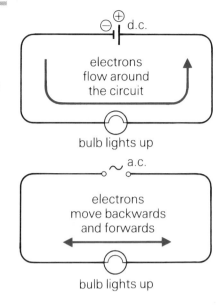

Looking at a.c. ⬢

A **cathode ray oscilloscope** (CRO) can show what is happening to the electricity in the wires carrying an alternating current. The CRO turns the a.c. signal into lines on a screen. The voltage in one wire rises and falls – this wire is called the **live wire**. The voltage in the other wire appears to remain constant – so this wire is called the **neutral wire**.

This changing cycle has a similar effect to switching the terminals on a battery – current is driven first one way then the other (from neutral to live, then live to neutral).

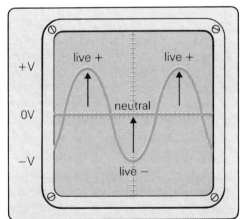

▼ *a.c. on a cathode ray oscilloscope.*

The three wires

Mains electricity needs two wires to work, but three wires to be safe. These wires are:

● *Live wire* – this carries the alternating voltage that will drive the current (once connected).
● *Neutral wire* – this is the 'base line': current flows backwards and forwards between this wire and the live wire.
● *Earth wire* – this is the safety wire which helps to protect you from dangerous 'short-circuits'.

The wires are made from copper, because this is a good conductor of electricity. They are covered with flexible plastic, which is a good insulator.

It is a matter of life and death that these wires are connected up the right way, so they are colour-coded. In household equipment, the plastic is coloured brown for live, blue for neutral and yellow-green for earth. The three wires are then covered with an extra layer of insulating plastic for safety.

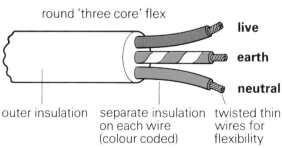

round 'three core' flex

live
earth
neutral

outer insulation   separate insulation on each wire (colour coded)   twisted thin wires for flexibility

Safety first

If the live wire carries the signal, which returns through the neutral wire – why bother with any others? A kettle connected to just live and neutral would work, so what use is the earth wire?

So long as everything *is* working perfectly, the earth wire has no use. But if a fault occurs in the other two wires, the earth wire could save your life!

What's the danger?

Think about an old metal kettle with just live and neutral wires – say a loose live wire touches the metal of the kettle. This makes the metal of the kettle 'live'. As soon as you touch the metal of this kettle, your body completes a circuit between the live wire and the 'zero volt' planet Earth. All the current flows through you, giving you an **electric shock**.

But copper wire is a much better conductor than your body, your shoes or the carpet. The copper in the earth wire provides a much easier path for any stray current escaping from the live wire. If all metal parts which you might touch are connected to an earth wire, any shock will short-circuit to Earth through the earth wire instead of through you.

Wiring a plug

Plugs have a strong plastic or rubber case for insulation. The pins are made of brass as it is hardwearing as well as being a good conductor of electricity. The wires have a small piece of insulation removed so that they can be screwed tightly to the pins, and the whole cable is clamped in place so that they cannot be pulled out.

The wires must be connected to the correct pin, as shown. The plug has a **fuse** (see page 12). This 'blows' if there is a short-circuit, breaking the circuit and so switching off the electricity. The fuse value must be the one recommended for the equipment used.

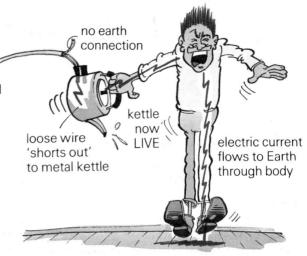

An unconnected earth wire can lead to a nasty shock . . .

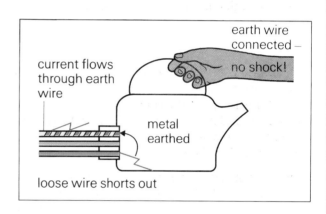

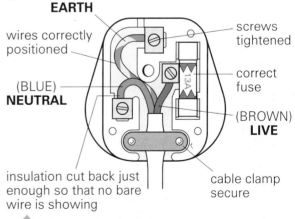

A correctly wired plug.

1
a What are the names of the three wires used in mains electricity?
b How are they colour-coded for household appliances?

2 Decribe how an earth wire could save your life if a fault occurred.

3 Give two reasons why brass is used for the pins in a plug.

4 Describe the movement of an electron around:
a an a.c. circuit
b a d.c. circuit.

5 *Safe as houses?*

How to treat electric shock.

Just how electrically safe is your home?

We use electricity so much that we often take it for granted and forget just how dangerous it can be.

Consider this incident: 'As the kettle started to boil, Peter reached across from the sink and pulled at the plug. The next thing he knew, he was lying on the floor on the other side of the kitchen!'

Do you know anyone who has had an electric shock? If they were able to tell you about it, they were lucky!

What shocks do

Electric shocks make your muscles contract. This can sometimes clamp your grip on the live equipment, but normally 'throws' you away. Shocks also affect the heart – either stopping it completely or causing it to beat irregularly. Even this can lead to brain damage within 2 to 4 minutes if no action is taken.

What to do

In case of electric shock *switch off the mains supply* and then apply emergency first aid if you know how. Get someone to phone for an ambulance.

(For short courses in emergency first aid, apply to your local branch of the St John Ambulance Brigade.)

Killer in the kitchen

Peter should have switched off the socket, not pulled the plug, but his main problem was wet hands!

Safety regulations state that power sockets should not be fitted in bathrooms or too close to sinks in kitchens. Why is that?

Your body has a fairly low resistance because of all the water it contains. Your only protection is if there is high resistance between your skin and the source of the current, or between you and the ground. Dry hands have a high resistance (and some shoes have a very high resistance) so 'dry' shocks are generally mild. But if your hands are wet a much better electrical contact is made, the resistance is lowered and more current flows – so the shock can be dangerous. And if your feet are wet too you are in danger of getting a fatal shock.

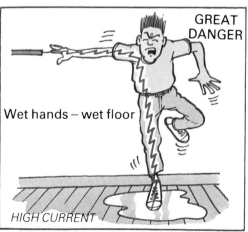

Be a safety sleuth!

Some common causes of electrical accidents are obvious enough – if you know what you are looking for! Watch out for . . .

1. Sockets too close to sinks.

2. Electrical flexes that have become split or frayed. This can happen in time to the wires of vacuum cleaners, irons, kettles, or anything else that is moved around a lot.

3. Wires trailing across heat sources. This often happens in the kitchen.

4. Wires trailing across floors where people could trip over them.

5. Overloaded sockets. Too many plugs in one socket could overload the wiring and cause a fire (see page 12).

6. Power appliances running from lighting circuits. This overloads the wiring too.

Another problem

Page 9 shows a correctly wired plug. Wiring a plug is an everyday activity – yet one that needs a lot of skill and patience if it is to be done safely! Some attempts will simply not work, or else will 'blow' as soon as they are plugged in. But others would appear to work yet would lead to long-term dangers.

If the live and neutral wires are reversed, the equipment will still work, but could still be 'live' and give a nasty shock – even when switched off! Switches (and fuses, see page 12) must always be in the live wire.

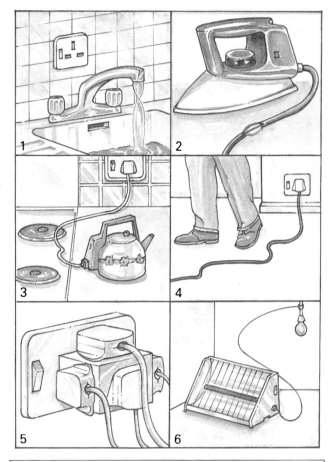

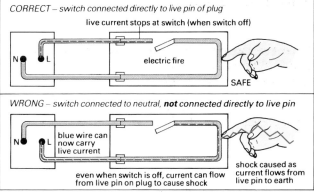

CORRECT – switch connected directly to live pin of plug
live current stops at switch (when switch off)
N   L   electric fire   SAFE

WRONG – switch connected to neutral, **not** connected directly to live pin
N   L   blue wire can now carry live current
even when switch is off, current can flow from live pin on plug to cause shock
shock caused as current flows from live pin to earth

A safe alternative

Some modern equipment with metal surfaces does not have an earth wire – but it is safe to use. Why? This is because all the parts which use the current are completely sealed off from the outside by a double layer of plastic. This **double insulation** means that there is no risk of shock even if there is a faulty live wire. So there is no need for an earth wire.

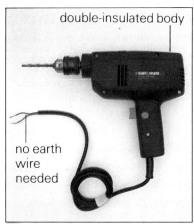

double-insulated body

no earth wire needed

1 Your friends say it doesn't matter if live and neutral wires are reversed. Explain to them why it does.

2 A customer has written to your firm of electricians requesting you to install a power point in his bathroom. Write back and explain why this is not possible.

6 Fuses, circuit breakers and RCDs

Fuses

Plugs have fuses, even stereos have fuses. We know they are for 'safety' and 'protection', but what are they? What do they do? How do they work?

The flow of electricity can make things hot – that's how electric fires and light bulbs work. Fuses also use this principle. A fuse is a wire made of a special metal which, if too much current is passed through, will get hot and melt (or 'fuse'). This then breaks the circuit and so switches off the current – we say that the fuse has 'blown'. Fuse wire can be made to take different, standard currents before melting. The general rule is that thick wire can take a larger current than thin wire. This is because thick wire has more room for electrons to flow, and so has a lower resistance.

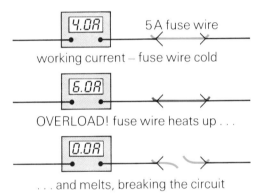

Which fuse?

To choose the correct fuse wire for the job, you need to know the 'working current' of the equipment. A three-bar electric fire can take nearly 13 amperes (13A), so a 5A fuse would blow as soon as the fire was switched on! The rule of thumb is to choose the next standard fuse rating *above* the working current.

	Working current	Fuse
3–bar fire (3 kW)	12.5 A	13 A
hairdrier (750 W)	3 A	5 A
100 W bulb	0.4 A	2 A

4.0A — 5A fuse wire

working current – fuse wire cold

6.0A —

OVERLOAD! fuse wire heats up . . .

0.0A —

. . . and melts, breaking the circuit

What do they protect?

Fuses melt if overloaded, but they have to heat up first. So if a fault occurs, the delicate electronics in your stereo could be damaged by heat *before* the current was switched off by the fuse. More importantly, fuses react far too slowly to protect you from an electric shock.

Fuses are in fact there to protect the **wiring** in your house. This, too, can get hot if too much current passes through it – hot enough to set fire to the house in extreme cases. That's why you are told not to overload your circuits with lots of adaptors plugged into one socket.

When a house is wired, different sized cables are used for different jobs: thick cables for power circuits, thinner ones for lighting (as bulbs use less current). The problem is that (especially in older houses) people forget and wire new

Overloading a socket can lead to fire.

power sockets into the old *lighting* circuit! Only the correct fuse can stop overheating and possible fire. So why not just use thick cables for everything? The answer is simple – cost!

Changing fuses

The **cartridge fuses** used in plugs are very easily replaced once the back of the plug has been removed. Household fuses in the **fuse box** are trickier, as a new length of the correct fuse wire must be screwed into the terminals.

Always switch off the current before changing a fuse, and *never* try to replace a fuse with a piece of wire or metal foil – even as a temporary measure. Unless you have discovered and corrected the fault that made the fuse blow in the first place, it will probably blow again. If you were to complete the circuit without a proper fuse, when the power comes on any surge of current could now continue unchecked, causing major damage or fire.

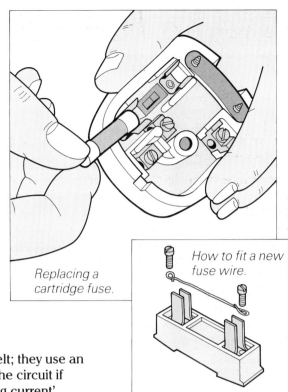

Replacing a cartridge fuse.

How to fit a new fuse wire.

Circuit breakers . . .

Changing fuses (often in the dark!) is such a fiddly business that they are often now replaced in the fuse box by **circuit breakers**. These don't melt; they use an *electromagnetic* effect (see pages 14–17) to break the circuit if overloaded and, like fuses, come in pre-set 'working current' ratings. Unlike fuses, however, the circuit can be restored at the push of a button.

▼ *Industrial circuit breaker.*

. . . can be lifesavers!

But, like fuses, circuit breakers are still too slow to save your life. The damage done by a shock depends on the *size* of the current and *how long* it passes for. If only the reaction time of these devices could be reduced enough, electricity could be made totally safe. Now, thanks to microelectronics, it can be done . . .

Normally, the current flowing in the live wire is exactly the same as that in the neutral wire. If a fault occurs, and some of the current flows back through you, however, this balance is upset. **Residual current devices (RCDs)** are designed to detect such an imbalance and to switch off the current within milliseconds – fast enough to save your life!

1 Explain how a fuse will stop a current overload.

2 Which fuse (2 A, 5 A or 13 A) would you fit for:
  a 3 kW kettle
  b a 100 W stereo
  c a 750 W vacuum cleaner?

3 What are fuses designed to protect? What can happen if house wiring is not correctly fused?

4 Describe how RCDs can save your life.

7 Magnets and electromagnets

Thousands of years ago, the Chinese discovered that pieces of a special kind of iron ore always pointed north if hung from a string. Nowadays we use a compass to find our way about, but the principle is the same as both compass needles and pieces of lodestone are **magnets**.

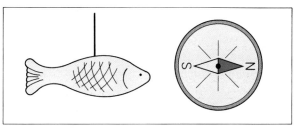

Magnetic tricks

Magnets have many interesting properties. They will pull pieces of iron or steel towards them but do not affect other materials – even other metals, such as copper or aluminium. Also, this force of attraction is not spread out evenly, but is concentrated near the ends, which we call the **poles** of the magnet. You can see this if you dip a magnet into iron filings.

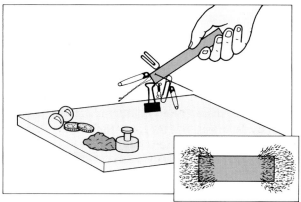

When a magnet is freely suspended, it always comes to rest with the same pole facing north. So this is called the 'north-seeking pole' (or **north pole** for short) and the other is the **south pole**. If the north pole of one magnet is brought near the south pole of another, the two magnets will attract each other. But if two north poles are brought together they push each other away.

The rule is: *like poles repel; unlike poles attract.*

If you have a compass you can use this rule to find which pole of a magnet is which.

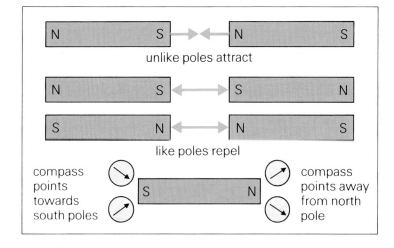

unlike poles attract

like poles repel

compass points towards south poles

compass points away from north pole

Magnetic fields

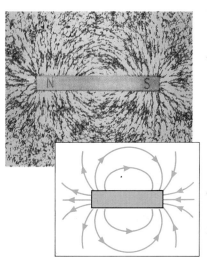

All of these things happen because a magnet is surrounded by a **magnetic field**. The pattern of this field can easily be seen if iron filings are shaken around a magnet. In a simplified diagram of this, a series of **lines of force** are marked which show how the north magnetic pole of a small compass would be moved.

The Earth has its own magnetic field, which is why compasses point north! (So what must the *magnetic* polarity of the *geographic* north pole be?)

These **permanent magnets** can be very useful – but they do have their limitations. They can't be made very large and, more importantly, they can't be switched off.

Switchable magnetism

A coil of copper wire will have no effect on a compass needle – until an electric current is passed around it. It then behaves just like a magnet, with poles and a magnetic field.

The more turns of wire there are, the stronger the magnetic field. But it is the flowing electricity, not the wire, that causes this effect. That's why these devices are called **electromagnets**. If the current is increased, the field becomes stronger; if it is reversed, the field is reversed; and, most importantly, if the current is switched off, the field is lost!

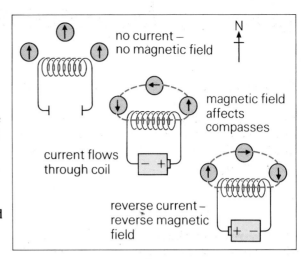

Just add iron

Long coils of wire like this are called **solenoids**. When current flows, their external magnetic field is just like that of a bar magnet. But they also have lines of force running through the coil. If an iron bar is placed inside the coil, it concentrates these lines of magnetic force and makes the electromagnet stronger.

Pure iron does not retain any magnetism when the current is switched off – but a steel bar does. So pure iron is called magnetically 'soft', and is ideal for using as a core for electromagnets. Because steel stays magnetic after being in a solenoid, it is magnetically 'hard'. This means solenoids can be used to make permanent magnets made of steel.

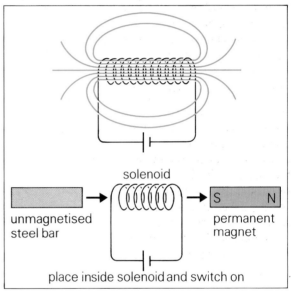

solenoid

unmagnetised steel bar → (solenoid) → S   N permanent magnet

place inside solenoid and switch on

Useful electromagnets

So, electromagnets can be made as strong as you like by:

● increasing the number of coils
● increasing the current
● winding the coils around a 'soft' iron core.

And, most importantly, they can be switched off.

Electromagnets have very many uses, from the 'heavy duty' versions that lift cars in scrapyards to the delicate and complex ones that control the picture on your TV.

---

1 Give five properties of permanent magnets.

2 What advantages do electromagnets have over permanent ones?

3
a Suggest an advantage of being able to turn off an electromagnet.
b Would an electromagnet with a steel core be suitable for such a use? Explain your answer.

8 Electromagnets at work

Buzzers and bells

Electromagnetic 'switchability' is put to good use in electric buzzers and bells. A simple buzzer can be made from a coil, an old nail and a piece of springy steel, as shown. When the circuit is completed, the coil becomes a magnet and so pulls the steel down onto it. But this breaks the circuit! So the steel springs back again, restoring the circuit, and the process is repeated. This continuous 'make and break' causes the steel to vibrate and so a buzz is heard. But if a hammer is connected to the steel spring and a gong is carefully positioned – the buzzer becomes a bell!

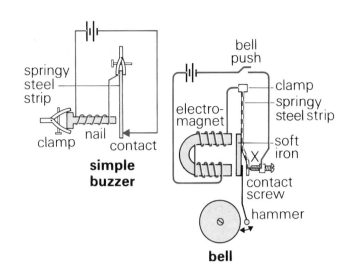

simple buzzer

bell

Relays

Electromagnetic effects can also be used to throw switches. In a **relay**, the electromagnet pulls down an iron plate which, in turn, pushes two electrical contacts together. This 'switching at a distance' can be very useful – it once formed the basis of our automatic telephone exchanges.

A relay device can also save money when making cars. The starter motor of a car takes a very high current (up to 100 A), so it needs very thick cables – which are very expensive. One way of starting the car would be to run thick cables to carry a high current from the battery to the ignition key switch to the starter motor – using a lot of expensive cable! A cheaper way is shown in the diagram – this uses thin, low-current wires to energise a relay, which *then* switches on the high current needed by the starter. All that is now needed is a short, thick wire from the positive terminal of the battery. (Cars employ the sneaky trick of using the metal body of the car to complete the circuit! This is called an **earth return**.)

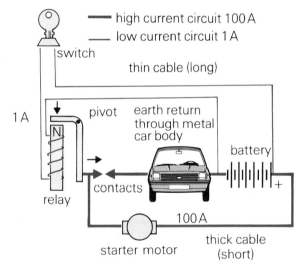

Repulsion, too

If you put an electromagnet next to a permanent magnet, you can get attraction and repulsion, just as you can with two permanent magnets. But with an electromagnet, you can reverse the effect of the force simply by reversing the current. You can also increase the force by increasing the number of coils or increasing the current.

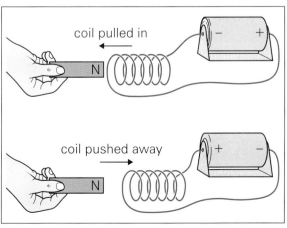

Making a noise

A **loudspeaker** uses this idea to convert electricity into sound. The amplifier in a radio or CD player sends out a variable electrical current, which matches the original sound. This goes to the loudspeaker, where it passes through a coil of wire, held loosely in the field of a strong magnet. The varying electrical signal makes the coil vibrate. The coil is attatched to a paper cone which vibrates too. That makes the air vibrate – which you hear as sound!

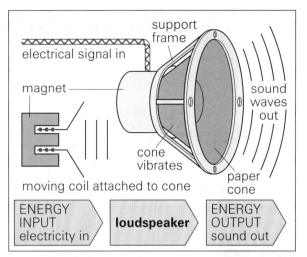

Move and measure

A similar effect is used to measure current in a **moving coil** electrical meter. Here, current flowing through a flat coil forms an electromagnet, which tries to turn in a magnetic field. But the coil is also attached to a spring that opposes this movement: the more it turns, the more the spring pushes back. The bigger the current, the bigger the force, so the greater the current in the coil, the more it turns. This movement can be made to move a pointer across a scale.

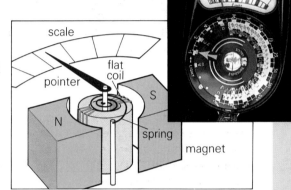

In a spin

Coils will only turn in a magnetic field until they are 'lined up' with it. But the direction in which the coil turns depends on the direction of the current. If you could reverse the current just at the critical moment, you could make the coil continue to turn . . .

Electric motors work in just this way, switching the current automatically. The current is fed in through carbon brushes which make contact with metal half-rings. These reverse the current in the coil every half turn. In commercial motors many turns of wire are used around a soft iron core, and the permanent magnets are replaced by more electromagnets to give a stronger field.

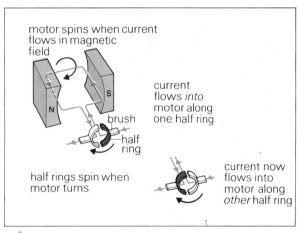

Diagrams show how an electric motor works

1 How can electromagnets be made stronger?

2 Describe, step by step, how an electric bell works.

3 Why is it an advantage to use a relay on a car starter motor?

4 A coil of wire is gently pulled towards a magnet when a current passes through it. How could you:
 a increase the force of attraction?
 b make the magnet repel the coil instead?

5 Explain how a loudspeaker turns electrical energy into sound energy.

6 How is the coil of an electric motor made to keep turning?

9 Generating electricity

What's the opposite of a motor?

In an electric motor, electrical energy (from a battery, for example) is turned into kinetic energy – the energy of motion. This process can be reversed.

If you connect the motor to a bulb and make it move, it will light the bulb. It has become a **generator** of electricity. How does this work?

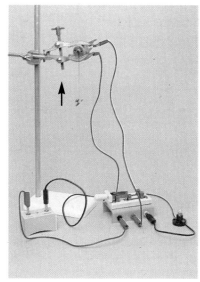

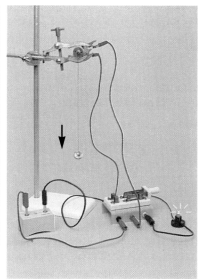

A motor running normally uses electrical energy...

...but a motor forced to turn generates electricity!

Moving through a field

In simple motors, a wire passing through a magnetic field moves when a current passes through it.

If you reverse this process and move a wire though a magnetic field, it creates (**induces**) a potential difference (voltage) across the wire. If there is a complete circuit, this voltage makes a current flow through the wire. This is called an **induced current**.

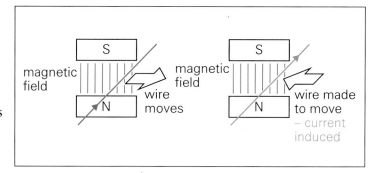

Coil it up

As with all electromagnetic effects, you can increase the effect by using a coil of wire instead of a single strand. The more coils you have, or the larger the area of the coils, the larger the induced voltage. A stronger magnet will also increase the size of the induced voltage.

It doesn't matter if it's the magnet or coil that moves – so long as there is movement. The size of the induced voltage also depends on the speed of movement.

And just as you can reverse a motor by reversing the current, the direction of the induced current depends on whether you push the magnet into the coil or pull it out!

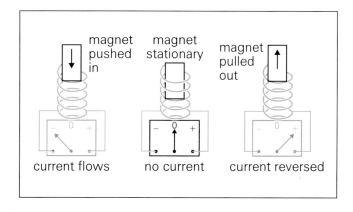

Spin it

Real electricity generators use a similar set-up to a motor, with a coil spinning in a magnetic field. But this does not produce a simple current. Electricity is generated when the wires cut across the magnetic field. Look at what would happen as the wire goes through one complete turn:

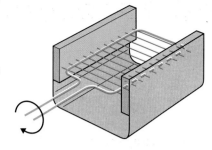

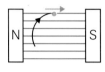

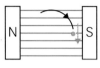

*1. The wire cuts **up** through the field. A current is induced.*

2. At the very top of the circle, the wire runs parallel to the field. No current!

*3. The wire cuts **down** through the field. A current is induced in the opposite direction!*

4. At the very bottom, the wire runs parallel to the field. No current!

As with motors, practical generators use many turns of wire around soft iron cores, and very strong magnetic fields are provided by electromagnets rather than permanent magnets. Generators also have to be very large to give the massive electrical energy output that is needed from power stations.

Generators make a.c. ◆ Ⓗ

So the current induced in a coil of a generator flows backwards and forwards with every turn. This is how the alternating current (a.c. – 'mains') you use at home is produced!

In order to get this current out from the generator without twisting and breaking the wires, a system of rings and brushes is used, similar to those on a motor. But this time, two continuous **slip rings** are used, so that the current taken out remains as a.c.

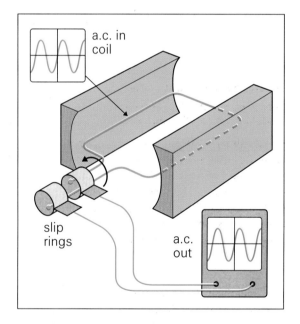

---

1 In what way is a generator the opposite of a motor?

2 What effect do the following have on the current induced when a wire moves through a magnetic field?
   a moving twice as fast in the same direction
   b moving in the opposite direction
   c using a coil with 5 strands of wire

3 Explain, with diagrams, how and why the induced current varies when a coil spins in a magnetic field.

4 Why does a generator need to have slip rings if you want to get a.c. from it?

5 List the ways in which you could increase the size of the current produced by a generator.

10 Charges at work

Creating static charges

Static charges (which you learned about earlier) can build up on insulators if they are rubbed together. Some materials, such as nylon or polythene, tend to pick up extra electrons and so become *negatively* charged. Others, such as ebony or glass, tend to lose electrons and so become *positively* charged.

If similarly charged rods are brought together, they repel each other, while oppositely charged rods attract each other. The rule is: *like charges repel; unlike charges attract*.

How can a comb pick up a paper?

A freshly rubbed comb will pick up pieces of paper, and a rubbed balloon will stick to a wall. So what makes these rubbed (charged) objects attract uncharged ones?

You need to remember that *everything* contains electric charges, but usually they are in balance. When a charged object is brought near, however, this balance can be upset enough to allow attraction to occur.

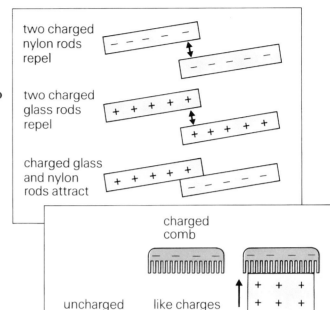

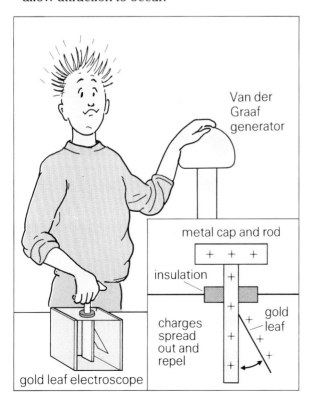

Van der Graaf generator

metal cap and rod

insulation

charges spread out and repel

gold leaf

gold leaf electroscope

Useful static repulsion

You may have seen experiments using a machine called a Van der Graaf generator, which can build up very large electrostatic charges. If a volunteer stands on an insulated plate and puts a hand on the charge dome, he or she will get a very hair-raising experience!

This happens because the charge spreads out all over the surface of the body and every single hair gets the same charge, and so *pushes away* its neighbour. This idea is put to work in electrostatic paint-spraying. Here, every droplet of paint gets the same charge and so keeps apart from its neighbour, giving a very smooth spray and finish.

Repulsion effects can also be used to detect charges. In a gold leaf electroscope, a thin strip of gold leaf is attached to a metal bar in an insulated box. If the cap is charged, this charge spreads out and causes the gold leaf to rise by electrostatic repulsion.

Making static flow

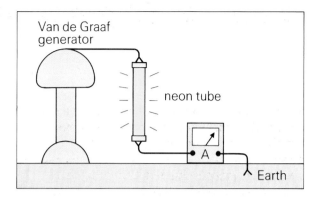

The charged dome of a Van der Graaf generator may reach such a high voltage that it will spark to Earth – through you if you get too close! It can easily be made to discharge to Earth through a wire and a neon tube – making the tube light up as the charge flows to Earth. A current can be detected in the wire by any sensitive meter. Why? Don't forget that current electricity is just flowing electrical charge!

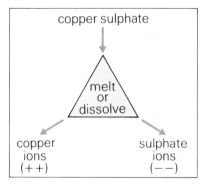

Using current to overcome static

Many compounds of metals are **ionic**. That means they are made up of positively charged bits and negatively charged bits that are held together by electrostatic attraction. (Charged particles are called **ions**.) If these compounds are melted or dissolved in water, however, these ions separate and may be torn apart by a direct current in a process called **electrolysis**.

Electroplating

If two wires are connected to a d.c. source and dipped into copper sulphate solution, the negative wire (the **negative electrode** or **cathode**) gets coated with fresh, metallic copper. This is because the copper in the solution has a positive charge and so is pulled towards the negative cathode. Here, the extra electrons cancel out the charge on the copper ions, and a **plating** of metallic copper is deposited on the cathode. Various other metal **electroplatings** can be made if you carry out electrolysis of the right solutions.

An electric current is just a flow of electrons: the larger the current and/or the longer you leave it flowing, the more metal you get from the solution. This method is used in industry to purify copper by electrolysis.

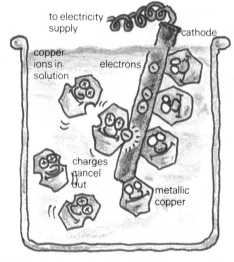

Electrolysis – using electricity to separate metals from their compounds.

1 What feature of static electricity is similar to a feature of magnetism?

2 How could you show that static electricity can have the same effect as current electricity?

3 Find out three different metals which are used for electroplating. Give a use for each one of your electroplated metal coatings.

4 'Sulphate' ions are negative. Which electrode will they be drawn to, the positive or the negative?

11 Measuring electricity

Mastering the units

You've read about amps and volts but, like many people, you may still be rather muddled and confused about them. So what is the difference?

Amps flow . . .

We use **amps** or amperes (A) as a measure of the *rate of flow* of electric current – the number of units of charge which pass every second. (The standard unit of charge is called a **coulomb**.)

low current   high current

To use a water model again, compare a waterfall in winter flood to the same waterfall as a summer trickle. The height of the fall is the same, the speed at which the water falls is the same. The only difference is the rate of flow – the amount falling every second.

. . . volts hurt!

We use **volts** (V), on the other hand, as a measure of the amount of *energy* carried by each unit of charge. This tells us how much work can be done by the current.

In a water model, compare the energy and possible effects of a bucket of water tipped from the top of a door to one dropped from the top of a skyscraper! So the number of volts tell us about the 'push' on the electrons, or the 'kick' of energy that they carry – or, on you, how much they hurt!

low voltage   high voltage

How does resistance fit in?

current and voltage go up and down together!

the resistance/current see saw

BOING

In simple circuits, *the relative size of the current flowing depends on the resistance*. A low resistance will allow a high current to flow, while a high resistance will allow only a low current to flow – a sort of see-saw (*inverse*) relationship.

But in a given circuit, *the actual size of the current also depends on the voltage*. In this case, however, the current rises as the voltage rises and falls as it falls – a more *direct* relationship.

The resistance of a circuit is measured in **ohms** (Ω) – it is calculated by dividing the voltage by the current.

Circuits

In a simple circuit there is just one loop, so the flow of electrons (the current) is the same all the way around it. This is called a **series** circuit.

Another common type of circuit has two or more separate branches. Like a river splitting and flowing around an island, the current in the main wire is split between the branches, only to recombine before returning to the 'pump'. This is called a **parallel** circuit.

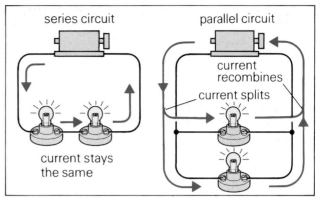

ammeter in series

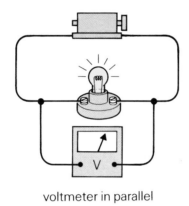

voltmeter in parallel

Measuring

Current is measured using an **ammeter**. A circuit must be broken and the ammeter put in, in *series*, to measure current, as *all* the current must flow through the meter.

Voltage is measured with a **voltmeter**. Voltage readings are easier to take, however, as the voltmeter leads need only be connected in *parallel* across the points to be tested.

Sharing the voltage

If you measure the voltage across separate components arranged in a series circuit, you will find that the voltage has been 'shared out' between them. If the components are all the same, they will all get equal voltage 'shares'. If they are different, the voltage will vary, depending on their resistance. The larger the resistance, the bigger the voltage 'share'.

In a parallel circuit, however, all the components get the same voltage as that provided by the power supply.

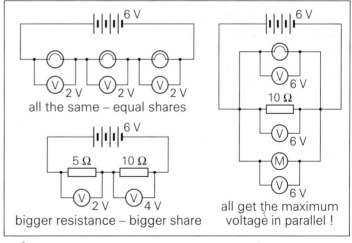

These diagrams use the symbols you met on page 7.

---

1 Explain, in words, the difference between current (in amps) and voltage (in volts). Think up your own models to help you.

2 Try to describe, in words, the relationships between current, voltage and resistance.

3 How do series circuits and parallel circuits differ? Draw diagrams and give examples.

4 Describe how you would practically measure voltage and current.

12 Plugging into electricity

From the power station . . .

Power stations are energy converters (transducers).

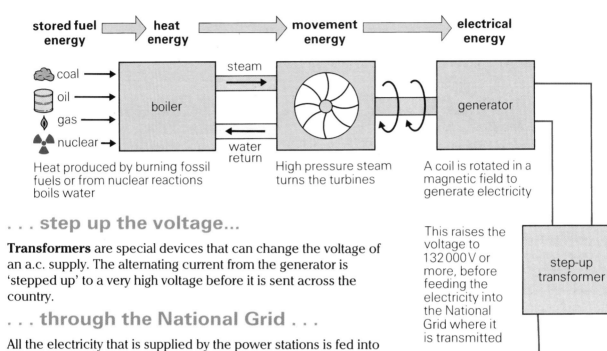

stored fuel energy ⟹ heat energy ⟹ movement energy ⟹ electrical energy

coal →
oil →
gas →
nuclear →
boiler

steam →
← water return

generator

Heat produced by burning fossil fuels or from nuclear reactions boils water

High pressure steam turns the turbines

A coil is rotated in a magnetic field to generate electricity

. . . step up the voltage...

Transformers are special devices that can change the voltage of an a.c. supply. The alternating current from the generator is 'stepped up' to a very high voltage before it is sent across the country.

. . . through the National Grid . . .

All the electricity that is supplied by the power stations is fed into the 'energy highway' that spans the country – the **National Grid**. This allows regional variations in supply and demand to be balanced out.

. . . into step-down transformers . . .

These step the voltage down to suitable working levels – sometimes several thousand volts for industry, but 230–240V for the home. Some energy is lost in these transformers: if you live near one that 'hums' a lot you can listen in to this wasted energy!

This raises the voltage to 132 000V or more, before feeding the electricity into the National Grid where it is transmitted

step-up transformer

cables of aluminium reinforced with steel

very high voltage needs very high levels of insulation

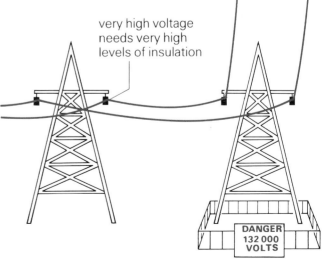

DANGER 132 000 VOLTS

. . . for everyone to use

In this country nearly everyone makes use of electricity for lighting at home and at work. Many people use it for cooking, heating and thousands of different types of electrical equipment. There are many specialist uses:

- *Manufacturing* – Extracting and refining various metals; powering robots to make cars.
- *Transport* – Electric motors in London Underground trains; various railway trains.
- *Business* – For communications and computers (such as in the Stock Exchange).
- *Leisure* – Floodlights at sporting events; power for video games and for fairground rides.
- *Broadcasting* – Transmitting radio and TV programmes.
- *Health* – Monitoring life-support machines in intensive care.
- *Education* – Computers . . . and school bells!

Why is electricity so expensive?

Electricity is a secondary source of energy – unlike coal, oil or gas, we have to manufacture it. This process involves many energy changes. Each change uses up a little bit of the energy, with the result that the overall system 'wastes' nearly two-thirds of its energy. Even then, there are further losses in the National Grid itself. No wonder electricity is expensive!

As you can see, electricity is 'Big Business', affecting nearly every aspect of our lives. We take it for granted – but could you imagine life without it?

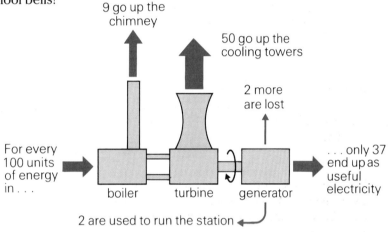

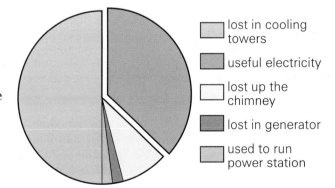

1 a Transformers 'waste' some energy. How can you tell?
   b Some energy is lost from the National Grid cables. Do you think more or less would be lost if a lower voltage was used? (Hint: why bother with transformers?)
   c The cables use steel for strength. Why do they use aluminium?

2 a What do you think are the five biggest advantages of having electricity? In each case how could people cope if there was no electricity?
   b What do you think are the five disadvantages of electricity?
   c Explain if you think the advantages outweigh the disadvantages.

3 Why is electricity so expensive?

13 *Clever tricks with a.c.*

The amount of **power** used by an electrical circuit is found by *multiplying the voltage and the current*. So the same amount of power could be delivered by:

- high voltage and low current, or
- low voltage and high current.

Sometimes we need high voltage, sometimes high current – wouldn't it be useful if we could change from one to the other? With a.c. we can – using a **transformer**.

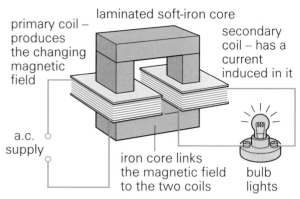

primary coil – produces the changing magnetic field

laminated soft-iron core

secondary coil – has a current induced in it

a.c. supply

iron core links the magnetic field to the two coils

bulb lights

How transformers work

On page 19 it was described how an electric current is produced in a generator, by moving a coil in a magnetic field – with the magnetic field staying constant all the time. But exactly the same effect can be obtained if the coil stays still and the field moves.

Pass a direct current through a coil and it becomes an electromagnet, with a magnetic field from its north to south pole. But pass a.c. through a coil and this field must switch backwards and forwards as the current reverses.

Put these ideas together and what do you have? A transformer!

Transforming voltages

The strength of an electromagnet is controlled by the number of turns of wire. The effect of a transformer depends on the ratio of the *number of turns in the primary and secondary coils*. If the secondary coil has four times more turns than the primary coil, the voltage from the secondary coil will be four times greater. If the number of coils were four times less, the voltage would be reduced down by a factor of four.

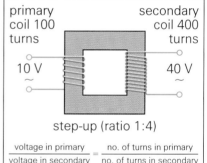

primary coil 100 turns

secondary coil 400 turns

10 V ~

40 V ~

step-up (ratio 1:4)

$$\frac{\text{voltage in primary}}{\text{voltage in secondary}} = \frac{\text{no. of turns in primary}}{\text{no. of turns in secondary}}$$

'Step-up' for the Grid

The cables used to carry electricity across the country on the National Grid are made of steel-reinforced aluminium. Metals such as aluminium are good conductors as some of the electrons from their atoms can move relatively freely through the metal as a whole. But the cables used for the grid may be hundreds of kilometres long. If the a.c. supply produced by the generators in a power station was sent straight out onto the National Grid, nearly all its energy would be lost as it gently heated up the cables!

To overcome this problem, transformers are used to raise the voltage of the a.c. supply. If the voltage is multiplied by a thousand, the current is reduced to a thousandth of what it was. As it is the flowing current that causes heating in a wire, stepping up the voltage like this reduces the heating effect and makes the transfer of energy across the Grid much more efficient.

'Step-down' and heat-up

Heating effects are most efficient at the 'high current' end of the power see-saw. Electric welders use a **step-down transformer** which has just a few, thick wire turns in the secondary coil to produce a very high current.
If this short circuits across pieces of metal, the heat produced is great enough to cause local melting, welding the pieces together.

Welding in progress during the assembly of concrete mixers.

Sega game system with mains adapter plugged in.

Step-down and save money!

Modern electronic equipment such as stereos, radios and computers, run on low-voltage d.c. supplies. These can be provided from batteries but, as those of you with portable cassette players will know, batteries soon run out and are expensive to replace. Mains electricity is much cheaper.

Mains adaptors can be used either built-in or separate for most electronic equipment. These adaptors use a step-down transformer to reduce the mains voltage to a suitable low voltage. But this is still a.c., so something else must be done . . .

Semi-conductor diodes

So far we have talked of conductors, insulators and resistors, but not all materials fit neatly into these categories. Indeed, all of our transistor and microchip technology depends on a group of materials, including silicon, which have much more complex properties and are known as **semi-conductors**.

One of the simplest semi-conductor devices is the **diode**. This lets current flow in *one* direction, but acts as an insulator if the voltage is *reversed*. Diodes can therefore be used as one-way valves, to protect equipment from an accidentally reversed voltage that might otherwise damage it.

This one-way effect can also be used to turn a.c. to d.c. – so you'll also find diodes in any mains adaptor.

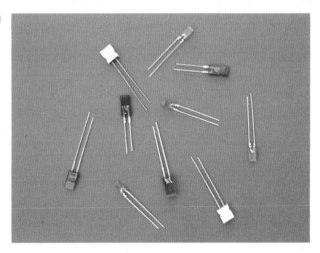

A selection of modern electronics diodes.

1. Compare the way a transformer works with what happens in a generator.

2. What is a step-up transformer? How is it used in the National Grid?

3. What is a step-down transformer? How is it used in an electric welder?

4. What are diodes? How do they:
   a protect equipment
   b change a.c. to d.c.?

14 Electricity by numbers

Power and current

When a current passes through a wire, some of the energy is lost as the wire heats up. The amount of energy transferred every second (the **power**) is found by multiplying the current and voltage together.

Power = potential difference × current
(watts, W)   (volts, V)   (amps, A)

For example, a 240 V mains electric kettle that takes a current of 12.5 amps has a power of:

power = 240 V × 12.5 A = 3000 W (3 kW)

▲ *3KW in action.*

Lamps and diodes

If you measure the current readings across a filament lamp at different voltages, you get a curve instead of a straight line! The gradient – and therefore the resistance – gets larger as the voltage increases. This is because the tungsten filament gets hotter and hotter as the voltage increases (it glows brighter and brighter). The resistance of tungsten, unlike carbon, changes with temperature. As it gets hotter, the resistance increases.

Diodes behave like carbon resistors if they are connected up correctly. But if you reverse the voltage, almost no current flows.

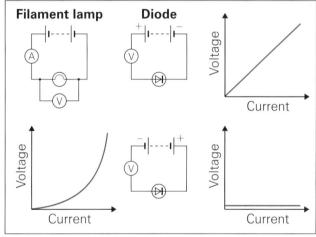

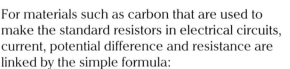

▲ *Voltage/current graphs for lamps and diodes.*

Example: If $V = 10$ V and $I = 2.5$ A, the resistance is given by:

$$R = \frac{V}{I} = \frac{10}{2.5} = 4 \text{ ohms}$$

Volts, amps and ohms ⬢

For materials such as carbon that are used to make the standard resistors in electrical circuits, current, potential difference and resistance are linked by the simple formula:

$$\text{resistance } R \text{ (in ohms)} = \frac{\text{potential difference } V \text{ (in volts)}}{\text{current } I \text{ (in amps)}}$$

(The symbol I is used for current.)

If you plot the current flowing through one of these resistors at different voltages, you get a straight line graph. The **gradient** of this graph gives the resistance in ohms. So for this type of resistor, the resistance stays constant. A higher resistance gives a steeper line, with a higher gradient. A lower resistance gives a less steep line.

Thermistors and LDRs

These useful devices have resistances that vary in a definite way. The resistance of a **thermistor** changes with temperature, getting lower as the temperature increases. That means, for a given circuit, more current will flow if the temperature increases. Thermistors can be used as 'electronic thermometers' to build thermostats or fire alarms or for use with computer data logging. **Light Dependent Resistors** (**LDRs**) show a similar effect with light. Their resistance drops as more light falls on them.

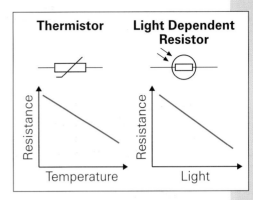

Which fuse?

Mains electrical equipment should be protected by a fuse. Fuses come in different current ratings. You need to know how much current flows through the equipment when it is working normally, and then use the next higher fuse rating. But how can you tell how much current is being used, without using an ammeter?

Mains equipment is usually marked with its **power rating** in watts. Light bulbs may be 60 or 100 W, hairdriers 500 W and electric fires 2 or 3 kW, for example. As you know that mains electricity runs at 240 V, you can work out the current that is used from the rearranged formula:

$$\frac{\text{current } I}{\text{(in amps)}} = \frac{\text{power } W \text{ (in watts)}}{\text{voltage } V \text{ (in volts)}}$$

Example:
A hairdrier is rated at 500 W so:

$$\text{current} = \frac{500\,\text{W}}{240\,\text{V}} = 2.1\,\text{A}$$

Choose a 3 A fuse.

Example: A coil of resistance wire can be used as a simple heater for science experiments. It can be used to investigate the energy needed to heat up different liquids.

Energy

The higher the voltage, the greater the amount of energy that is carried by a given amount of electric charge. These are linked by the equation:

$$\begin{array}{ccc} \text{energy transferred} = & \text{voltage} & \times & \text{charge} \\ \text{(In joules, J)} & \text{(in volts, V)} & & \text{(in coulombs, C)} \end{array}$$

If the current is 1 amp, 1 coulomb of charge flows. So:

$$\begin{array}{ccc} \text{total charge} = & \text{current} & \times & \text{time} \\ \text{(coulombs, C)} & \text{(amps, A)} & & \text{(seconds, s)} \end{array}$$

Putting these two equations together gives:

$$\begin{array}{cccc} \text{Energy transferred} = & \text{voltage} & \times & \text{current} & \times & \text{time} \\ \text{(joules, J)} & \text{(V)} & & \text{(A)} & & \text{(s)} \end{array}$$

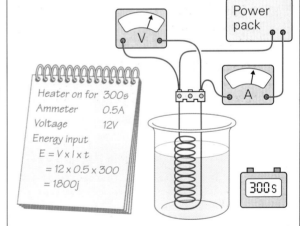

1 a Why does the gradient of a voltage/current graph for a light bulb get steeper as the voltage increases?
b A bulb passes 0.1 A at 5 V, but only 0.15 A at 10 V. Calculate the resistance in each case.

2 Electrical equipment can be damaged if the batteries are fitted the wrong way round. How can a diode prevent this damage?

3 What is the resistance in ohms in the following examples?
a current = 3 A, voltage = 12 V
b current = 0.25 A, voltage = 240 V
c current = 12 A, voltage = 240 V

4 In a given circuit, a thermistor passed 0.1 A at 20 °C and 0.2 A at 50 °C. At what temperature would the current be 1.5 A?

5 a What fuse would you use for a 750 W mains vacuum cleaner?
b How much energy would this use in 5 minutes?

15 *For you to do*

1 Angie set up a circuit to test whether different things conducted electricity or not. A piece of copper made the bulb light up.

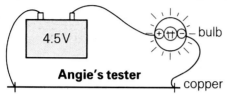

Angie's tester

a Is copper a conductor or insulator?
b Would the bulb light up if the copper was replaced by:
  i   a penny   iv a matchstick
  ii a gold ring v   a rubber
  iii a plastic comb vi an iron nail?

2 **a** Denzil set up a circuit as shown. His paper-clip switch had three positions, A, B and C.

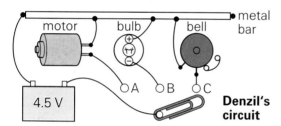

Denzil's circuit

Which position would:
  i   ring the bell
  ii spin the motor
  iii light the bulb?

b Freda set up a circuit using a battery, a buzzer, three lengths of wire and a switch. The buzzer came on only when the switch was turned on. Draw a picture of her circuit.

3 Which of the energy changers shown below is designed most efficiently to change:
  a sound to electricity
  b motion to electricity
  c electricity to motion
  d electricity to light
  e chemical energy to electricity?

Energy changers: lightbulb, battery, electric motor, microphone, generator.

4 Which circuit diagram below could represent:
  a a simple torch
  b a light with a dimmer switch
  c a two-bar fire with separate switches
  d a variable-speed motor

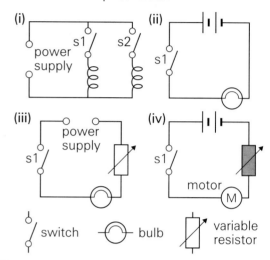

5 If two cells make each of the two bulbs glow to 'standard brightness', would the bulbs in the circuits shown glow brighter, the same, dimmer, or not at all?

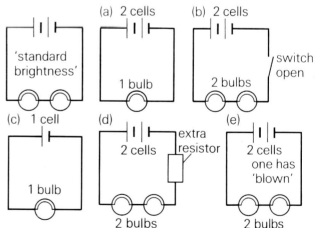

6 An electromagnet can be made from coils of wire connected to a d.c. power supply.
  a Suggest three ways to make a simple electromagnet stronger.
  b What happens to the magnetic field if:
    i   the current is switched off
    ii the current is reversed?

7 a If current is passed along a wire in a magnetic field, a force acts on the wire which can make it move.

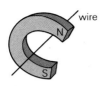

What happens to this force if:
  i the current is increased
  ii the magnetic field is reversed?

b If a direct current is passed through a coil of wire in a magnetic field as shown, what will happen to it? (Draw a diagram to show how it ends up.)

8 a Explain how the split rings in a d.c. motor allow the coil to continue to spin.

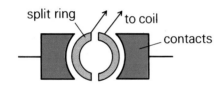

b In an old electric motor, only 70% of the electrical energy was turned into kinetic energy. Suggest two ways in which the rest of the energy may have been 'lost'.

9 Use $P = I \times V$ to calculate the working current of the electrical devices shown.

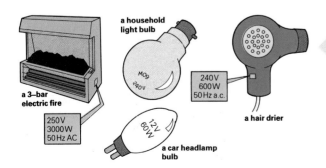

a 3–bar electric fire   250V 3000W 50Hz AC

a household light bulb   M09 240V

a hair drier   240V 600W 50Hz a.c.

a car headlamp bulb   12V 60W

If fuses come in 2 A, 5 A and 13 A sizes, which would you use for these four devices?

10 a A test circuit was set up as shown, using a low resistance, 24 V power supply, an ammeter and a 1 metre length of resistance wire.

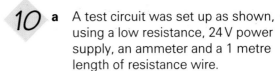
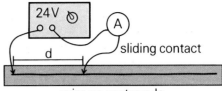

wire on metre rule

The current was measured for different lengths of wire. The results were:

length of wire (*d*)	33 cm	50 cm	1 m
current	2.25 A	1.5 A	0.75 A

Plot a graph of these results. From the graph:
  i what current would you expect for a 75 cm length of the same wire?
  ii what current would you expect if the wire was 2m long?

b Use the formula $V = I \times R$ to calculate the resistance of the 1 m length of wire.

c Find the 'missing values' in the following table of resistors:

	R1	R2	R3	R4	R5
voltage (volts)	?	42	63	112	?
current (amps)	0.5	3	?	?	0.01
resistance (ohms)	200	?	21	1120	1000

11 Describe step-by-step how electricity is generated in a coal-fired power station, transmitted across the National Grid, and used to light your classroom. Explain the energy changes and processes involved, indicating where useful energy is lost from the system and what steps are taken to minimise this loss.

12 A transformer has 1000 turns in its primary coil and 50 turns in its secondary coil. If the primary voltage is 240 V, what is the secondary voltage?

NEW MODULAR SCIENCE
for GCSE

MODULE   *Energy*

Spread

Cover photograph *Kariba hydroelectric station dam, Zimbabwe*

1 What is energy?

The reason for change

Energy is needed to make anything happen – it makes the sun shine, it makes cars and buses move, it even keeps you alive!

For something that is so important in our lives, energy is very hard to explain. We know we have to 'save it' if we want to keep our bills down. We know that the glucose in a Mars bar is 'for energy'. If somebody is very active we might say that they are 'energetic'. But exactly what is energy? Where does it come from? What kinds of energy are there? Whatever it is, it certainly comes in a lot of disguises!

Energy helps you work rest and play.

The sun sends out **light** energy and **heat** energy.

Fridges remove **heat** energy from food. This makes the food cold.

Gas contains *stored* energy. This turns to **heat** energy when you burn it.

Electric lights give out **light** energy and **heat** energy.

Food contains *stored* energy.

Petrol contains *stored* energy.

1 Make a list of all the different kinds of energy shown in the three scenes on these pages.

2 For each of these kinds of energy, try to list the ways in which we can use them.

3 Write a sentence or two to explain what you now think energy is!

Radios use **radio wave** energy, boosted by **electrical** energy, to make **sound** energy.

Loudspeakers can give out lots of **sound** energy.

Moving things have **kinetic** energy

Things that are high up have gravitational **potential** energy.

Stretched springs (or elastic) contain *stored* energy.

Coal contains *stored* energy. This turns to **heat** energy when it burns.

TVs use **electromagnetic** energy boosted by **electrical** energy to give out **light** and **sound** energy.

Living things use energy all the time - even when resting.

Batteries have *stored* **electrical** energy.

Radio waves have **electromagnetic** energy.

If you looked up the word 'energy' in a science dictionary, you would find something like 'energy is the capacity to do work'. But what does work mean? Work in this sense can mean making anything happen.

Energy is often stored in energy sources, such as fuels and batteries. But in many cases the energy from these sources is changed into another form of energy before it is used. Whatever form it's in, energy is useful stuff. You can find out more about energy by reading through this module.

2 Active energy, stored energy

Lots of energy

Though there are many different types of energy, it is possible to sort energy into two main forms. Some types are **active** and so are more obvious. Light can be seen, sound can be heard, heat can be felt. A moving object clearly has energy, too.

But where is the energy in a piece of coal, a sausage, a wound spring, a battery or a rock on a hillside? The energy here is **stored**, and only appears when something happens to make it *change* into active energy.

From stored to active

Potential energy is stored in the rock due to its position at the top of the hill.

As the rock rolls down the hill, its potential energy changes to kinetic energy.

Some stored energy is called *potential* energy because it has the '*potential* to do work'. For example, things that are high up have gravitational **potential** energy. If they are not held in place they will fall downwards because of the pull of gravity. As they fall, they lose this potential energy, which is turned instead into energy of motion, called **kinetic** energy.

Other energy 'stores'

Energy can also be stored in things that have been bent, squeezed or stretched.

A bent bow has stored energy – when it is released, this turns into the kinetic energy of the moving arrow. This is similar to the energy stored in a stretched spring or elastic.

The wound spring in a clockwork motor stores energy in much the same way. A spring metal strip is coiled tightly by winding a key, or by turning the wheels. When released, the metal tries to straighten out. This releases the stored energy, causing the wheels to turn – releasing kinetic energy.

Because these ways of storing and releasing energy all involve *mechanisms*, this type of stored energy is called stored **mechanical** energy.

Stored chemical energy

Some materials have energy locked up in the chemicals from which they are made. Perhaps the simplest example of this is coal. A lump of coal may not seem very energetic, but just try burning it to make it react with the oxygen in the air! A lot of energy is given out in the form of **heat** and **light** energy. Materials like this – such as wood, coal, oil and gas – are called **fuels**.

The food we eat reacts in a similar way inside our bodies. The energy released keeps us warm and also provides the energy we need for life – food is like a fuel for our body!

At a barbeque, chemical energy stored in the charcoal is released as heat energy. The cooked food also releases its stored chemical energy – inside your body.

Batteries also contain stored chemical energy, but this time the chemicals react to give **electrical** energy. This is a particularly useful type of energy as it can be easily turned into many other types of energy, such as light, sound, heat...

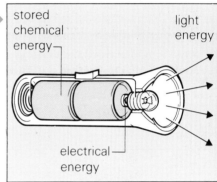

From active to stored

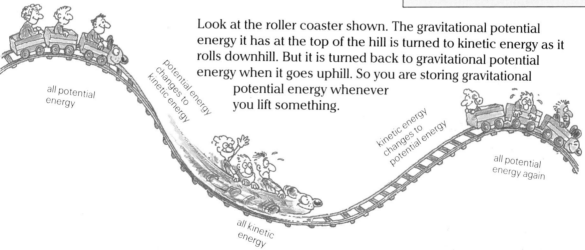

Look at the roller coaster shown. The gravitational potential energy it has at the top of the hill is turned to kinetic energy as it rolls downhill. But it is turned back to gravitational potential energy when it goes uphill. So you are storing gravitational potential energy whenever you lift something.

A similar process happens in a car, but involves electricity. When a lead–acid (car) battery is connected to the headlamps, the energy stored in the battery is turned into electrical energy and then into light energy. But once connected to a battery-charger, electrical energy is pushed back into the battery, refilling the energy store!

1 List some examples of active and stored energy.

2 What are **two** main types of stored energy? For each, try to explain how the energy is stored.

3 What type of energy does stored mechanical energy usually turn into?

4 What types of energy can stored chemical energy turn into?

5 How can active energy be turned back into stored energy?

3 Heat energy on the move

How heat energy moves

Given enough time, heat energy will flow from a hot place to a cool place until the temperatures have levelled out. How long it takes for this 'levelling' to occur will depend on the **temperature difference**, and also on the **materials** involved. Some let the energy flow quickly; others slow it down. To understand how best to use them, we first need to know about the three ways in which heat energy can move: **conduction**, **convection** and **radiation**.

Conduction

When you first prod a fire with a metal poker, one end could get 'red hot' while the other end stays cool enough to hold. But after a while, the heat energy moves steadily along the poker, each bit of material being heated in turn by its neighbour. This is the way heat passes through *solids* – it is called **conduction**.

Metals are generally good **conductors** – and some are very good. A copper 'poker' would give you burnt fingers in minutes. Not all solids are good conductors. Plastic and wood are used in saucepan handles because they do *not* conduct heat well. Poor conductors are called **insulators**.

Heat moves in three different ways – which one will make these balloons rise?

▲ *A metal soon conducts heat all along its length – but liquids are very poor at conducting heat. The hot water at the top cannot transfer heat to melt the ice.*

boiling water at 100°C

gauze to trap ice

ice at 0°C does not melt

▲ *The heater is at the bottom of a kettle so that heat energy can be carried upwards by convection.*

Convection

Although liquids are poor conductors, they will let heat travel in a different way. This happens when a liquid (or a gas) is heated from below. First the liquid at the bottom is heated directly by *conduction*. This *hot* liquid **expands** and 'floats' up through the cooler liquid.

In this way, heat energy is carried up and away from the 'hot spot', into the cooler parts of the liquid (or gas).

This process is called **convection** – and this flow of liquid is called a **convection current**.

Radiation

Conduction and convection both need a material which can transfer heat energy – solids for conduction, liquids or gases for convection. So how come we feel heat from the sun, which reaches us through 150 million km of the empty vacuum of space? The answer is that the energy reaches us as **infrared radiation**, which is like light and radio waves. You can feel these infrared waves when you warm your hands in front of an electric fire. All objects radiate energy. The hotter they are, the more energy they radiate.

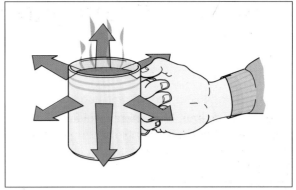

A mug of hot coffee radiates energy into the room – that's why it cools down.

Home heating on the move

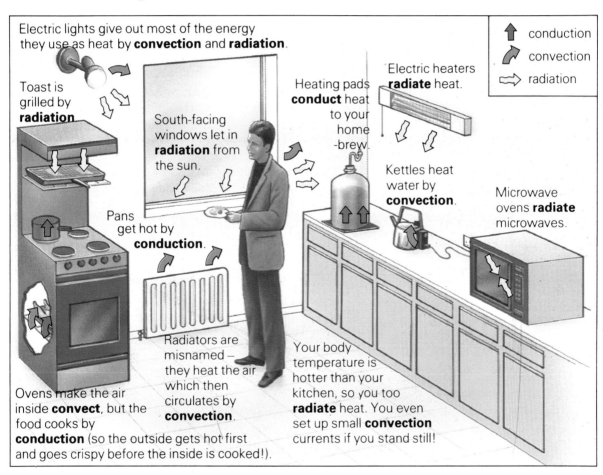

Electric lights give out most of the energy they use as heat by **convection** and **radiation**.

↑ conduction
↗ convection
⇨ radiation

Toast is grilled by **radiation**

South-facing windows let in **radiation** from the sun.

Pans get hot by **conduction**.

Radiators are misnamed – they heat the air which then circulates by **convection**.

Ovens make the air inside **convect**, but the food cooks by **conduction** (so the outside gets hot first and goes crispy before the inside is cooked!).

Heating pads **conduct** heat to your home-brew.

Electric heaters **radiate** heat.

Kettles heat water by **convection**.

Your body temperature is hotter than your kitchen, so you too **radiate** heat. You even set up small **convection** currents if you stand still!

Microwave ovens **radiate** microwaves.

---

1 What are the three ways in which heat can move?

2 **a** What materials (if any) are needed for each heat transfer?
b Describe how the heat energy moves in each case.

3 Why can't heat from the sun reach us by conduction or convection?

4 List examples of conduction, convection and radiation that you use in your home.

4 Stopping heat from moving

plastic/cork – good insulator, doesn't conduct heat away; stops convection of hot air above liquid; blocks radiation.

double-walled – allows vacuum to be made.

hard case – protects fragile glass walls.

hot drinks stay hot

(or cold drinks stay cold)

vacuum – no solid, liquid or gas, so there is no conduction and convection.

silver surfaces – reflects radiation back into flask.

seal point – where air was removed when making vacuum.

A vacuum flask can keep heat in – or keep it out – by stopping conduction, convection and radiation.

Marathon runners can get very cold when they stop running. 'Space blankets' help to stop them radiating heat energy.

Stopping conduction and convection

Like any gas, air is a very poor conductor. If it can be stopped from moving around (and so convecting), air can make a good and cheap insulator. That is how clothes and fur help to keep us and animals warm. Even the tiny hairs on our bodies stand up when we're cold, to try to trap more air and so keep us more insulated. A similar effect is given by air trapped between the sheets of paper used to wrap our fish and chips.

Other natural insulators, such as cork, trap air in tiny pockets or bubbles. Expanded polystyrene, fibre glass, string vests and foam rubber all insulate in this way.

Don't waste it!

Heat energy is only useful if it can be kept where it is wanted. If heat energy moves away from such places, it is wasted – and this can be expensive!

To insulate properly we have to stop all three methods of heat transfer. The classic example of this is the vacuum flask.

Stopping radiation

Matt black surfaces do not reflect light – they absorb it. They also absorb radiated heat energy. So objects with matt black surfaces are easy to heat up by radiation – they are **good absorbers** – which is why a black coat feels hot on a sunny day. But matt black surfaces are also **good radiators** of heat energy. If a black object is hotter than its surroundings, it will radiate heat energy and cool down very quickly.

In contrast, smooth, silver surfaces reflect light, which is why you can see your reflection in a mirror. In the same way, smooth, silver surfaces reflect radiated heat energy. This means that objects with silver surfaces are not easy to heat up by radiation – they are **poor absorbers**. But they are also **poor radiators**, so a hot silver object will not radiate heat energy very well and so will stay hot much longer.

That's why your Chinese take-away stays hot in its shiny aluminium container – the inside surface doesn't absorb much heat energy from the food, and the outside surface doesn't radiate much heat energy out.

'Space blankets' are thin silvery plastic sheets. These can help to keep in your body-heat if you are out in cold weather.

The fur of the arctic fox slows down convection – and its white colour reduces energy loss by radiation too!

Insulating materials for the home

Once insulated from the house, the loft gets cold. So water tanks and pipes must be **lagged** – wrapped in fibreglass or foam – to prevent the water from freezing.

Because heat rises by convection, much heat energy is lost through the roof. But a layer of fibreglass just 10cm thick can reduce that loss by more than three-quarters.

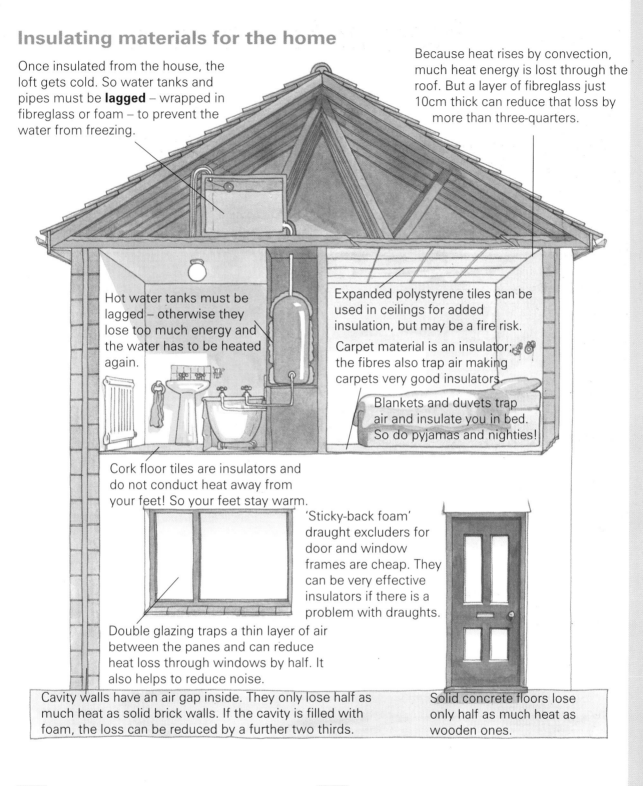

Hot water tanks must be lagged – otherwise they lose too much energy and the water has to be heated again.

Expanded polystyrene tiles can be used in ceilings for added insulation, but may be a fire risk.

Carpet material is an insulator; the fibres also trap air making carpets very good insulators.

Blankets and duvets trap air and insulate you in bed. So do pyjamas and nighties!

Cork floor tiles are insulators and do not conduct heat away from your feet! So your feet stay warm.

'Sticky-back foam' draught excluders for door and window frames are cheap. They can be very effective insulators if there is a problem with draughts.

Double glazing traps a thin layer of air between the panes and can reduce heat loss through windows by half. It also helps to reduce noise.

Cavity walls have an air gap inside. They only lose half as much heat as solid brick walls. If the cavity is filled with foam, the loss can be reduced by a further two thirds.

Solid concrete floors lose only half as much heat as wooden ones.

1 How does a vacuum flask stop conduction, convection and radiation?

2 Why does take-away food come in aluminium containers? Why does the food stay hot?

3 Make a list of the different insulators used to keep a house warm.

4 Draw a plan of your own home. Show how heat energy may escape and suggest ways to stop the heat loss in each case.

5 Energy in the home

What's is used for?

The main uses of energy in the home are for heating, lighting, cooking and for electrical appliances. The electrical appliances you use are up to you. But in Britain, everyone needs some form of heating, lighting and cooking. And there is more than one way of doing each.

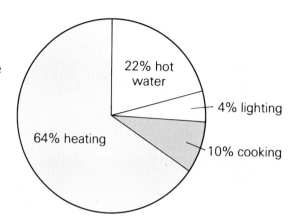

Energy used in the home for heating, cooking and lighting.

Which energy source?

Coal was once the main fuel used for home heating, but coal fires can be difficult to light and have to be 'topped up' with fresh coal at regular intervals. Coal fires also produce a lot of smoke and soot, plus gases that cause acid rain. Very little coal is used like this today.

coal
(cheap)

oil
(cheap)

natural gas

electricity
(cheap at night)

Oil has to be brought in in large tankers and then has to be stored safely at home. But central heating systems can then run automatically, with the oil piped in from the storage tank. Many homes (and more offices, schools and factories) use oil as their main heating fuel.

Gas was first piped into houses in the last century, for gas lighting. Today, most homes have 'natural gas' piped in. Gas is the most popular fuel for central heating systems, and is also widely used for cooking.

Electricity also comes directly into houses, through the 'mains' cables. It can be used directly for heating in ovens, kettles and electric fires. It can be expensive to heat a whole house like this, however. Electricity is also used for lighting and running 'electrical gadgets' – from vacuum cleaners to computers!

Different fuels used in the home.

£1 produces less electricity than other energy sources.

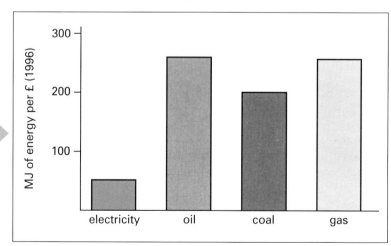

Why electricity?

We buy coal by the tonne, gas by the therm, oil by the gallon, and electricity by the **kilowatt hour**. This means it's not easy to compare these energy sources to see which is the cheapest. But if you work out the energy in each as the number of **megajoules** (MJ) which you get for each pound of money, you can see that electricity is in a class of its own – by far the dearest!

Despite the cost, we use so much electricity because it's just so convenient. It is easy to convert it into any other form of energy we might need – at the flick of a switch!

Spend money to save money! ◆H

It costs money to produce the heat energy needed to warm a home. In time, all of this heat escapes – that is why a home eventually gets cold. If any of this heat escapes too quickly, then money is wasted along with the heat. So even a small reduction in the amount of heat wasted can mean big savings.

Let's consider a home with a heating bill of £300 a year. If 10% of the heat can be kept in for longer, then the heating bill will be reduced by £30. But how much money should be spent on insulation? It all depends on which type of insulation is chosen...

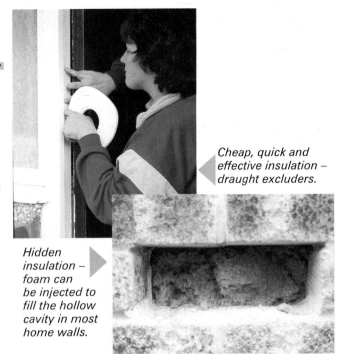

Cheap, quick and effective insulation – draught excluders.

Hidden insulation – foam can be injected to fill the hollow cavity in most home walls.

Heat escapes through...	Percentage of heat escaping	Cost of heat escaping	Possible insulation	Reduction in heat escaping	Cost of insulation	Years to recover cost	Comments
Walls	35%	£105	foam in cavity walls	35%→14%	£315	5	needs experts
Roof	25%	£75	fibre glass in loft	25%→5%	£180	3	cheap, easy to do
Draughts	15%	£45	draught excluders	15%→6%	£54	2	very chaep very easy
Windows	10%	£30	double glazing	10%→4%	£216 or £1800	12 or 100	do-it-yourself or expert fitted

More than just money

There are other considerations besides the cost. Many people like to have open fires instead of modern forms of heating. But a central heating system can be operated by timers which make heating a home very easy and convenient – the choice is yours!

1 Give two reasons why gas is such a popular fuel for home heating.

2 Why is electricity used so much, despite being so expensive?

3 Which form of insulation is cheapest and easiest to put in?

4 Make a list of the advantages and disadvantages of the different types of home heating.

5 If you had £400 to spend on insulation, how would you spend it? Explain your answer.

6 Explaining energy transfers

Everything is made of particles

Everything is made of particles that are always on the move!

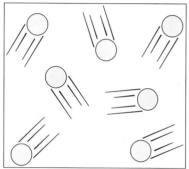

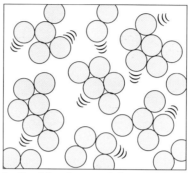

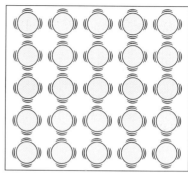

In a gas, the particles are separated and are whizzing about at high speed.

In liquids, the particles are packed closely together but they are still moving.

In solids the particles are closely packed and joined together. They cannot move out of position, but they are still vibrating.

Movement and temperature

How much the particles are moving depends on how hot the substance is. When you heat something up you are transferring energy to the particles. This makes them move faster. The higher the temperature, the faster the particles are moving on average.

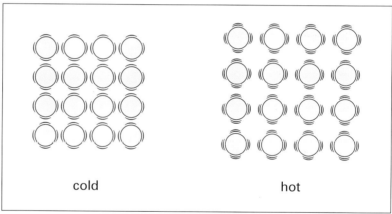

cold   hot

The faster the particles vibrate, the more they spread out – that's why things expand when they are heated.

Explaining conduction...

If you heat one end of a metal rod, the energy passes along the rod by conduction (see page 38). How can this happen?

All atoms have tiny charged particles called **electrons** whizzing around them. In metals, some of these electrons are 'loose' and can move from atom to atom. When you heat a metal, these 'loose' electrons move faster. This means they have more kinetic energy. They spread out from the atoms that are being heated directly, colliding with the nearby particles and making them move faster too. In this way, the energy spreads through the solid.

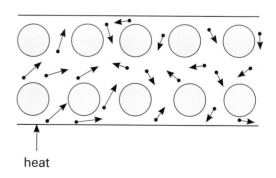

heat

... convection...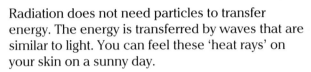

When the particles in a substance move more, they spread out a little, taking up a little more space – the substance **expands**. It now takes up a bigger volume but it still has the same mass, so its density goes down a little.

If you heat a liquid or gas from below, the hot part expands and so becomes less dense. This less dense material then floats up through the cooler, more dense material around it. Cooler material is drawn in to take its place, this is then heated and so starts to rise in its turn, and so on.

In this way, all of the liquid or gas is heated directly, as it swirls around in convection currents like this.

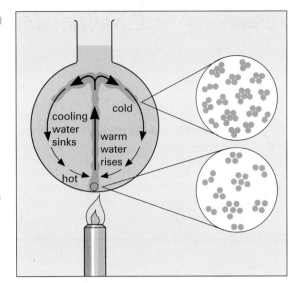

... and radiation

Radiation does not need particles to transfer energy. The energy is transferred by waves that are similar to light. You can feel these 'heat rays' on your skin on a sunny day.

You can detect radiation like this using sensors, too. A light sensor that is triggered by a 'white hot' piece of metal still shows a reading when the metal has cooled down enough to stop glowing.

Rough or matt black surfaces are good at absorbing radiation. The radiant energy makes the particles vibrate more – they get hotter. But black surfaces are also good radiators of radiation. If they are hotter than the surroundings they will give out radiation. When this happens, the particles slow down, and the material gets cooler.

Smooth silver surfaces do not absorb radiation; instead they reflect it away. But smooth silver surfaces are poor radiators too.

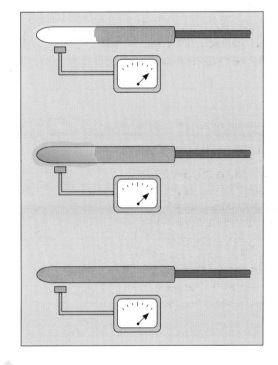

1 Describe what happens to the particles in a solid when it is heated.

2
  a Describe how energy is conducted along a metal rod.
  b Why are most non-metals poor conductors?

3
  a Why do most materials expand when heated?
  b Describe how a convection current develops when water is heated from below.

4 Some hot water tanks have immersion heaters near the top of the tank to give a small amount of hot water very quickly. How do they do this?

5 Why do you feel hot if you wear black clothes on a sunny day?

6 Why do marathon runners wrap themselves in silver blankets before and after a race?

7 Paying for electricity

How much energy?

How much electrical energy you use depends on the power of the electrical appliances you have, and how long they are switched on for.

Most electrical appliances have an information plate on them that gives important information including the **power rating** in **watts (W)**. Energy is measured in **joules (J)**. To find out the energy you use, you must multiply the power by the time in seconds.

energy (joules) = power (watts) × time (seconds)

For example, If you switch on a 100 W bulb for one minute:

energy = power × time = 100 W × 60 s = 600 J

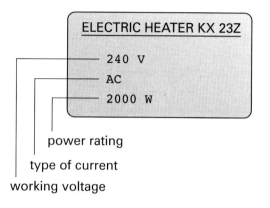

ELECTRIC HEATER KX 23Z

240 V — type of current
AC
2000 W — power rating

power rating
type of current
working voltage

The power ratings of some common appliances

bulb	100 W
radio	10 W
toaster	250 W
hairdrier	350 W
Hoover	500 W
kettle	2 kW
electric fire	3 kW

The 'unit' of electricity

As you can see from this example, a joule is rather a small amount of energy, compared to the amounts used at home for lighting and heating. The electricity suppliers use a much bigger unit called the **kilowatt hour**. This is the amount of energy used by a 1 kW (1000 W) electric fire in one hour. In joules:

energy = power × time = 1000 W × (60 × 60)s

= 3 600 000 J

= 3.6 megajoules (3.6 MJ)

Paying the bill

All the electricity coming into a house or flat passes through a special meter which records the number of kilowatt hour 'units' used. This meter is read every 3 months and a bill is prepared based on the number of 'units' that have been used.

One unit costs approximately 7p.

Example

meter reading	43 675 units
previous reading	42 063 units
used this quarter	1612 units

Cost = 1612 × 7p = 11 284p = £112.84

Electricity Bill

Customer: M STIRRUP

Current meter reading	43675
Previous meter reading	42063
Units used this quarter	1612
Cost per unit	£0.07
Payment due	£112.84

Running costs

You can use the cost of one 'unit' to work out the running costs of different electrical appliances. Some are very cheap: a small (10 W) radio could run for 100 hours for just 7p, while a 100 W light bulb could run for 10 hours.

Appliances using motors have 'mid range' costs. A 250 W food mixer could run for 4 hours, a 500 W vacuum cleaner for 2 hours for 7p.

Anything that uses electricity for heating will be more expensive. A 'one bar' (1 kW) fire will cost 7p per hour, while a 'three-bar' (3 kW) fire will cost 21p an hour. An electric cooker with all grills and hotplates full on might cost as much as much as 35p an hour.

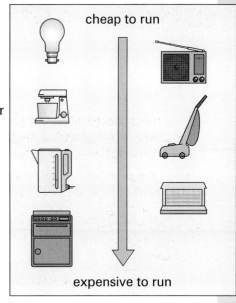

Value for money?

Electrical heaters are expensive to use, but they are convenient as you can just plug them in where you need them. They also make good use of the electricity, as nearly all the electrical energy is turned into useful heat energy.

This is not true of all electrical appliances. When you switch on a food mixer, for example, you want the electrical energy to turn into kinetic energy as the motor turns. But food mixers can be noisy, and the motor warms up as it runs. Some of the energy has turned into sound energy and heat energy instead. That means that it is 'wasted' as far as you are concerned.

Light bulbs are particularly bad from this point of view as you want the electricity to turn into light – but most of it actually turns into heat energy. For every pound you spend on electricity for lighting using ordinary light bulbs, you only get 8 pence-worth of light, as 92 pence-worth of the energy turns to 'wasted' heat energy!

Whatever the energy change, there is always some energy that does not end up in the form you want, and so is effectively 'lost'. This 'lost' energy usually ends up as heat energy, and so warms up the surroundings. In this form, it is too 'spread out' to be of any more use.

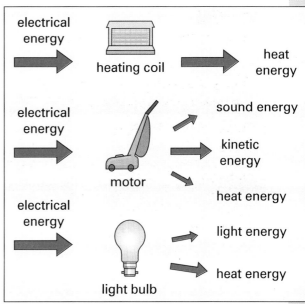

Some energy changes with their energy 'losses'.

---

1. How many joules of energy are used by:
   a. a 60 W bulb in 2 minutes?
   b. a 100 W bulb in one hour?
   c. a 1 kW fire in 20 minutes?

2. How many kilowatt hour 'units' are used by:
   a. a 100 W bulb for 1 day?
   b. a 500 W vacuum cleaner for half an hour?
   c. a 3 kW fire for 8 hours?

3. Work out the cost (to the nearest penny) for each of the examples given in question 2.

4. If the old meter reading was 96 423 and the new meter reading is 98 000, what will the bill be if electricity costs 7p a unit?

5. Fluorescent tubes give you 30 pence-worth of light for every pound you spend on electricity. Why do you think schools and offices use them instead of light bulbs?

8 Energy change efficiency

Efficiency... or not!

Electric heaters convert most of the electrical energy they use into 'useful' heat energy, while light bulbs change only a fraction of the electrical energy they use into 'useful' light (see page 46). Another way to put this is that electric heaters are **efficient** energy changers, while light bulbs are **inefficient** energy changers. You can work out the efficiency of any energy change using the formula:

$$\text{efficiency} = \frac{\text{useful energy output}}{\text{total energy input}} \times 100\%$$

Here are some examples.

For a bulb:

100 J of electrical energy gives only 8 J of light energy:

$$\text{efficiency} = \frac{8}{100} \times 100\% = 8\%$$

– that is, very inefficient!

Lift it up

An electric motor turns electrical energy into kinetic energy. If a motor is used to lift a bucket of water, for example, this kinetic energy is then turned into gravitational potential energy in the water.

To calculate the amount of potential energy that has been stored up, you can use the formula:

gravitational potential energy (p.e. in joules) =

weight (w in newtons) × height (h in metres)

For example, 10 kg of water has a weight of 100 N. If this is raised by 80 cm (0.8 m):

$$\text{p.e.} = w \times h = 100 \times 0.8 = 80\,\text{J}$$

If it took a 10 W electric motor 10 seconds to lift this water, the energy used by the motor would be:

$$\text{energy} = \text{power} \times \text{time} = 10\,\text{W} \times 10\,\text{s} = 100\,\text{J}$$

So the efficiency would be:

$$\text{efficiency} = \frac{\text{output (the p.e. gain)}}{\text{input (energy used by motor)}} \times 100\%$$

$$= \frac{80}{100} \times 100\%$$

$$= 80\%$$

Electric motors are designed to be efficient in this way.

This system converts electrical energy into gravitational potential energy.

Drop it back

If you let the bucket of water drop back, it will spin the motor as the gravitational potential energy turns back to kinetic energy. A motor spun like this will act as a generator, producing electricity as it turns. But ordinary motors are not designed to work this way, so they are not so efficient. You may only get 20 J of electricity from the 80 J of potential energy that are changed as the bucket of water falls. The remaining 60 J are effectively 'lost' from the system. They turn into unwanted heat energy.

$$\text{efficiency} = \frac{\text{electricity output}}{\text{loss of p.e. (input)}} = \frac{20}{80} \times 100\% = 25\%$$

Hydroelectric power stations work like the 'falling bucket' experiment. Falling water is used to turn a generator and make electricity (see page 53). Here the generators are designed to be as efficient as possible, however!

*You can measure the energy used by an electrical circuit directly by using a **joulemeter**. This works like a household electricity meter.*

Efficiency in the power station

In some power stations fossil fuels are burnt to make steam which spins generators and makes electricity.

The system is not very efficient. For every 100 J of stored chemical energy in the fuel that you start with, only 37 J of electrical energy are produced. That's just 37% efficient!

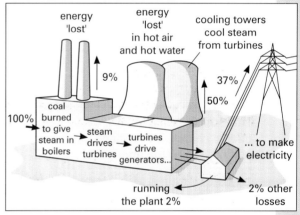

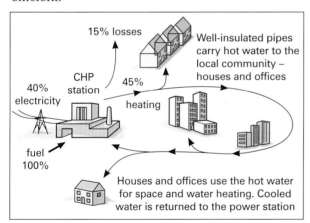

In a conventional power station, most of the wasted heat energy goes up the chimneys or cooling towers. But in a **combined heat and power** (CHP) plant it is used to make hot water, which can then be pumped out to heat factories, schools, hospitals or even homes. In this way up to 85% of the energy in the fuel can be put to good use, making it more than twice as efficient as a conventional power station.

---

1 Mrs Smith weighs 600 N. The shop lift takes her to the first floor which is 5m above the ground floor.
  a How much gravitational potential energy has she gained?
The lift motor is rated at 6 kW and the journey takes 10 seconds.
  b How much energy is used?
  c How efficient is this use of the lift?
  d Why do you think the efficiency is so low? (The lift takes up to 10 people.)

2 A cubic metre of water weighs 10 000 N.
  a If it falls 10 m, how much gravitational potential energy does it lose?
  b If this amount of falling water generates 90 kJ of electrical energy in a hydroelectric plant, how efficient is the system?

3 Draw pie charts for the energy outputs in a conventional power station and combined heat and power station. Clearly mark the 'useful' part.

9 What powers the power station

Power to the people

In an industrial country like Britain, there is a large demand for electricity. In all, there are 81 power stations (**generating plants**) in Britain. That's enough to power 500 million light bulbs!

Although these generating plants use different energy sources, most of them use a long 'energy chain' like this.

But is it efficient?

The trouble is that every energy change is less than perfect. Not all the energy released by the energy source ends up as electricity. A lot ends up as waste heat that goes up the chimneys and into the air.

For every 100 J of 'stored energy' that start the journey, 63 are wasted and only 37 J end up as electrical energy. Because of this, electrical energy, though very useful, is an expensive way to get our energy!

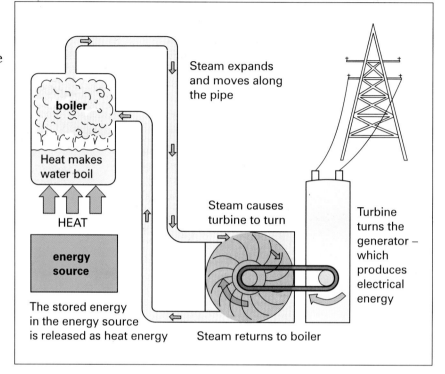

Steam expands and moves along the pipe

boiler

Heat makes water boil

HEAT

energy source

The stored energy in the energy source is released as heat energy

Steam causes turbine to turn

Steam returns to boiler

Turbine turns the generator – which produces electrical energy

The power station energy chain:

chemical ▶ heat ▶ movement ▶ electrical
energy   energy   energy   energy

Using fossil fuels

There is another problem with these power stations. Many of them use **fossil fuels** – coal, oil or gas. Fossils fuels are formed from the remains of plants or animals over millions and millions of years. The problem is that we are using them up a million times faster than they formed! In just a few decades, they will all run out, and they cannot be replaced. Fuels like this are called **non-renewable** fuels.

Some power stations use nuclear fuels instead of fossil fuels, but even these will run out eventually. Scientists need to find energy sources that will not run out.

How can they do this? Plants may have the answer...

Coal is a fossil fuel that formed from plants millions of years ago.

Plants trap sunlight

Plants are fuel factories! Plants use the energy from sunlight to build up chemicals such as sugar from carbon dioxide and water. This happens in the green leaves in a process called **photosynthesis**.

The plants do this for themselves, but animals like us 'steal' these chemicals for food, as they are energy stores – body fuels.

Plants also make wood in this way. Wood has been used as a fuel for thousands of years.

A fuel factory in action.

Burning wood

When you burn wood, you get the trapped sunlight energy back! Could burning wood be the answer to our energy needs?

Some forests should not be burnt! The rain forests are already in danger and so they must be protected. In any case, rainforests take too long to grow. If their wood was used, that would run out as well!

Grow your own

But some trees grow very fast. They can be planted as a crop – just like wheat or cabbages! Farmers can plant trees and harvest them for fuel year after year. This is a **renewable** source of energy that will never run out – as long as the sun shines!

Farmers are already growing trees as a fuel crop in Cornwall, and power stations there are being built to run on 'wood chip' fuel instead of coal or oil. Could this be the energy source of the future?

Rainforests should not be burnt!

1 List the energy changes that take place in a coal-burning power station.

2 Why is electricity such an expensive way to get energy at home?

3 a Name the fossil fuels.
  b What is the problem about using fossil fuels to make our electricity?

4 a In what way is a plant a 'fuel factory'?
  b Where do plants get the energy to do this?

5 You get lots of energy when you burn wood. Where did this energy come from originally?

6 How can trees be used to give a renewable source of fuel for power stations?

10 Supply and demand

Keep going, don't stop

Electrical energy is very useful, but it is expensive to produce. One reason for this is that oil- or coal-burning plants have to be kept running 24 hours a day! If shut down for any time, the boilers have to be cooled slowly and carefully to avoid damage. A period of maintenance is then needed, followed by an equally slow warm-up period when they are put back into service.

The National Grid

Over a long term, the slow cooling and start up of plants is not too much of a problem. This is because Britain has an energy 'highway' system – the **National Grid**. For example, as overall demand falls in the summer, a plant at Southampton can be shut down for a few months. In the meantime that region can 'feed' off the rest of the National Grid.

'I want it now!'

The main difficulty in organising a national distribution of electricity is the ever-changing demand for electricity. At night, most of the country stops work, goes to bed – and demand for electricity drops like a stone!

But the generating plants can't just be switched off, so what can be done with all the 'surplus' electricity at night? There are two main ways of tackling the problem – either use more electricity at night or build power stations that respond more quickly.

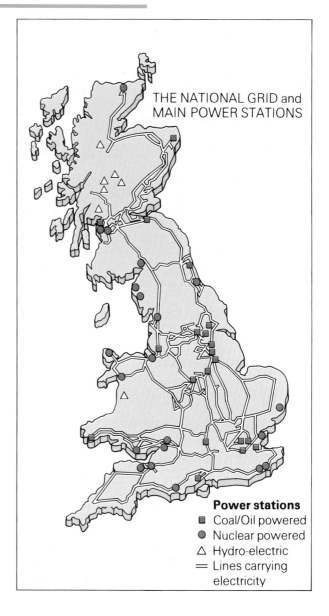

THE NATIONAL GRID and MAIN POWER STATIONS

Power stations
- ■ Coal/Oil powered
- ● Nuclear powered
- △ Hydro-electric
- ═ Lines carrying electricity

Buy now, use later!

As many people use electricity for home heating, it's a good idea to try to store the electricity as heat. **Night storage heaters** are connected to a separate payment meter that only works at night. Because electricity is plentiful at night, it is sold off at 'bargain' rates! Night storage heaters use this cheap electricity to heat up special bricks inside the heater. This heat stays stored in the bricks all through the night. This stored energy is then slowly released into the house the following day. But despite plenty of publicity, this has not really made much of a dent in the problem. This is because the main demand for electricity is when people are awake – working, cooking and watching TV. There is no way most people will do these things all night instead!

Hydroelectric plants

These do not use an energy source which produces heat – so they do not have long cool-down and warm-up periods.

Water high in the mountains has lots of gravitational potential energy which turns to kinetic energy as it flows downhill. This can be harnessed to turn turbines, spin generators and so produce electricity.

In countries with high mountains and lots of rain, like Scotland and Wales, high valleys are often dammed and their water is channelled through pipes to turbines to generate electricity.

A hydroelectric plant can be shut down or started up in minutes rather than days so they are very useful plants to include in the National Grid. Hydroelectric plants in mountainous areas of Britain can be used to supply electricity all over the country. Another advantage to these plants is that the rain comes free! So not only are they flexible but they are cheap to run too!

The natural conditions here in the north of Scotland – high valleys and plenty of rain – are ideally suited to the building of hydroelectric plants like this one.

A combined effort

The Cruachan Dam holds back a vast lake high in the hills of Argyll, Scotland. This is the potential energy storehouse. It is added to by rainfall over the hills (which is common!) but it also has another way of filling.

During the peak daytime demand in electricity, the plant acts as in a 'traditional' hydroelectric plant. Water falls through tubes the size of railway tunnels to the generating hall – a great cavern cut from solid granite deep in the mountain. There it is used to drive the special turbine-dynamos which then feed electricity into the National Grid – all within minutes of starting the plant up.

But the water does not flow away – instead it is kept in a lower reservoir. At night, the National Grid is full of surplus electricity, but few people are awake to use it. Now the machinery goes into reverse. The turbine-dynamos become motor-pumps which push water back up into the upper reservoir – storing some of the unwanted electrical energy as potential energy. This water can then be used to generate electricity in the normal way – such as during the next day when everyone is awake and at work.

At what times will sudden increases mean that the National Grid will need electricity from Cruachan? ▼

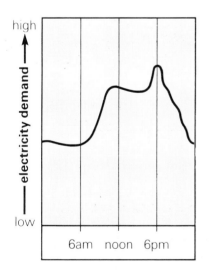

1 Why can't power stations simply be switched on and off depending on demand?

2 Why are electricity companies keen to sell 'cheap' electricity at night?

3 **a** What is the big advantage of a hydroelectric power station?
   b If they are so good, why don't we have more of them?

4 Describe how a 'pumped storage' system works.

11 Back to the sun

What's the alternative?

With non-renewable fossil fuels running out, one day we will have to rely on other sources of energy. It may seem a long way off, but if we start using other sources of energy *now*, the remaining fossil fuels will be used less quickly. The other sources of energy may be able to fill the role of a fossil fuel as an *energy* source. But most of them will not be able to produce a ready supply of *chemicals* to make plastics and other materials. This is why we must use our remaining fossil fuels wisely.

Nuclear power is one option, but what other sources of energy are available in the world around us? We must look for renewable energy sources that will not run out.

Solar energy

Vast amounts of energy pour down onto the earth from the sun every day - a staggering 15 000 times as much as our technological society uses! The problem is, of course, that it is spread out over the entire 'daylight' face of the globe. It also tends to be at a peak where it is least needed – in the desert and at sea. Even so, it can be the equivalent of a one-bar electric fire on every square metre of the surface. No wonder too much sun can burn!

Trapping the sun's energy

Solar furnaces use mirrors to concentrate the sunlight onto one spot. This can produce temperatures of up to 4000°C, which can be used to drive a generating plant, or directly as a heat source for industry.

Solar panels

A 'gentler' way of using solar energy involves solar panels to heat our homes. These use sunlight to heat water in long pipes on the roof. These are painted black to absorb the energy (see page 40).

Even in cloudy Britain, this method could keep a house warm (and even provide hot water) for most of the year. In midwinter, it would need to be supplemented with other forms of heating, but it would still keep the fuel bills down!

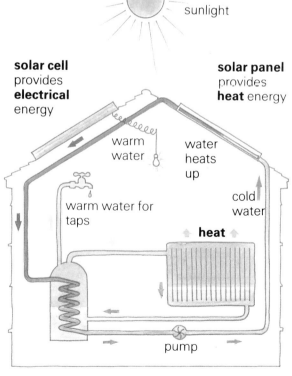

sunlight

solar cell provides **electrical** energy

solar panel provides **heat** energy

warm water

water heats up

warm water for taps

cold water

heat

pump

Solar cells

How can we tap into this 'free' energy to make electricity? Many things use **solar cells**, which produce electrical energy directly from sunlight. You may have seen calculators that are powered in this way. The problem is that it is very expensive to make large solar cells that can provide enough electricity to turn motors or heat buildings, for example.

One place that this is not a problem is in space! Communications satellites cost millions of pounds to build, and then millions more to launch them. The heavier they are, the more it costs to blast them into orbit around the earth. They need a reliable yet lightweight source of energy to keep them working day after day, year after year. They use huge banks of solar cells which are unfolded in orbit and pointed towards the sun. Their high initial cost is balanced out by the savings made in putting them in orbit, compared to other, heavier energy sources.

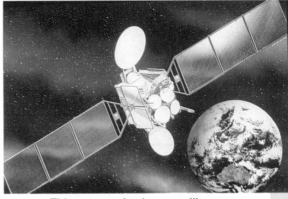

This communications satellite uses solar cells.

Plant power!

Plants absorb energy from sunlight and lock it up in chemicals. Scientists in the USA are developing a type of cactus that produces an oily sap which can be refined like crude oil. In Brazil, oil is scarce but sugar cane grows in abundance. The sugar is fermented to make dilute alcohol. This is concentrated by distillation to give industrial alcohol. This is then used in cars as '**gasohol**', instead of petrol!

Using the weather

A large proportion of the solar energy heats up the air, causing it to move around as strong winds. The energy in wind can be seen by the scale of destruction left by a hurricane. The **wind** has also been used for centuries to grind corn and to pump water. Modern windmills use propeller-like blades which drive generators and so generate electricity. These may seem a perfect, environmentally-friendly answer to our needs for electricity. There are now some 'wind farms' in use on windy ridges in the south-west of England. But if you wanted to replace an ordinary power station by a wind-farm like this, it would have to be vast! Would people be quite so happy with wind-generators if the landscape was covered with them?

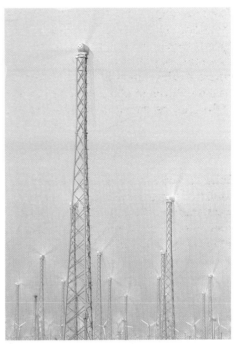

This vast wind-farm in California, USA provides some of the electricity used by the city of Los Angeles.

1. List *five* alternatives to fossil fuels. Include one that provides a useful chemical.

2. a Why are solar cells not always a 'practical solution'?
   b Why is this not a problem for satellites?

3. How does a solar furnace work?

4. How can the weather be a source of energy?

5. Why can't all power stations be replaced by wind-farms?

12 Moon and earth power!

Tidal power

Anything that is moving has kinetic energy which, in theory at least, can be turned into electrical energy. Moving water and waves caused by the wind can be used to generate electricity on a relatively small scale, but much larger water movements are caused by the pull of the moon – the **tides**. Twice a day the sea level around the coastline rises and falls by several metres, moving billions of tonnes of water up and down. This moving water can be used to spin turbines and drive generators. The potential for electricity production is enormous – and it will never run out!

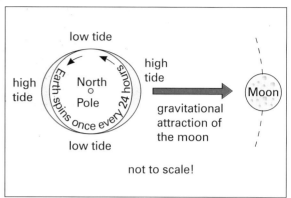

The tides are produced by the gravitational pull of the moon (and to a lesser extent the sun).

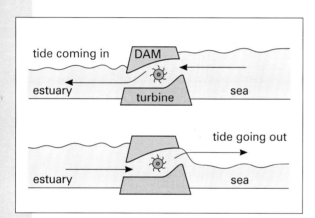

The Rance estuary

Some of this energy has been tapped in the Rance estuary, near St Malo in Brittany, France. The Rance estuary is a funnel-shaped inlet similar to (but smaller than) the Thames estuary in England. At high tide water flowed in from the open sea, and at low tide it flowed out again.

The estuary now has a barrage (long dam) built across it to restrict this flow. When the tide comes in, it has to force its way through turbines, which spin generators to produce electricity. When the tide goes out, the water flows back, spinning the turbines the other way and generating more electricity.

The Severn barrage?

Britain has one of the best sites in the world for such a tidal power station. The tides are funnelled into the long narrow estuary between south Wales and south-west England. If a barrage was built across this, the moving water could be used to generate enormous amounts of electricity with no fuel costs!

Unfortunately there are many problems with this scheme. Building the barrage would be an incredibly difficult and expensive project – similar in scale to the Channel Tunnel. It would stop shipping using the estuary. It would also have a major environmental impact on life in the estuary, as fish such as salmon would not be able to migrate freely from the sea to the rivers to spawn. There are no simple solutions!

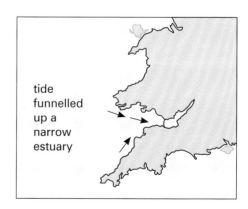

Geothermal energy

Another possible source of energy is the earth itself. As you go deeper into the crust of the earth, the temperature rises. This makes life hot and sticky for deep miners – but it is also another source of renewable energy that we can exploit.

In some places there are very hot rocks quite close to the surface – hot enough to boil water. In Yellowstone Park in Wyoming, USA, groundwater is boiled by these rocks and is forced up and out as **geysers**.

It is possible to tap this **geothermal** energy by driving boreholes deep into the rocks. Cold water is pumped down into the hot rocks, where it gets so hot that it boils. The steam then forces its way back up to the surface through other boreholes. It is then collected and used to drive turbines and spin generators, just as it would in a conventional power station.

There she blows! Uncontrolled geothermal power in action as the 'Old Faithful' geyser erupts. ▶

Where does this energy come from?

If you could slice the earth in half, it would look a bit like a soft-boiled egg! The thin crust covers hot and soft rock, which in turn surrounds a molten core. Why is the earth so hot inside, like this?

The earth contains many radioactive elements such as uranium in its rocks. As they slowly break down over millions of years, they release energy into the earth. But the crust of the earth acts like a blanket, insulating the rocks beneath and trapping the heat energy. So the inside of the earth is acting like an enormous but very slow nuclear reactor! (see page 59)

In Mexico, New Zealand, Italy and Iceland geothermal power stations like this are in use. ▶

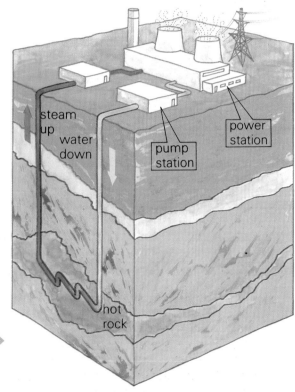

1 Describe how the moon creates the tides.

2 **a** What kind of energy does tidal water have when it has been lifted up at high tide?
   b What kind of energy does it have as it falls to a lower level when the tide goes out?

3 How is the tidal energy tapped in the Rance estuary in France?

4 Make a list of the benefits and drawbacks of building a barrage across the Severn estuary to generate electricity.

5 How is the energy in hot rocks extracted and turned into electricity in a geothermal power station?

6 Where did all the heat energy inside the earth come from?

13 Nuclear energy

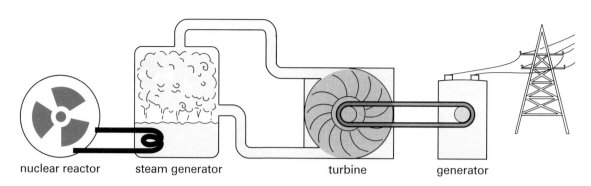

nuclear reactor   steam generator   turbine   generator

Nuclear power stations

Most power stations work by boiling water and using the steam produced to spin turbines and so turn generators. In conventional power stations, the water is heated by burning fossil fuels: coal, oil or gas. In nuclear power stations, the water is boiled in a different way, but the steam produced is then used in the same way, to spin turbines and so turn generators.

radioactive → ENERGY   smaller atoms

decay

Uranium – a large, unstable atom

The difference is in the way that nuclear fuels produce heat energy. They do not burn like coal, oil or gas. Instead, they break down on their own by a process called **radioactive decay**. This produces vast amounts of heat energy, but can be difficult to control and produces a lot of dangerous **radioactive waste**.

About 10% of British electricity is produced in this way. In some countries, such as France, the figure is much higher. The advantage is that whereas fossil fuels will run out in just a few decades, the reserves of nuclear fuels are much larger.

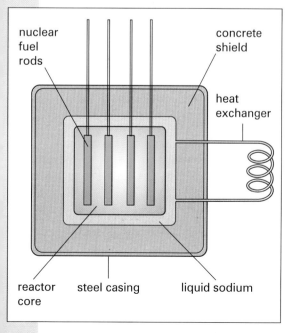

nuclear fuel rods

concrete shield

heat exchanger

reactor core   steel casing   liquid sodium

How does it work?

Everything is made up of atoms. Normally, these atoms do not change. When you burn a fuel, the atoms just rearrange themselves, combining with oxygen from the air. But some atoms, such as uranium and plutonium, are unstable and naturally break down. When this happens, they split into two smaller atoms, giving off vast amounts of energy. This type of radioactive decay is called **nuclear fission**.

At the core of a nuclear power station is the **nuclear reactor**. In this, rods of specially prepared uranium or plutonium are brought close together. This sets off a reaction which generates vast amounts of heat energy. This is then carried away from the reactor core by liquid sodium, which is then used to boil the water, and so on.

Because these nuclear reactions produce harmful **nuclear radiation**, the reactor has to be surrounded by great thicknesses of concrete and steel. The whole process has to be carefully controlled to keep it working safely.

Nuclear problems

Nuclear fuels can produce vast amounts of energy, so why don't we use more of them? The answer is complicated, but one reason is that these same nuclear reactions are responsible for the horrors of nuclear weapons, such as those that destroyed Hiroshima. We know that nuclear radiation can kill in large doses, but even at low doses it can cause cancer and other problems.

In power stations, this enormous power and its dangerous radiation are carefully controlled, but accidents can happen. There have been radiation leaks at nuclear power plants all over the world. In the worst accident so far, a serious fire at the Chernobyl plant in Russia caused a very large leak of radioactive material.

▲ A radioactive cloud spread out from the Chernobyl plant after the 1986 incident.

Nuclear waste

There is also a great problem about what to do with the waste material from nuclear power stations, as it is still highly radioactive. Some of it can be reprocessed into fresh nuclear fuel, but the rest has to be stored safely for hundreds or maybe even thousands of years. There is an international debate about how to do this. Bury it in deep mines? Dump it in the sea? Fire it into space? All these methods have been considered.

Even the power stations themselves are a problem. They were expensive to build but, once running, produced relatively cheap electricity. However, many have now reached the end of their 'working lives'. Their reactors and all the protective concrete are now highly radioactive, and it will cost a vast amount of money to make them safe. These high 'decommissioning' costs were not considered when the reactors were first built.

Trawsfynydd power station in Wales has now closed down and has to be made safe.

Back to the sun?

The sun is a gigantic nuclear reactor too, but it works in a different way. In the sun, small hydrogen atoms are fused together to make helium. This **fusion** reaction also produces vast amounts of energy, but the materials themselves are not radioactive. H-bombs use this fusion reaction, but scientists have not found a way to control it for generating electricity yet. If (or when) they do, the energy crisis will be over.

1 In what way are nuclear power stations 'steam powered'?

2 How do nuclear fuels differ from fossil fuels in the way they are used to heat water?

3 Why do nuclear reactors have to be surrounded with steel and concrete?

4 Why don't we simply switch to nuclear power stations as the fossil fuels run out?

5 It used to be thought that nuclear power produced 'cheap' electricity. Why is that not the case?

6 How might the sun hold the key to our future energy needs?

14 The nuclear debate

A tricky question

The nuclear debate has no easy answers. It is related to how we use energy now – and how we plan to use it in the future. The important thing is to understand exactly what both sides are talking about. . .

WE NEED IT!
Fossil fuels will run out. 'Alternative' energy sources are unproven on a large scale. We have large amounts of nuclear fuels already, and we know that it can provide all the energy we need. Once fusion is perfected, we will have limitless energy at our disposal!

STRICT LAWS
The laws are very strict about the levels of radiation allowable in nuclear plants. There is often more radiation in places such as Dartmoor or Aberdeen, which are built on granite.

DEMAND IS INCREASING
More and more energy is being used. People want a more comfortable lifestyle.

IT'S CHEAP
Nuclear reactors in Britain produce electricity more cheaply than 'traditional' power stations.

IT IS SAFE
Even including Chernobyl, there have been fewer accidents and injuries to workers in nuclear plants than in 'traditional' power stations. Look how dangerous coal mining is by comparison! What about the miners killed by accidents and by lung disease? The chance of a major accident at a nuclear power plant in Britain is tiny. Whenever problems have arisen, the built-in safety systems have always worked. Chernobyl was the results of a whole series of 'human errors' that could never have happened here. In fact, Chernobyl has so highlighted the dangers that it will probably never happen again anywhere in the world.

IT'S ALL UNDER CONTROL
If all the electricity used by one person in their entire life was generated using nuclear fuels, the total amount of waste fuel would be about the size of a cricket ball! From a coal-fired plant, there would be tonnes of toxic chemical waste to dispose of – not to mention the nasty waste gases and the 'acid rain' they produce.

TERRORISTS COULD USE ANYTHING
A bucket of cyanide from the local factory thrown into the reservoir could kill thousands, too! Unfortunately, terrorists could use almost anything if they wanted to. It's something we have to live with, and try and guard against.

Organise a 'nuclear debate' in your class.
Each side should prepare its
case in advance. Use newspaper
stories to support your ideas.

WE DON'T NEED IT!
The 'alternative' energy sources
have not had as much money spent
on their development as the
nuclear reactors. If we conserve
our fossil fuels, there will be
plenty of time to perfect the new sources.
And they do no harm to the
environment. What's more,
they will last forever – and are free!

DANGEROUS RAYS!
Nasty rays come from radioactive
materials like nuclear fuel and
waste. These can cause cancer and
other long-term problems.

CUT DEMAND!
It's easy, just get people
to insulate their homes.
That would reduce demand.

NO IT'S NOT
The latest coal-fired power stations will be
cheaper – and we've still got lots of
coal left. Rivers, wind and tides can provide
cheap *safe* power too!

IT IS DANGEROUS!
However good the system, there is always the possibility of human error,
as Chernobyl showed only too clearly. It may not have gone up like an
atomic bomb, but it spewed its radioactive waste into the atmosphere. It
caused untold damage to the local environment. It also spread with the
winds across frontiers and seas. It fell with the rain on Welsh hills,
contaminating the sheep and making their meat inedible for many
months. And who knows what the long-term effects will be? How many
will die untimely deaths of cancer? Will the lives of children yet unborn be
affected? The risks are just too great to take.

DANGEROUS WASTE!
The waste from nuclear reactors
remains dangerous for hundreds of
years or more. Storage problems
are bad enough now, but if we went
over to nuclear fuels altogether
we would be buried in nuclear
waste. There is much more than
just waste fuel – there's disused
equipment, tonnes upon tonnes of it,
all radioactive. How could we leave
such a menace to our children and our
childrens' children?

TERRORISTS COULD USE IT
Nuclear waste contains plutonium.
This is also used to make atomic
bombs! What is there to stop a
terrorist group getting hold of
this and making a bomb of their
own? Or spreading it around the
cities to make them uninhabitable?

1 In central heating systems, water is heated in a 'boiler', by burning gas or oil. This hot water is then piped around the house.

a What energy change is occurring in the boiler?

Some of this very hot water is used to heat up a separate 'hot water supply' for washing. The diagram shows how the hot water in the tank is heated.

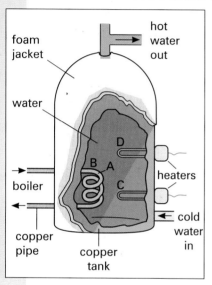

foam jacket
hot water out
water
D
B A
C
heaters
boiler
cold water in
copper pipe
copper tank

b How does the heat energy get from A to B?

c How does this then heat up all the water in the tank?

This tank also has two identical electrical heaters, which can be used to give hot water when the main central heating system is switched off.

d When heater C is switched on, what energy change is occurring?

e How does C heat up the tank of water?

If heater D only is switched on, you get hot water much more quickly than with C, but you only get half as much. It costs about 25p to heat up the full tank of water using the electric heater.

f Think of two reasons why you may want to use heater D only.

g Why does heater D only heat up the 'top half' of the tank?

Most hot water tanks are covered with a thick layer or jacket of foamed plastic.

h Why is this outer layer or jacket important?

i How does it work?

2 If you keep tropical frogs in a tank, you have to keep them warm. This can be done by using a hood with a low power light bulb in it.

a How does a light bulb help to keep the tank warm?

For every 100J of electrical energy used by the bulb, you only get 8J of light.

b How much heat energy do you get?

A light bulb is only 8% efficient as a source of light.

c How efficient is it as a heater?

John thought he'd save money by replacing the light bulb in his tank with a fluorescent tube, as the advert said he would get four times as much light for the electrical energy he used.

d Why should he be worried about his frogs if the weather turns cold?

3 Sally weighs 400 N.

a How much gravitational potential energy does she store in her body when she climbs up the stairs to the first floor, which is 10 m above the ground floor?

Sometimes Sally takes the lift to the first floor.

b How much gravitational potential energy does she store when she goes to the first floor by the lift?

The lift uses a 10 kW motor and takes 4 seconds to reach the first floor.

c How much energy does it take to do this?

d How efficient is the lift when it carries Sally to the first floor?

The lift can take five people at the same time, with a total weight of 2000 N. It still takes 4 seconds to get to the first floor.

e How efficient is the lift when it is fully loaded like this?

f If Sally can climb the stairs in 10 seconds, how much useful power does she generate?

4 Farmer Goodlife has decided to become self-sufficient for energy on his farm on the south-west coast of England. He needs a renewable fuel source that he can use for cooking and heating, but he will also need to find a way to generate electricity for lighting and running his washing machine, refrigerator and so on.

a Suggest as many ways as you can that he could become 'self-sufficient' like this. For each idea, decide whether it would be easy or hard to do, and whether it would be relatively cheap or very expensive.

He decided to build a solar panel to provide hot water and help to keep the farm warm.

At first he used shiny new copper pipe pinned onto a black board and connected up to the water system.

b This did not work very well. Why not? After some thought, he covered the black board with silver foil and painted the copper pipe matt black before pinning it back in place. Finally, he covered the panel with two sheets of glass, with a small air gap between them. It now worked very well indeed.

c Explain how each of the changes he made helped to improve the way his solar panel worked.

5 Large towns have many problems, but two important ones are:
i) how to get rid of all the waste that people throw away, and
ii) how to provide enough electricity to meet the demand.
Many local authorities are now looking to a solution that helps to solve both of these problems. Conventional power stations burn fuel in a furnace to produce heat energy to make the steam that turns the turbines and spins the generators. So why not burn the rubbish as a fuel in a power station? Much of the rubbish we throw away is either paper (made from wood) or plastic. Both of these contain a lot of stored energy.

a How does burning waste like this help to solve two problems that are faced by local authorities?

b How do wood and plastic compare to coal and oil in terms of the stored energy they contain?

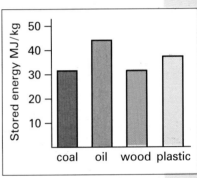

c How does burning waste help to 'buy time' before the fossil fuels run out?

Burning household waste like this can lead to the release of tiny amounts of chemicals called dioxins into the air. These chemicals are deadly poisonous. They are formed in tiny amounts like this whenever wood is burnt, such as on bonfire night. Scientists calculated that burning rubbish in well run power stations produces only one thousandth of the amount of dioxins that would be a health hazard. But these power stations are often built in urban areas, as that makes it easy to collect the rubbish to burn. Some people are worried that a source of pollution like this is built 'on their doorstep'.

d List the advantages and disadvantages of burning rubbish as a fuel.

e A rubbish-burning power station is going to be built in your area. Write a letter to the local paper, either in support of the power station or against it. Support your point of view with clear arguments, countering any opposing views where possible.

Index

NEW MODULAR SCIENCE
for GCSE

MODULE — *Humans as Organisms*

Spread

Cover photograph *Start of the London marathon*

1 This is your life

What is special about living organisms?

What makes living organisms different from non-living things? You can find the answer to this question by examining what organisms *do* and the *processes* that take place inside them. Look at these photographs. How can you tell which are living organisms and which are not?

This crystal grows by using the materials that surround it. Is it living material?

What does this marmot have in common with the flower it is eating? In what ways do they differ?

Are these pebbles or beans? How could you tell which could be living material?

What changes take place when something dies?

Keeping you alive

You are an example of a living organism. Like all living organisms you are able to carry out seven **life processes** that keep you alive. These processes take place not only in the human body but in all organisms – animals and plants.

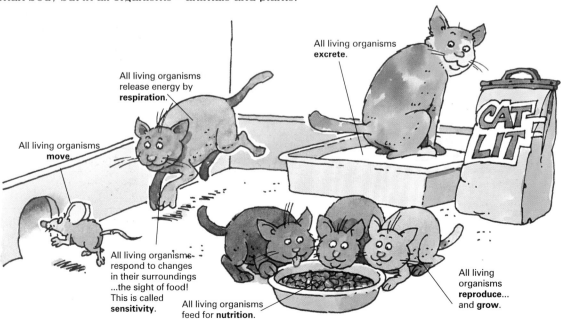

All living organisms release energy by **respiration**.

All living organisms **excrete**.

All living organisms **move**.

All living organisms respond to changes in their surroundings ...the sight of food! This is called **sensitivity**.

All living organisms feed for **nutrition**.

All living organisms **reproduce**... and **grow**.

Living building blocks

Your body, like all other organisms, is made up from millions of tiny **cells** in the same sort of way as a house is made of bricks – cells are the building blocks of your body. The cells making up each part of your body look similar because they are **specialised** to carry out a particular job. Cells come in different shapes and sizes but can you see any features that they have in common?

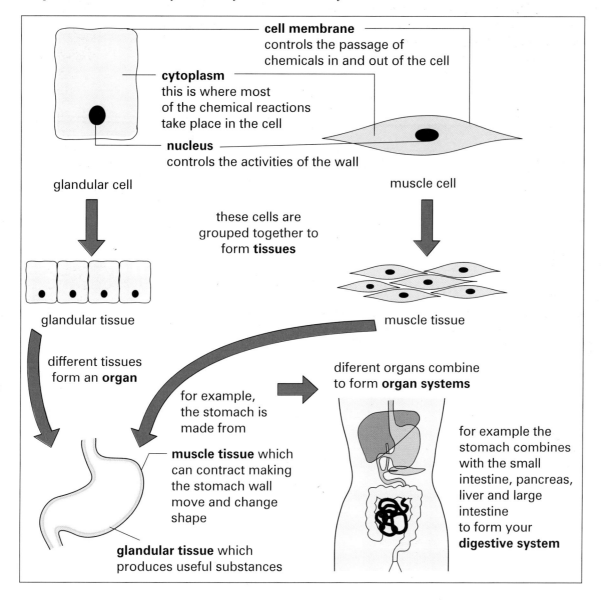

cell membrane
controls the passage of chemicals in and out of the cell

cytoplasm
this is where most of the chemical reactions take place in the cell

nucleus
controls the activities of the wall

glandular cell

muscle cell

these cells are grouped together to form **tissues**

glandular tissue

muscle tissue

different tissues form an **organ**

diferent organs combine to form **organ systems**

for example, the stomach is made from

muscle tissue which can contract making the stomach wall move and change shape

glandular tissue which produces useful substances

for example the stomach combines with the small intestine, pancreas, liver and large intestine to form your **digestive system**

---

1 Make a copy of this table and then complete it to show some human organ systems.

2 Name the structures that are usually present in all cells.

3 Find out which **two** structures are often found in plant cells but never in animal cells.

System	Examples of organs
circulatory system	heart, arteries, --------, -----------
-----------	brain, eyes, ears
digestive system	--------, ---------, --------

2 Healthy eating

Chemicals for dinner!

Do you have any idea what is in the food you eat? Your food provides you with the energy and different chemicals that you need to keep your body working properly. Scientists divide these chemicals into three main types: carbohydrates, fats and proteins.

Look at the table below to find out which foods contain carbohydrates, fats and proteins. Can you find any foods that you eat a lot?

Carbohydrates	Fats	Proteins
High content		
RICE, Biscuits, CRISPS	CRISPS	
BAKED BEANS, Potatoes, Cheese	Cheese	BAKED BEANS, CRISPS, Biscuits, Lentils
Low content		
	BAKED BEANS, MILK, RICE	MILK, RICE

The body's fuel

Carbohydrates are your body's main fuel. They are to your body what petrol is to a car. The energy contained in carbohydrates can be released quickly and used by your body, especially by your muscles. The more active you become the more you will use carbohydrate to supply the energy. For example, when you are running, your body is fuelled almost entirely from carbohydrates. Because you cannot store much carbohydrate in your body you need to eat enough of them daily.

Butter, margarine, meat and most fried foods contain a lot of fat.

Stores of energy

Fats contain more than twice the amount of energy that carbohydrates do but their energy cannot be released quickly. This means that they make good energy stores. The excess food that you eat is stored as fat. Your body can store an almost unlimited amount and use it again later.

The body's building materials

Proteins provide the raw materials that your body needs to build new cells and repair damaged ones. It is essential to include some protein in your diet to provide your body with a regular supply of growth material.

Meat, eggs, cheese, beans and nuts all contain proteins.

The hungry and the greedy

You need to eat the right amounts of food to remain fit and healthy. Eating too little, eating too much or eating the wrong kinds of food can result in **malnutrition** – bad nutrition. In some developing countries malnutrition is a constant problem because it is difficult to obtain a variety of foods, or even enough food.

Malnutrition occurs in developed countries as well, but the main reason is *eating too much*. Over 40% of adults in the UK are overweight and are likely to suffer health problems as a result.

The tables below each picture show what three people eat in a typical day. Who has the best diet and why?

Daily food intake provides:	
Energy	18 600 J
Carbohydrate	270 g
Fat	180 g
Protein	58 g

Daily food intake provides:	
Energy	9 300 J
Carbohydrate	196 g
Fat	48 g
Protein	28 g

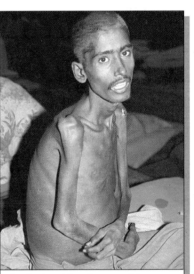

Daily food intake provides:	
Energy	2 100 J
Carbohydrate	45 g
Fat	2 g
Protein	6 g

1 a Which *two* diets in the pictures above are likely to cause health problems?

b Explain how each of these two diets can be improved.

2 The pie charts opposite show the diets of two 12-year-old girls. One girl lives in the UK and the other in Mali, a drought-prone African country. Explain which girl has the healthier diet.

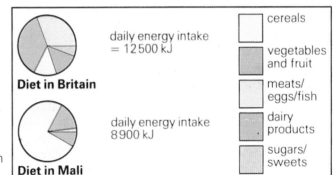

daily energy intake = 12 500 kJ

Diet in Britain

daily energy intake 8 900 kJ

Diet in Mali

cereals

vegetables and fruit

meats/ eggs/fish

dairy products

sugars/ sweets

3 Cutting food down to size

Getting food to where it is needed

What happens to food after you have chewed it and swallowed it? When it leaves your mouth it goes to your stomach and to other parts of your **digestive system**. The job of this system is to break down food into small molecules so that it can pass into your bloodstream.

Sometimes during hospital treatment patients get the food their bodies need without having to eat and digest anything. The foods they need go directly from a drip feed into their bloodstream. These foods are then taken to all the cells of the body. These drips often contain glucose, a simple sugar which will dissolve in the blood. Glucose provides the energy patients need to get better.

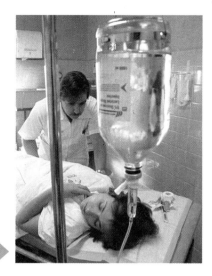

Glucose from this bottle flows down a drip feed, through a needle in the patient's arm and passes into their blood.

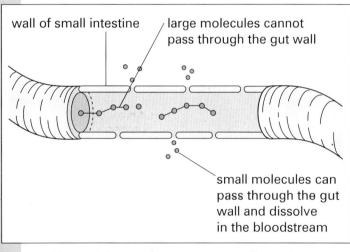

wall of small intestine

large molecules cannot pass through the gut wall

small molecules can pass through the gut wall and dissolve in the bloodstream

Simple foods

Once substances are in your blood they can travel to every cell. The food you eat must get from your gut into the blood vessels that surround it.

But your food is not usually made up from small molecules that can dissolve in blood. For example, starch is a very large insoluble molecule. It has to be broken down into smaller molecules before it can pass out of your gut and dissolve in your blood.

Small molecules like glucose and amino acids can pass out of your gut and into your bloodstream.

Breaking down your food

Your body produces special substances that can help to break down the food you eat. These substances are called **enzymes**. The enzymes in your gut break down the large molecules in your food to small molecules. For example, starch is broken down into smaller molecules called glucose. Glucose molecules are so **small** that they can pass through your gut wall, and they are **soluble** and can dissolve in your blood.

Complex molecules (such as starch) are gradually broken down by enzymes into simple molecules (such as glucose).

enzymes break down part of the large molecule

other enzymes then break down the parts to smaller parts...

... until the whole molecule has been broken down into smaller molecules

The stages of digestion

The process of breaking down large food molecules into smaller molecules is called **digestion**. It starts at the entrance of your gut – the **mouth** – and continues as food moves along the gut to other organs. First, the food in your mouth is chewed. This breaks it up into small pieces. Some enzymes also mix with the food while it is being chewed.

Then the chewed food is swallowed and moves down the **gullet** into the **stomach**. While it is in the stomach the food is churned up and more enzymes and other digestive juices are added.

After a while the partly digested food leaves the stomach and enters the first part of the **small intestine** where more digestive juices are added to it from the **pancreas** and **liver**. Digestion is completed as food moves through the small intestine.

The end products of digestion are all small, soluble substances which can pass into the bloodstream.

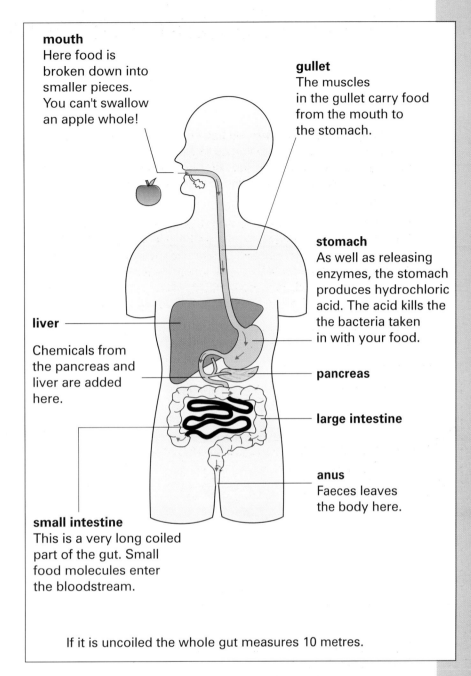

mouth
Here food is broken down into smaller pieces. You can't swallow an apple whole!

gullet
The muscles in the gullet carry food from the mouth to the stomach.

stomach
As well as releasing enzymes, the stomach produces hydrochloric acid. The acid kills the the bacteria taken in with your food.

liver
Chemicals from the pancreas and liver are added here.

pancreas

large intestine

anus
Faeces leaves the body here.

small intestine
This is a very long coiled part of the gut. Small food molecules enter the bloodstream.

If it is uncoiled the whole gut measures 10 metres.

Removing waste

By the time food reaches the **large intestine** all the products of digestion will have been absorbed into the blood, leaving behind the substances in food, such as fibre, which cannot be digested. Water is then absorbed from the undigested material to form semi-solid waste called **faeces**. This waste is removed from the body through the **anus**.

1 List in order the parts of your gut that food passes through.

2 Copy and complete the following:
During digestion .... molecules are .... into small molecules. Only small molecules can pass through the .... and dissolve in the blood.

4 Speeding things up

Speeding up reactions

If you are carrying out a science investigation and want to speed up a chemical reaction, how do you do it? Most reactions can be speeded up by heat. There are thousands of reactions taking place inside your body which occur very effectively at body temperature.

You can also speed up a reaction by adding a **catalyst**. A catalyst is a substance that makes a reaction go faster, but is not changed itself. Living organisms have very efficient catalysts called **enzymes** that make reactions inside your body extremely fast. The reactions that keep you alive could not occur without enzymes.

Making big molecules smaller

The breakdown of large molecules into smaller molecules during digestion is speeded up by enzymes. Much of the food that you eat is in the form of long molecules (such as starch) which have to be broken down so that they can be absorbed into your bloodstream. As food passes along the gut different digestive enzymes are released on to the food to break it down. Each organ in the digestive system carries out a particular part of digestion by producing enzymes that break down specific types of food.

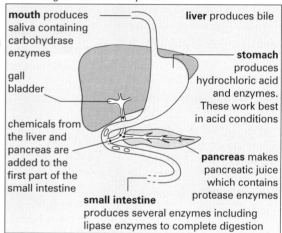

Secretions from different organs enable digestion to take place.

mouth produces saliva containing carbohydrase enzymes

liver produces bile

gall bladder

stomach produces hydrochloric acid and enzymes. These work best in acid conditions

chemicals from the liver and pancreas are added to the first part of the small intestine

pancreas makes pancreatic juice which contains protease enzymes

small intestine produces several enzymes including lipase enzymes to complete digestion

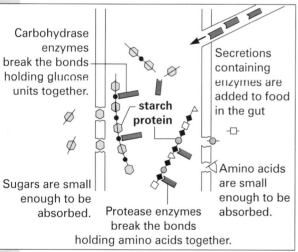

Carbohydrase enzymes break the bonds holding glucose units together.

starch protein

Secretions containing enzymes are added to food in the gut

Sugars are small enough to be absorbed.

Protease enzymes break the bonds holding amino acids together.

Amino acids are small enough to be absorbed.

The right tools for the job

Each kind of food molecule requires a specific kind of enzyme to break it down, just as a certain key will only open up one type of lock. Protein-splitting enzymes will only break down proteins – they have no effect on starch or fats. You can see from this diagram that enzymes break down long chain molecules into their smaller units.

The table summarises the main digestive enzymes at work in the human gut.

Name of enzyme	Where from	What the enzyme works on (substrate)	Products of digestion
protease	stomach, pancreas, small intestine	proteins	amino acids
carbohydrase	saliva, pancreas, small intestine	starch and other carbohydrates	glucose
lipase	pancreas, small intestine	fats	fatty acids, glycerol

Big drops to little droplets

The liver produces **bile** which is stored in the **gall bladder** before it is released into the small intestine. One effect of bile is to neutralise the acid that is added to food while it is in the stomach. This provides the optimum pH for the enzymes in the small intestine to work effectively.

Bile also breaks large drops of fat into tiny fat droplets – a process called **emulsification**. The total surface area of a lot of small droplets is greater than the surface area of the original big drops (see page 78). So there is more surface for the lipase enzymes to act on.

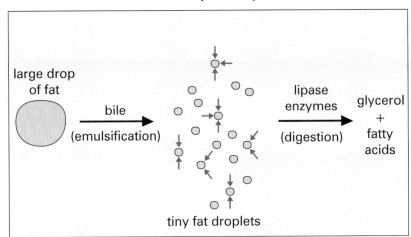

Many fat droplets means a large surface area for lipase enzymes to work on.

Investigating enzyme activity

The diagram opposite shows how a group of students designed an investigation to find out the effect of pancreatic juice on proteins. The protein they used was egg white (albumen).When the test tubes were first set up and shaken, the contents of all the tubes were cloudy. The observations and measurements the students made are shown in the table below.

Tube 1

2 cm³ hydrochloric acid

2 cm³ pancreatic juice

5 cm³ albumen

Tube 2

2 cm³ sodium hydrogencarbonate (alkali)

2 cm³ pancreatic juice

5 cm³ albumen

Tube 3

2 cm³ sodium hydrogencarbonate (alkali)

5 cm³ albumen

Tube 4

2 cm³ sodium hydrogencarbonate (alkali)

2 cm³ boiled pancreatic juice

5 cm³ albumen

Time (mins)	Appearance of test tube contents			
	1	2	3	4
5	cloudy	cloudy	cloudy	cloudy
10	cloudy	clear	cloudy	cloudy
15	cloudy	clear	cloudy	cloudy
20	cloudy	clear	cloudy	cloudy
25	clear	clear	cloudy	cloudy
30	clear	clear	cloudy	cloudy

1
a What reaction causes some of the tubes to go clear?
b In which tube does the reaction occur most rapidly? Explain why the reaction is fastest in this tube.
c Explain the results obtained for tube 4.

 Explain why the digestion of fats by lipase enzymes is more rapid after the fat has been mixed with bile.

 Why does chewing help digestion?

5 Getting food into the body

Pushing food along

The gut is surrounded by layers of muscle. The action of these muscles helps to break up the food into small pieces so that enzymes can more easily act on the food. You can hear food being churned up when your stomach rumbles. The gut muscles also push food along by a wave-like action called **peristalsis**. This action pushes food along in rather the same way that toothpaste is squeezed out of a tube.

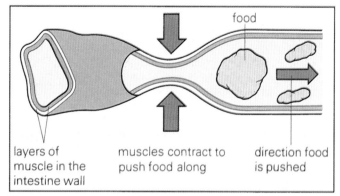

layers of muscle in the intestine wall

muscles contract to push food along

direction food is pushed

*The action of **peristalsis** pushing your food along the gut.*

What happens to digested food?

Once foods have been broken down to form small soluble molecules the process of digestion is complete. Molecules of digested food are small enough to be absorbed through the gut wall.

They are also soluble so that they will dissolve into the bloodstream which transports them to all parts of the body.

tiny blood vessels (capillaries)

muscular wall of intestine

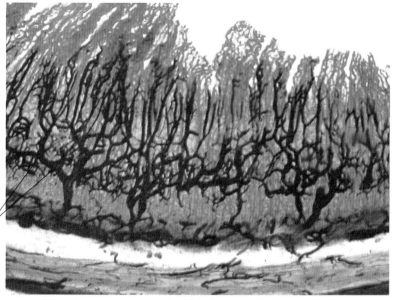

What features can you in this photograph that make the gut wall very efficient at absorbing food?

Getting food into the body

The small intestine is very efficient at taking in digested food because its structure is ideally suited to the job of absorbing food:

● it is long so that there is a large area for absorbing food,

● its inner surface contains thousands of tiny folds called **villi** which produce a huge surface area for the food to pass through,

● each villus contains many tiny blood vessels (capillaries) to carry away absorbed food,

● each villus is very thin so that absorbed food can easily reach the blood stream.

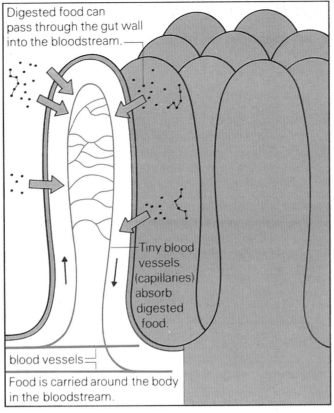

Digested food can pass through the gut wall into the bloodstream.

Tiny blood vessels (capillaries) absorb digested food.

blood vessels

Food is carried around the body in the bloodstream.

The small molecules of digested food pass through the cells lining each villus, then through the walls of capillaries and into the bloodstream. Here the food molecules dissolve in blood **plasma** – the liquid part of blood. Blood is transported to all parts of the body along a network of blood **vessels**.

Each villus (plural villi) contains many tiny blood vessels to carry away absorbed food.

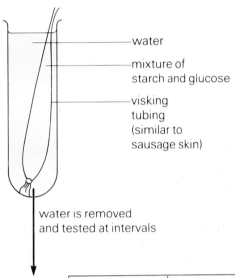

water

mixture of starch and glucose

visking tubing (similar to sausage skin)

water is removed and tested at intervals

Making a gut model

You can find out how food molecules pass through the gut wall by making a model of the gut. The model is made from visking tubing, which is similar to the gut in the way that it allows only small molecules to pass through it.

The diagram opposite shows how a group of students used visking tubing in an investigation. They put a mixture of starch and glucose inside the tubing and then placed the tubing in a tube of water. The students tested the water surrounding the visking tubing at intervals for starch (iodine test) and glucose (Benedict's test). The table shows their results.

	2 min	20 min
Iodine	solution stays deep red	solution stays deep red
Benedict's test	solution stays blue	solution becomes brick red

1 Use the results of the model gut investigation to answer the following:
  a What food substance (if any) is present in the water surrounding the tubing after   i) 2 min?
      ii) 20 min?
  b i) Which of the two substances used cannot pass through the gut wall?
      ii) How does the body change this substance so that it can be absorbed?

2 In the same investigation what part of the body is represented by
  i) the visking tubing?
  ii) the distilled water?

3 Cellulose is a carbohydrate made from long chain molecules. Your body does not produce an enzyme that can break down cellulose. Predict what you think will happen to the cellulose you eat as part of your diet.

6 The breath of life

Glucose is used up by your body to give you energy.

Gasping for breath

When you start to run you may be relaxed but soon you become red-faced, gasping for air and tired! In very long races 'drink stations' are provided. Glucose drinks provide runners with more energy. But the runners also need oxygen from the air.

Oxygen and glucose react together in your body to release **energy**. This process is **respiration**. Activities such as running will use up lots of energy from respiration. **Carbon dioxide** and **water** are produced as by-products of respiration. Here is an equation which summarises the respiration process:

Glucose + oxygen ➡ carbon dioxide + water + energy

Exchanging gases

The job of your **breathing system** is to get fresh supplies of air containing oxygen into your **lungs** and to get rid of carbon dioxide that your body produces. The diagram opposite shows your breathing system. Study this diagram carefully. Notice the three main parts:

● a series of **air passages** which connect your lungs with the outside air,

● **gas exchange** tissues made from millions of tiny air sacs called alveoli,

● **breathing structures** made from bone and muscles.

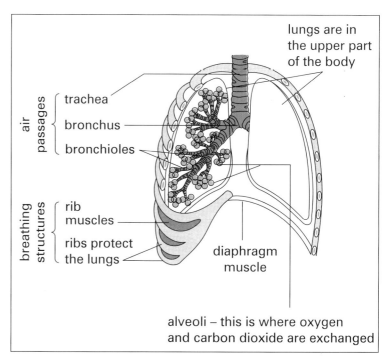

air passages
- trachea
- bronchus
- bronchioles

breathing structures
- rib muscles
- ribs protect the lungs

lungs are in the upper part of the body

diaphragm muscle

alveoli – this is where oxygen and carbon dioxide are exchanged

The breathing system.

Take a deep breath

Place your hand on your chest for a few minutes. You can feel your **breathing movements** – your chest goes up and then down, forcing air in and then out of your lungs. The diagram explains how these breathing movements are brought about.

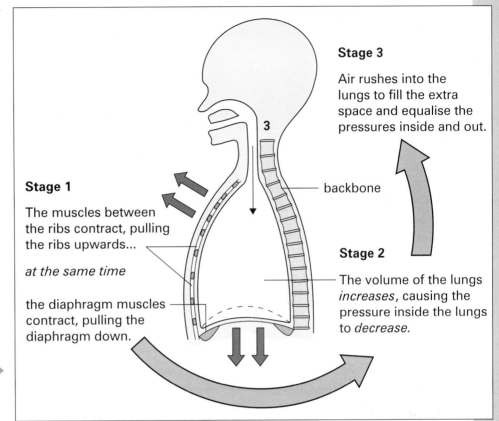

Stage 3

Air rushes into the lungs to fill the extra space and equalise the pressures inside and out.

backbone

Stage 1

The muscles between the ribs contract, pulling the ribs upwards...

at the same time

the diaphragm muscles contract, pulling the diaphragm down.

Stage 2

The volume of the lungs *increases*, causing the pressure inside the lungs to *decrease*.

Sequence of events when you breathe in.

Deep breathing

As you become more active your body needs more energy. To provide more energy you start to respire more rapidly. This means that you need to get more oxygen into your body. The results below are taken from an investigation to find out how a student's breathing changed as she increased the number of bench step-ups she did, in one minute.

Activity	Volume of each breath (cm³)	Number of breaths taken per minute
Rest	500	18
20 step-ups per min	750	25
50 step-ups per min	1200	34

1 List in order the parts of your body that air passes through when you breathe in and then out.

2 Explain when you breathe in
 a how the volume of the chest is increased and
 b how this increased volume draws air into your lungs.

3 Use the results from the breathing investigation to answer the following.
 a State *two* changes in your breathing pattern that take place as you become more active.
 b From the table calculate the total volume of air taken in at rest and during each exercise.

7 A fair swop

Getting oxygen

You breathe because you need the oxygen from the air to release energy from the food you eat. Your breathing system and your circulatory system make sure that every cell in your body gets the oxygen it needs. By breathing, you not only take in the oxygen you need, you also get rid of the waste products of respiration. When you breathe you exchange your waste for what you need – a fair swop!

Gas	Inhaled air	Exhaled air
Oxygen	20%	16%
Carbon dioxide	0.04%	4%
Water vapour	a little	a lot
Nitrogen	78%	78%

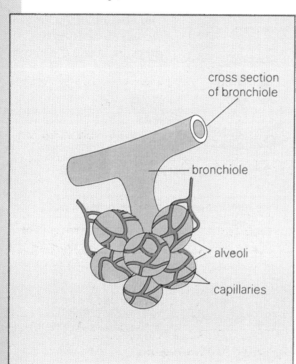

Oxygen diffuses out through the walls of the alveoli into blood vessels called capillaries.

Increasing surface area

Each bronchiole leads to a bunch of tiny alveoli (singular: alveolus). Having many tiny air sacs provides the lung with a much larger surface area than if it were one very large air sac.

Five balloons can have the same volume, but a larger surface area, than one large balloon.

Exchanging gases

Your lungs are highly efficient at providing the oxygen that keeps you alive and active and at removing carbon dioxide. This is called **gaseous exchange** and it takes place by a process called **diffusion**. Oxygen and carbon dioxide diffuse easily between the air in your lungs and your blood. This is because the alveoli in your lungs are highly specialised for exchanging gases. The alveoli in your lungs

- provide a very **large moist surface** for exchange,
- are **richly supplied with blood** capillaries to transport gases to and from the lungs, and
- have **very thin membranes** so gases move only a short distance.

Each small balloon has a volume of 200 cm³ and a surface area of 165 cm²

Volume = 1000 cm³ surface area = 480 cm²

A close relationship

You can see in the diagram on page 78 that each alveolus has a **network of fine capillaries criss-crossing its surface**. The air and blood are separated only by very thin membranes. Because of this the air in each alveolus is very close to a large amount of blood.

Oxygen dissolves in the water lining the alveolus and then diffuses through the membranes into the blood in the capillary. Oxygen diffuses from the alveolus, where it is in high concentration, to the blood, where it is in low concentration. Waste carbon dioxide diffuses from the blood into the alveolus and is then breathed out.

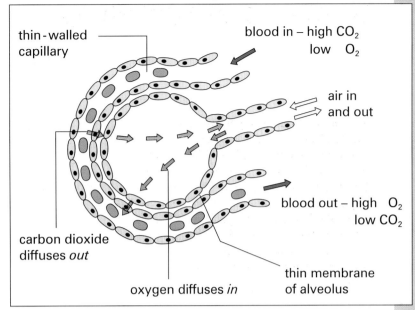

Exchanging gases in the alveolus.

Evidence of exchange of gases

The apparatus shown in the diagram opposite shows how inspired and expired air can be compared. Each flask contains hydrogencarbonate solution which changes from red to yellow when carbon dioxide is dissolved in it. What changes would you expect to see when someone breathes in and out through the rubber tube?

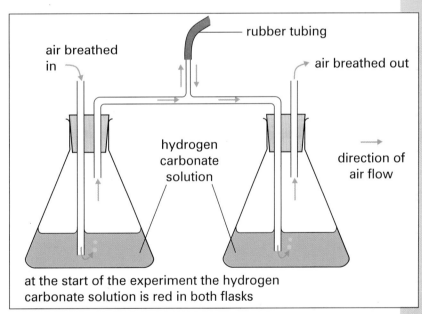

1 **a** Predict the colour of the solutions in each flask in the apparatus shown above after someone has breathed in and out several times.
   b If the same person repeated the experiment using fresh solution, What difference, if any, would you expect to see? Explain your answer.

2 List in order the structures that oxygen will pass through from when you breathe in until the oxygen reaches your blood.

3 Refer to the table on page 78.
   a Which gases show an increase in exhaled air?
   b Explain why the amount of oxygen in exhaled air is lower than in the air inhaled.
   c Explain how carbon dioxide passes from living cells into the blood.

8 Blood – supplying your needs

What does your blood do?

In many simple living organisms their body is made up of just one 'unit' called a cell. The chemicals that are needed for life are all inside this single cell. More complicated organisms have lots of cells. Complex organisms, such as humans, need to transport chemicals from one cell to another and their blood system does this job. An average 16-year-old needs about 4 litres of blood to transport everything around the body.

If people have lost blood in an accident they can be given **blood transfusions**. This means giving them some 'new' blood to 'top up' their blood supply. Look at this picture. There is a small plastic bag hanging on the right which contains blood. The blood flows down the tube, then through a needle in the man's hand and into his body.

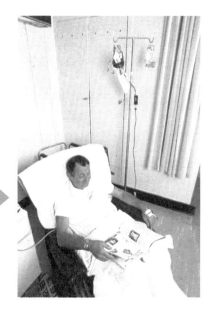

What is in your blood

Blood is a mixture of many chemicals and cells. These all have different jobs to do. In the diagram you can see what is in your blood and what the different things do.

Blood contains water, cells and lots of different chemicals.

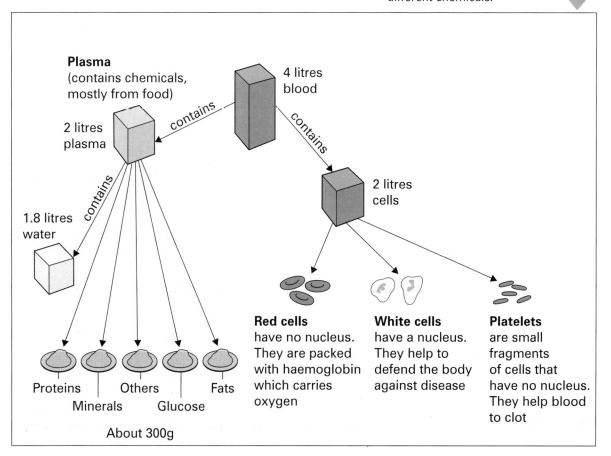

Plasma (contains chemicals, mostly from food)

4 litres blood

2 litres plasma

contains

contains

2 litres cells

1.8 litres water

contains

Proteins

Minerals

Others

Glucose

Fats

About 300g

Red cells have no nucleus. They are packed with haemoglobin which carries oxygen

White cells have a nucleus. They help to defend the body against disease

Platelets are small fragments of cells that have no nucleus. They help blood to clot

Transporting soluble substances

The liquid part of blood is called **plasma**. This liquid is mostly water with a large number of dissolved substances in it. Soluble substances are transported from one part of the body to another in the plasma. The main substances transported in plasma are:

- **carbon dioxide** which is produced in cells of body organs as they respire. The carbon dioxide is transported in plasma from body organs to the lungs and then breathed out.

- the **products of digestion** which are absorbed from the small intestine, dissolved in blood plasma and then transported to other body organs.

- **urea** which is a waste product produced in the liver from amino acids. It is transported in blood plasma from the liver to the kidneys and then removed from the body as urine.

Oxygen carriers

Blood contains an enormous number of red blood cells – every $1\,mm^3$ of blood contains about 5000 million red cells! Red blood cells transport oxygen from the lungs to body organs which need oxygen for respiration. Red cells are packed with a red pigment called **haemoglobin**. In the lungs haemoglobin combines with oxygen to form **oxyhaemoglobin**. As the blood flows through other body organs oxyhaemoglobin splits up into haemoglobin and oxygen.

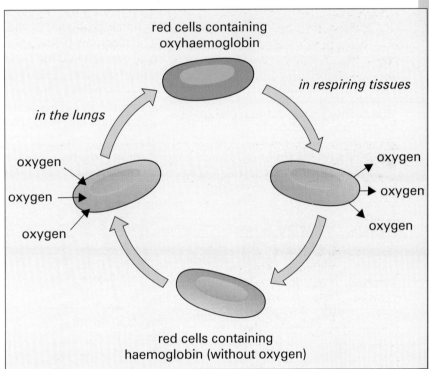

red cells containing oxyhaemoglobin

in respiring tissues

in the lungs

oxygen

oxygen

oxygen

oxygen

oxygen

oxygen

red cells containing haemoglobin (without oxygen)

1
  a How much water does your blood contain?
  b List *three* substances that are transported around the body in plasma.

2
  a Where in the body is oxyhaemoglobin formed?
  b A shortage of iron in the diet may lead to anaemia, a disorder which causes a shortage of red blood cells. Explain why people who are anaemic are often pale and tired.

3 The table below shows the number of red blood cells of people living at different altitudes. The air at higher altitudes contains less oxygen.

Height above sea level (metres)	Red cell count (per mm³)
0	5000
1500	6500
5400	7400

  a How does the red cell count differ between sea level and high altitudes?
  b Explain the benefit of this difference to people living at high altitudes.

9 On the beat

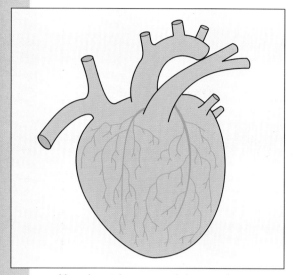

Your heart is a powerful muscular pump.

Life blood

Your blood provides all the organs of your body with the materials needed to stay alive and healthy. Blood flows around your body through a network of blood vessels which makes up your **circulatory system**. Your blood is kept flowing around this system by the action of your **heart**.

Pumping the system

Your heart is the circulatory system's pump. The pumping action is produced by the thick muscular walls of the heart. The diagrams below show the action of a single heart beat. You can see that the heart contains four chambers: two **atria** (singular: atrium) and two **ventricles**. When the muscles surrounding the atria and ventricles tighten (*contract*) blood is squeezed out. When these muscles *relax* blood enters the chambers.

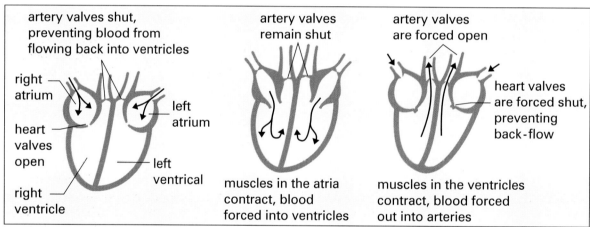

artery valves shut, preventing blood from flowing back into ventricles

right atrium

heart valves open

right ventricle

left atrium

left ventrical

artery valves remain shut

muscles in the atria contract, blood forced into ventricles

artery valves are forced open

heart valves are forced shut, preventing back-flow

muscles in the ventricles contract, blood forced out into arteries

The muscles of your heart must contract in a special order if your blood is to be pumped efficiently.

A double pump

If you follow the arrows in the diagram opposite you will trace the path of blood around two separate circulatory systems. Blood from the right-hand side of the heart is pumped to the lungs and then back to the heart. Blood from the left-hand side of the heart is pumped all around the rest of the body before returning to the heart. This is called a **double circulatory system** because blood travels through the heart twice as it is transported around the body.

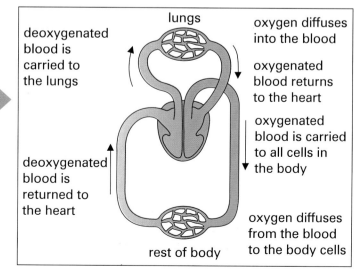

deoxygenated blood is carried to the lungs

deoxygenated blood is returned to the heart

lungs

oxygen diffuses into the blood

oxygenated blood returns to the heart

oxygenated blood is carried to all cells in the body

oxygen diffuses from the blood to the body cells

rest of body

Supply lines

Blood is carried around your body in three types of **blood vessel**.
This diagram shows how each type of blood vessel carries out its job.

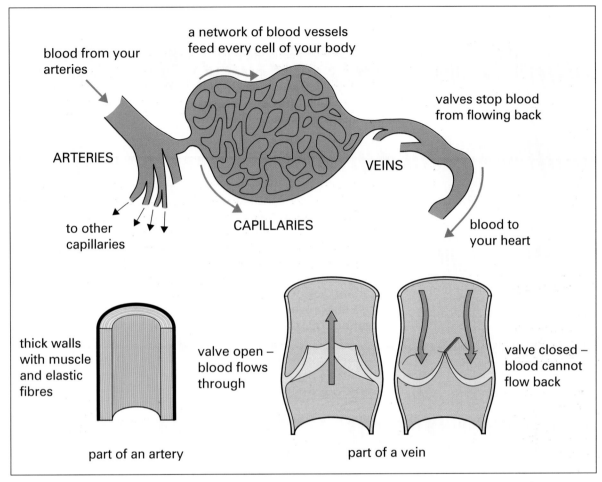

blood from your arteries

a network of blood vessels feed every cell of your body

valves stop blood from flowing back

ARTERIES

VEINS

to other capillaries

CAPILLARIES

blood to your heart

thick walls with muscle and elastic fibres

valve open – blood flows through

valve closed – blood cannot flow back

part of an artery

part of a vein

Blood flows from the heart to other organs of the body through **arteries**. As the blood flowing through arteries is under very high pressure, arteries have thick walls containing muscle and elastic fibres to withstand the pressure.

Arteries gradually divide to form smaller and smaller vessels and eventually form very narrow, thin walled, **capillaries**. The thin walls allow substances needed by cells to pass *from the blood*, and substances produced by cells to pass *into the blood*.

Capillaries gradually join up again to form **veins**. The pressure in veins is very low so blood flows much more slowly than in arteries. Veins have thin walls as they do not need to resist high pressure. They also have valves to prevent the blood flowing backwards.

1
a State two features of veins which are *not* found in arteries.
b Explain why each of these features of veins is needed.

2
a Name two substances that pass from the blood in capillaries into surrounding cells.
b Explain why each of these substances is needed by cells.

3
List, in order, the parts of the circulatory system that blood flows through from when it enters the right atrium.

4
a What prevents blood flowing back into the atria when the ventricles contract?
b What is meant by a 'double circulatory system'?

10 Releasing energy

Sources of energy

Many substances such as coal, natural gas and petrol have energy stored in them. This is why we use them as fuels. When these substances burn their stored energy is released quickly as heat. Living organisms use food substances as their fuel. **Glucose** is the main food used to provide your body with the energy it needs.

Fuels in the motorbike engine release energy quickly.

Releasing energy

Energy is released from glucose by a process called **respiration**. During respiration chemical reactions take place inside the cells of your body. When glucose reacts with oxygen, energy is released and carbon dioxide and water are produced as waste products. Because this process uses oxygen from the air it is called **aerobic respiration**. This process is summarised by the equation:

glucose + oxygen ➡ carbon dioxide + water + energy

Using energy

The energy that is released during respiration is used by your body to:

● build larger molecules from smaller ones,

● make muscles contract so that you can move,

● keep your body temperature steady even when you are in colder surroundings.

Energy from the bicyclist's food is released more slowly – Sometimes this feels like hard work!

Energy is needed...

...to make new molecules that help you to grow...   ...so that you can move...   ... and stay warm.

Respiration without oxygen

Sometimes your body cannot get enough oxygen. For example, during very strenuous activity such as sprinting, insufficient oxygen reaches muscles so aerobic respiration slows down and eventually stops. This also happens in other 'explosive' events such as throwing the javelin. To provide the energy that is needed, glucose is broken down without using oxygen. This is called **anaerobic respiration**. This process does not break down glucose completely, so less energy is released than in aerobic respiration and **lactic acid** is produced instead of carbon dioxide and water. This process can be summarised by the equation:

glucose ➡ lactic acid + energy

Getting into debt

Anaerobic respiration can only take place for a short time because the build-up of lactic acid stops muscles from working, by causing fatigue. After releasing energy in this way lactic acid has to be removed. This is done by using oxygen to break down lactic acid to carbon dioxide and water. After exercising you will need to keep breathing heavily to take in extra oxygen to remove lactic acid. We can say that during strenuous exercise you build up an 'oxygen debt' and when the exercise is over you have to repay the debt.

Energy is released without the use of oxygen during 'explosive' events such as throwing the javelin.

How much oxygen do you need?

Respiration takes place in all living cells. Oxygen is taken into your body as you breathe. The amount of oxygen that cells use depends on how much energy is needed. The table shows the amount of oxygen breathed in and the energy that is needed during various activities.

Activity	Amount of oxygen breathed in (litres per min)	Energy needed (kJ per min)
lying down	0.20	4
sitting	0.30	6
walking	1.50	30
jogging	4.00	80

1
  a What substance is used by the body to release energy?
  b What substances are produced as waste products from aerobic respiration?

2 Explain why aerobic respiration releases more energy than anaerobic respiration.

3 Give *three* ways of using the energy released from respiration.

4 Use the table above to answer the following.
  a Why does the amount of oxygen breathed in increase as the activities change?
  Olympic athletes use up to 200 kJ of energy during a 100 m race.
  b Using the data in the table, predict how much oxygen an athlete will take in during a 100 m race.
  c When the amount of oxygen taken by the athlete was measured it was found to be 0.5 litres. Explain why this measured value is different from your prediction.

11 Making the body work hard

In a race, a sprinter uses enough energy to boil one cup of water.

Why do you need energy?

You need energy to do *anything*. Energy is used to keep warm, to go for a walk and even to grow. You also need energy just to stay alive – even when you may believe you are doing nothing! The amount of energy you need depends on what you do.

Where do you get your energy?

You get your energy from the food you eat. This is because your food is made of special chemicals which have energy stored inside them. For example, there is a lot of chemical energy stored in foods such as pasta. Your body can release this chemical energy from the food. This energy is used for warmth, movement, growth, or even just staying alive.

If humans don't get enough of energy from their food, their health may suffer. A child would become very tired and would not grow much. An old person would feel cold all the time and could even die from getting too cold.

Energy for growth

You have grown in size and weight since you were born. As you grow, you use energy to help make the cells of which your body is made. Even when you have stopped growing you still need to make new cells to replace old ones as they die off. You can lose 4 million skin cells in a lesson! They just die and eventually fall off. So you need energy all the time to make new cells.

Energy to stay alive

At night while you are fast asleep, your body is still active. Breathing, repairing cells, fighting infections – these all involve important chemical reactions which keep you alive. Energy is needed to keep these reactions going. These important reactions carry on non-stop, so you need a constant supply of energy from food to stay alive. The table shows you that even when you sleep you use as much energy as the lightbulb in your room.

Activity		Energy used in 1 minute (measured in kilojoules)	
	Lying still	5 kJ	
	Sitting	7 kJ	
	Walking	10 kJ	
	Dancing	30 kJ	
	Running	44 kJ	
	Swimming	46 kJ	
	Skiing	64 kJ	cold water → hot water

Releasing enough energy

When you work hard your muscles need more energy – energy that is released from glucose. During respiration in muscle cells, glucose is combined with oxygen and carbon dioxide, water and energy are released. The energy that is released is used by muscles to move your body. More respiration takes place to release more energy when muscle cells are made to work harder. This uses up large amounts of glucose and oxygen. The table below shows some of the changes that take place in your body during strenuous exercise.

Measurements of breathing rate and heart beat, when subjects first at rest and then after hard exercise. ▼

	Number of breaths per min	Volume of each breath (cm³)	Pulse beats per min	Volume of blood leaving the heart after each beat (cm³)
At rest	18	450	72	65
After 10 min strenuous exercise	41	1050	90	120

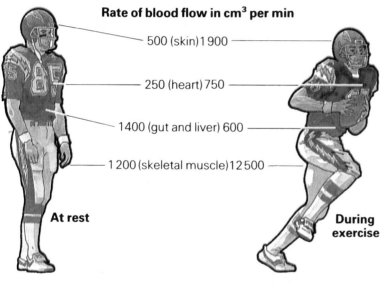

Rate of blood flow in cm³ per min

500 (skin)1 900

250 (heart) 750

1400 (gut and liver) 600

1 200 (skeletal muscle)12 500

At rest

During exercise

The rate of blood flowing to the main regions of the body increases as your work harder.

Getting in supplies

By breathing faster and deeper as you work harder you take in more air. Your heart also beats faster and harder to pump blood around the body faster so that hard-working muscles obtain more oxygen and glucose, and waste carbon dioxide is removed. These are not the only changes that take place in your body during exercise. The amount of blood flowing to various parts of the body also changes.

1 Energy is used for all kinds of movements. Write down two other things energy is used for.

2 a Where does your energy come from?
b Why do marathon runners eat lots of pasta before a race?

3 a Who do you think would use up most energy, someone who is sleeping or someone who is running? Why?
b Who needs more energy *in total* – two people dancing or twelve people sleeping?

4 Study the diagram above showing changes in the rate of blood flow.
a Which parts of the body show an increased blood flow during exercise?
b Use the data to explain why it is bad to exercise after a meal.

5 a Use the information in the table above to identify *three* changes that take place in the body during exercise.
b How much air is breathed into the lungs each minute during exercise?
c How much blood leaves the heart each minute at rest and during exercise?

12 Fit for life

Fit for what?

Many people spend time jogging, going to aerobics classes or to the local health club trying to get and stay fit. But what is fitness? Professional sports people need to be very fit to compete against others in their sport. They work very hard at improving their overall fitness. But everyone needs to be fit enough to carry out everyday activities such as mowing the lawn or carrying the shopping! Becoming tired and short of breath after climbing a few flights of stairs or lacking the energy to walk to the local shops are signs of being unfit and unhealthy. Do you think you may be unfit?

Fitness isn't just a measure of whether you can win an olympic medal! We all need to be fit to go about our daily activities – like doing the shopping!

Improving fitness

Exercising regularly improves your fitness. Any activity which gives you exercise is good for you. This is because exercise has several effects on the body. When you exercise regularly:

● your muscles become larger and able to work longer and harder.

● your heart muscle becomes stronger so that the blood is pumped around the body more efficiently.

● your breathing becomes more efficient and more air can be taken in with each breath.

● the risk of heart attacks and strokes decreases because of the improved circulation.

This table shows the effects of regular exercise on the body. (All measurements are taken when the person is at rest).

	Before getting fit	After becoming fit
Amount of blood pumped out of the heart during each beat (cm³)	64	80
Heart volume (cm³)	120	140
Breathing rate (no. of breaths per min)	14	12
Pulse rate	72	63

Some of these effects of regular exercise on the body can be seen in the table above. The measurements shown in the table are taken from the same person before and after several months of regular exercise.

Using pulse rates

You can see from the previous table that the resting pulse rate *decreased* as the person became fitter. In a fit person the pulse rate is often low. It increases during exercise and then it rapidly returns to normal. In an unfit person exercise makes the pulse rate go very high and it returns to normal only slowly. Measuring pulse rate before and after exercise is a good way to assess fitness because it indicates the efficiency of the heart and circulation.

This graph shows the pulse rates of two girls. Can you tell who is the fittest?

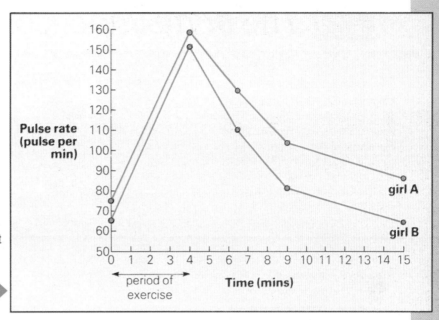

Stamina to keep going

The ability of your breathing system and lungs to supply oxygen and remove carbon dioxide is an important part of fitness. A good supply of oxygen improves stamina or 'staying power' so that you can keep running or walking without getting tired and puffed out.

The breathing rate and the volume of air taken in by a person during each breath can be measured using a **spirometer.** A trace is produced which shows the pattern of breathing and the amount of air taken by the person being monitored.

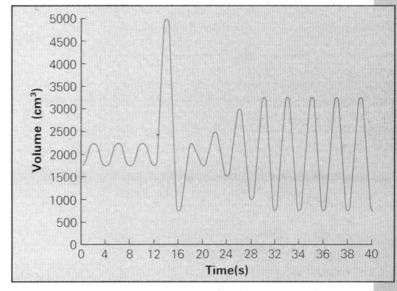

This spirometer tracing was made by a student who plays a lot of sport. He was asked to breathe steadily at rest, then to breathe in and out as deeply as possible and finally to breathe steadily while exercising.

1 What effect does exercise have on
a the size of the heart, and
b the strength of heart beat?
Explain your answer.

2 'Fitness makes breathing more efficient so that more air can be taken in with each breath. 'What evidence is there in the table opposite to support this statement?

3 **a** Use the graph of pulse rates to suggest which girl is the fitter.
b Give *two* reasons for your choice.

4 Use the spirometer trace above to calculate:
a how much *extra* air is taken in with each breath during exercise.
b the total amount of air that can be breathed into the lungs.

5 If a spirometer was used to measure the total volume of air that could be breathed in by a student who hardly ever takes exercise, how would the results differ from those shown here? Explain your answer.

13 Microscopic killers

Harmful microbes

Many diseases are caused when microbes such as certain bacteria and viruses get into the body. A person is more likely to develop a disease if large numbers of **bacteria** or **viruses** enter their body. This can happen by being in unhygienic conditions or by being in contact with someone who already has a disease. Once bacteria or viruses are in the body they reproduce rapidly and may release poisons called **toxins** which make you feel ill. The table below shows some diseases caused by microbes.

Type of microbe	Examples of diseases
Viruses	Flu, common cold, polio, chickenpox, measles, AIDS
Bacteria	Whooping cough, tuberculosis, tetanus, gonorrhoea

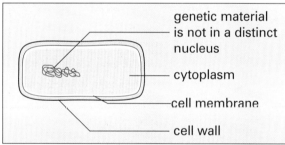

genetic material is not in a distinct nucleus

cytoplasm

cell membrane

cell wall

Structure of a bacterial cell.

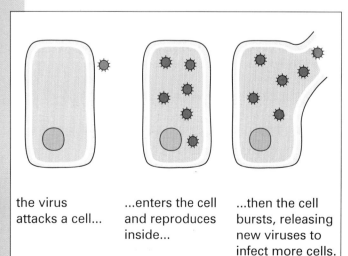

the virus attacks a cell...

...enters the cell and reproduces inside...

...then the cell bursts, releasing new viruses to infect more cells.

Viruses are very simple structures but have a deadly effect on living cells.

Would you buy your hot dog here? Large numbers of microbes can be found in unhygienic conditions.

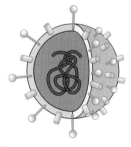

A flu virus. Viruses are very, very small, much smaller than bacteria. They can only reproduce inside living cells.

Coughs and sneezes

Influenza or flu is a disease caused by a virus. The virus is easily passed from person to person. You can catch flu by breathing in viruses from a person with the illness. The flu viruses then get into the cells lining your breathing passages. Once inside these cells the viruses take over. They cause the cells to make new flu viruses. Eventually the cells burst, releasing many new flu viruses which can infect more cells. Not surprisingly, this makes you feel ill – your temperature rises, your throat becomes sore, your muscles ache and you get a headache. Fortunately, your body defenses (see page 92) will destroy all the infected cells and viruses so that you will not need too much time off school!

Standards of living

The following article from The *Guardian* newspaper reports on a cholera epidemic. Read the article carefully to identify the cause of the disease, how it is spread, and how living conditions affect the spread of the disease.

Contaminating water

Cholera can spread at alarming speed where there is overcrowding and a lack of sewage treatment systems. The disease is spread when sewage from infected people is poured into rivers and the sea. More people are then infected by drinking contaminated water or eating contaminated food such as fish.

Troubled waters

CHOLERA is killing thousands of people a month in the developing world. Epidemics of the water-borne disease have broken out from South America to Africa and the Far East. Medical experts believe it can only be controlled by improving standards of sanitation. Yet many countries cannot easily afford public-health programmes.

At the end of January this year, cholera struck in Peru in the first South American epidemic this century. Schools in Peru were closed for an extra two weeks at Easter while the government built toilets as part of a programme to help control the epidemic, which had killed more than 1,000 people there by the start of May. But many schools could not even afford the building materials.

Up to 120 million people in South America are thought to be at risk. The United Nations predicts that 2 million will catch the disease before the end of this year.

Cholera is caused by a bacterium which lives in dirty water, sewage and contaminated food. Its chief symptom is severe diarrhoea. The disease spreads rapidly in places where standards of water purity, sanitation and health services are poor. The World Health Organisation has created a task force on cholera to coordinate attempts to control and eradicate the disease. The WHO has called the epidemic 'an unfolding worldwide tragedy'.

The Guardian, 18 June 1991

▼ *Cholera is a disease spread by dirty water.*

River water may be used to dispose of sewage

River water may be used as drinking water or to wash food or clothes

---

1 Give two examples of diseases caused by viruses and two examples caused by bacteria.

2 **a** Describe *two* features common to all viruses.
b Explain how viruses can damage cells.

3 Imagine you are an Environmental Health Officer and you have just inspected the conditions in the hot dog stand shown opposite. Write a report describing the health problems you have found.

4 **a** Explain how the microbe that causes cholera gets into the body.
b What is the effect of the toxin that this microbe produces?

5 **a** Explain why cholera is common in some developing countries and very rare in the UK.
b Describe the steps that can be taken to prevent the spread of this disease.

14 Body defences

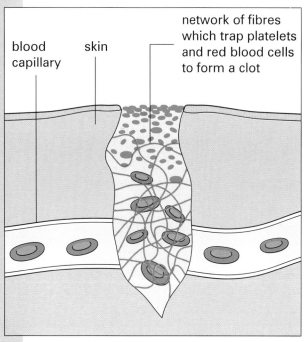

Blood clots to seal a cut through the skin.

blood capillary

skin

network of fibres which trap platelets and red blood cells to form a clot

cell releasing mucus

bacteria trapped in mucus get carried back to the throat

cilia

Cells lining the breathing passages protect against infection.

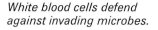

White blood cells defend against invading microbes.

Outer protection

Your body comes into frequent contact with harmful microbes without you becoming ill. This is because your body is very good at keeping micobes out. Your **skin** acts as a barrier stopping microbes getting into your body. If the skin is cut or damaged microbes may get in and cause infection. To prevent this happening your blood forms **clots** that seal any cuts. Blood clotting prevents entry of harmful bacteria and stops you losing too much blood.

Trapping microbes

Even though your skin prevents microbes getting in, some can still enter your body in the air you breathe. Your breathing passages are lined with specialised cells which have tiny hair-like projections called **cilia**. Other cells produce a sticky liquid called **mucus**. Bacteria and dust that you breathe in get stuck in the mucus. Then the cilia sweep the mucus and trapped bacteria back to your throat, where they can be swallowed.

Microbe-eating cells

If microbes do get into your body you have another line of defence – **your white blood cells**. These cells help to defend you against disease in three ways. They

- **ingest microbes** and then digest them,

- produce chemicals called **antibodies** that destroy microbes,

- produce other chemicals called **antitoxins** which counteract the toxins (poisons) made by microbes.

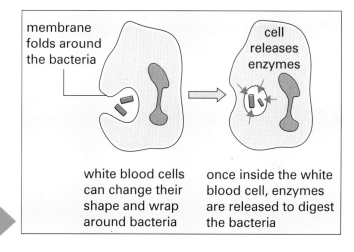

membrane folds around the bacteria

cell releases enzymes

white blood cells can change their shape and wrap around bacteria

once inside the white blood cell, enzymes are released to digest the bacteria

Life-long protection

When you have a disease microbes will be reproducing inside your body and may produce toxins which make you feel ill. Fortunately your white blood cells will be working hard to destroy the microbes and help you to recover. Once your white blood cells have destroyed a type of microbe you are unlikely to catch the same disease again. This is because your white blood cells are able to recognise the microbe if it gets into your body again and then produce antibodies much more quickly. This makes you **immune** to the disease for the rest of your life.

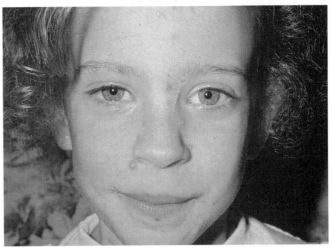

Illnesses like chickenpox make you ill because viruses damage your cells. Fortunately, white blood cells bring about recovery.

A quick sharp jab

You have probably been vaccinated against a number of diseases, such as whooping cough when you were a young child. You may have had your TB (tuberculosis) vaccination more recently or even be looking forward to it soon!

Vaccinations are given to protect you against certain harmful diseases. For example, the TB vaccination protects you against the bacteria that cause tuberculosis – a disease which can badly damage your lungs. The vaccination involves injecting a weakened form of the microbe that causes the disease into your blood. Because the microbes are weakened, or even dead, they do not cause illness but they make your white blood cells produce the antibodies that will give you immunity.

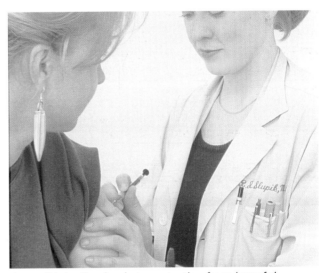

A small injection leads to protection from harmful diseases. The chemicals injected help you develop immunity to certain diseases.

1 Describe two ways that microbes are stopped from getting into your body.

2 Explain how white blood cells destroy microbes that have got into your body.

3 Explain why people catch some diseases, such as measles, only once.

4 The table below shows the number of people in the UK who caught measles in certain years.

1981	1984	1986	1988	1990
62 000	68 000	90 000	91 000	17 000

a In which year was measles at its highest?

b In 1988 a new combined measles, mumps and rubella vaccination was introduced. Explain the effect that this new vaccination had in protecting people from measles.

15 *For you to do*

1 The diagram below shows a group of cells found on the lining of the trachea (windpipe).

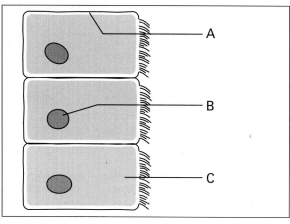

a Identify the parts of the cells labelled A, B and C.

b What name is given to a group of cells that have a similar structure and carry out the same job in the body?

2 The diagram below shows part of the lung where exchange of gases takes place.

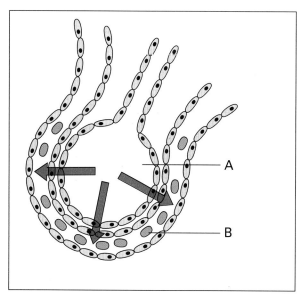

a Identify the structure labelled A and the type of cells labelled B.

b Name the gas which diffuses in the direction shown by the arrows.

c For what process is this gas needed?

3 The diagram below shows a type of cell found in the blood.

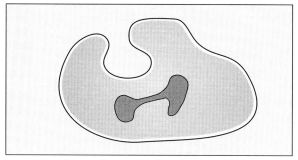

a State the type of cell shown.

b Describe *three* ways that this type of cell helps to protect the body from disease.

Once someone has a disease such as measles they become immune to it.

c What is meant by 'immunity'?

d Explain how someone develops immunity to a disease.

e Describe *two* ways by which your body prevents the entry of microbes.

4 The diagram below shows three organs which work together as part of the same organ system.

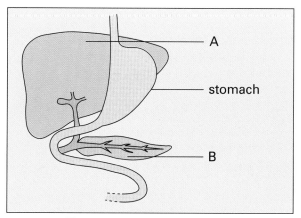

a To which organ system do these organs belong?

b Name the organs labelled A and B.

c i) Name the enzyme produced by the stomach.

ii) What type of food does this enzyme break down?

iii) What products are formed by this reaction?

5 The arrows in the following diagram show the direction of blood flow through the heart.

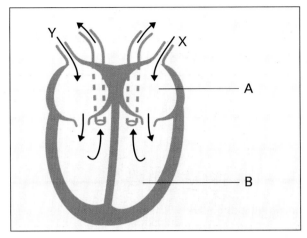

a What name is given to the structures labelled A and B?

b Where does the blood come from in the blood vessel labelled X?

c Describe *two* differences in the content of the blood in blood vessels labelled X and Y.

 a Make a copy and then complete the following table.

Part of the body	breathing in	breathing out
-----------	move up and out	move down and in
Diaphragm	-------------	relaxes (moves up)

b Explain how air is forced into the lungs when a person breathes in.

 7 The following structures (X, Y, and Z) can be found in blood.

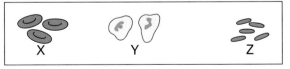

a Give the letter of the structure which:
  i) will increase at the site of bacterial infection such as a tooth abscess,
  ii) helps to form clots when the skin is cut,
  iii) contains haemoglobin.

b Sometimes people cannot make enough haemoglobin and develop a condition called **anaemia**. Explain why people with anaemia are often tired and seem to lack energy.

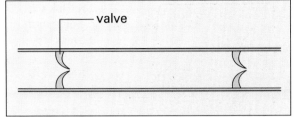 **8** The diagram below shows a type of blood vessel.

a What type of vessel is shown in the diagram?

b Describe the purpose of the valves shown in the diagram.

c Describe one other feature shown in the diagram that indicates what type of blood vessel it is.

9 The table below shows the percentage of overweight adults in the UK.

Age group	% overweight	
	men	women
20–29	25	21
30–39	40	25
40–49	52	38
50–59	49	47

a Which age group has the largest percentage of overweight people?

b Which age group has the largest difference between men and women who are overweight?

c What food in the body forms the extra weight?

NEW MODULAR SCIENCE
for GCSE

MODULE *Earth Materials*

Spread

Cover photograph *Satellite image of the Earth showing Europe at the centre*

1 Secondhand rocks

Rocks can get broken

What are beaches made of? Broken rocks! This is obvious in the big boulders that have crashed down from the cliffs. But look closely. Nearby there may be smaller pieces that have been worn smooth and round by the crashing waves. If the rock is hard, some pieces may be found as pebbles or gravel, too.

Many beaches also have sand and clay. This, too, is broken rock! Some rocks, like granite, contain the hard mineral quartz mixed up with other minerals such as feldspar. The air and rain gradually break down the feldspar to make clay. This releases the quartz crystals, which form the sand. There may be no granite nearby, so how did the sand and clay get on the beach?

Rocks break down to pebbles, sand or clay.

This river is red because of all the mud and sand from the desert it is carrying down to the sea.

River action

Rocks also get broken up in the mountains. In cold areas this is helped by frost action. Water gets into cracks in the rock. If it freezes at night it expands and pushes the crack open. The same action can burst house water pipes!

The rain then gets to work on the broken pieces, washing them into streams and rivers which carry them down to the sea. As the pieces move along, they get rolled and battered and worn, becoming smaller, smoother and rounder. They also crash into the river bed, wearing that away too! That's how a river cuts its valley.

The sea at last!

The Nile delta as seen from the Space Shuttle.

Most of the sediment carried by a river will eventually reach the sea, and here the river's power is lost and the river dumps its load of sediment. Now the sea takes over – wave action stirs and sorts out the sediment: fine clay is washed out to sea by even the weakest of currents, but any sand or pebbles are spread out along the beach.

If a very large amount of sediment is brought to the sea by a river, the sea may not be able to move it all. A great wedge of sand and mud (a **delta**) may build out into the sea as new land. The Nile delta is so big that it is easily seen from space. It is an important farming area in Egypt, where so much of the rest of the land is desert – no good for growing crops.

Layers on the sea-bed

Eventually, most of the pebbles, sand and clay brought in by the rivers end up in more or less horizontal layers – **beds** – at the bottom of the sea. These are separated by **bedding planes** – natural breaks that were once the sea-bed, and over which sea creatures may have left their scattered remains.

In time, these sediments will be buried and squashed by other layers that form above them. Over thousands or even millions of years they harden to form **sedimentary rock**, as the water is squeezed out and the fragments become cemented together.

*Pebbles form **conglomerate** rock – this is a bit like concrete, with the pebbles held together by a natural cement.*

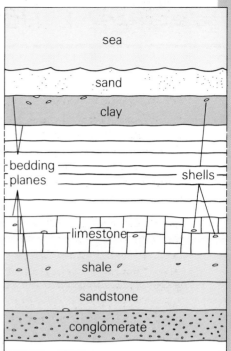

Sediment layers underneath the sea-bed.

*Sand forms **sandstone** – often soft, but some old sandstones can be very hard.*

*Squashed mud forms **shale** – this is flaky and often contains fossils. The layers shown here have been twisted up by movements in the crust.*

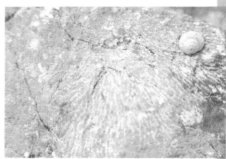

*Crushed shells form **limestone** – this also contains many fossils, such as the coral shown here.*

Fossils and limestone

The animal and plant remains trapped in the rocks may be preserved as **fossils**. Soft tissues usually rot away, so just the hard parts – bony skeletons, teeth or shells – are found as fossils.

Shells are made of calcium carbonate. If the broken fragments of enough shells collect together, they can make a new sedimentary rock on their own. This rock is called **limestone**.

1. a Where does the sand on the beach come from?
   b What carries the sand from the mountains to the sea?

2. How does water help to break rocks high in the mountains at night?

3. What is a delta? How does it form?

4. How is it that soft sediment can turn into hard sedimentary rock?

5. What kinds of sedimentary rock form from:
   a mud   b sand   c clay?

6. a What are the remains of shells found in the rock called?
   b What rock is made completely from shells?

2 The igneous rocks

Looking at granite...

Granite is a hard, speckled grey or pinky-grey rock. It forms the knobbly tors of Dartmoor and much of the Highlands of Scotland.

If you look closely, you can see that it is made of a mixture of tightly interlocking crystals. They include glassy quartz and grey or pink feldspar, arranged in a random pattern. The individual crystals are easy to see. They are several millimetres across.

You can easily see the crystals in granite.

The Giants' Causeway, Northern Ireland

You need a microscope to see the crystals in basalt.

... and basalt

Basalt is a hard black rock. It often forms thick layers that can cover large areas. Parts of Northern Ireland and the West Coast of Scotland are covered by basalt. In some places, the basalt has broken up into giant polygonal columns.

If you look closely at basalt, you will see little more than the odd lighter speckle in the dark rock. But if you cut a thin slice of the rock and look at it through a microscope, it seems very different. The rock is made of a mass of interlocking crystals, in a similar way to granite. But in basalt the crystals are too small to see without a microscope.

How did they form?

Crystals can grow when a solution evaporates. But granite and basalt are not soluble in water, so they could not have formed like this.

Crystals can also grow when a liquid cools and freezes. Both granite and basalt must have formed as molten rock cooled and set. Rocks that form in this way are called **igneous** rocks.

You can make **salol** crystals grow by carefully melting some salol in a tube and then pouring a few drops onto a microscope slide. If the slide is cold, the salol cools and sets rapidly and you get a lot of small crystals. But if the slide is warm, the salol cools more slowly. This time, you get fewer but larger crystals.

How does this explain the crystal sizes in rocks?

Volcanoes

The deeper you go underground, the hotter the rocks become. In many parts of the world, the rocks have got hot enough to melt – 1000 °C or more! If this molten rock reaches the surface, it pours out as **lava**. A volcano forms as the lava cools and turns to rock. Often the lava contains dissolved gas under pressure. This can sometimes make volcanic eruptions explosively dangerous – but very spectacular.

As the surface of the Earth is very cold – compared to molten rock – the lava cools very rapidly, so it has lots of tiny crystals. Basalt formed in this way too, which is why it has such small crystals!

A spectacular volcanic eruption.

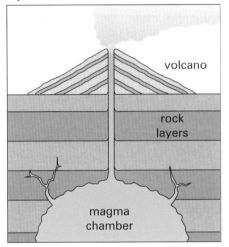

Most magma cools and solidifies underground.

What's underneath?

In places where there are active volcanoes and newly forming mountains, vast amounts of rock melt deep within the Earth's crust. Only a fraction of this reaches the surface of the Earth to form lava. The rest stays trapped deep within the crust.

Eventually this molten rock (**magma**) will start to cool and set. But it will take a very long time to cool down, as it is very well insulated (it is surrounded by hot rock). Because of this, the crystals have time to grow large. Granite forms when magma is trapped deep within the crust like this. That is why granite has large crystals.

How can we see it?

Igneous rocks that form on the surface of the Earth (the **extrusive** rocks) are easy to spot. But if granite formed deep within the crust, as an **intrusive** rock, how come you can see it at the surface now, on Dartmoor and in Scotland? The answer is that the rocks above have been steadily eroded away over millions of years.

The rocks of Scotland may have formed 40 km down in the crust, about 400 million years ago. That means that Scotland has been wearing away at the rate of 1 mm every ten years!

How long would it take to lose another 100 m off Ben Nevis?

1
  a Describe granite and basalt.
  b In what ways are they the same ?
  c In what ways are they different?

2
  a What are the two ways in which crystals can grow?
  b Which of these formed granite and basalt?
  c What are rocks that form in this way called?

3
  When you open a can of coke that has been heated or shaken, the contents squirt out everywhere. How does this compare to an erupting volcano?

4
  a Why does granite have larger crystals than basalt?
  b How come you can find granite at the surface?

3 All change

Earthquake!

In 1995, the people of Kobe were woken by a violent shaking. It was as if the ground was being shaken out like a rug beneath them. Japan had been hit by another powerful earthquake. The shock wave caused buildings and parts of the freeway system to collapse.

Parts of the Earth's crust are under enormous pressure. If the pressure gets too great, the rocks crack and move, sending out an earthquake shock wave. Sometimes you can see these cracks in the rocks. They are called **faults**.

◄ *Destruction in the streets - but it could have been much worse. An earthquake can be more powerful than a nuclear explosion!*

Going up

Given enough time, the effect of all this **tectonic** activity (earth movement) can be enormous. Sometimes after an earthquake, you can see that parts of the land have been pushed up. In places the seabed becomes dry land, for example. This may only mean a rise of a metre or two, but if it is repeated every few years for a million years or so, what was once the seabed can become a mountain! That is why you can often find fossil sea shells in rocks that are high in the mountains.

Going down

Rocks can go up – but they can also be forced down. Over millions of years, sediments can become buried deep in the roots of newly forming mountains. The heat and pressure can be so great there that once-hard rocks can be folded up like Plasticine.

The high temperatures also make the minerals in the rocks start to recrystallise. Limestone, for example, changes to marble, and any fossils it contained are lost. Rocks that have been changed like this are called **metamorphic** rocks.

The greater the temperature and pressure, the more and more extreme these changes become. This is most obvious with clay, which changes its appearance drastically as new minerals grow in the rock.

Metamorphic changes

Shale *is a soft, flaky sedimentary rock made from clay. It often contains fossils.*

If the pressure increases but the temperature is not too great, clay turns to **slate**. *All the minerals line up, which makes slate easy to split into thin sheets.*

If the temperature increases too, new minerals start to grow. Mica forms flat crystals which line up against the pressure. This makes a rock with wavy layers called **schist**.

The rock cycle

If the rock is heated too much, of course, it will melt. When this happens it forms **magma**. If this sets and cools you have an igneous rock again. This completes the cycle in which one rock type can change into another. The whole process may take hundreds of millions of years.

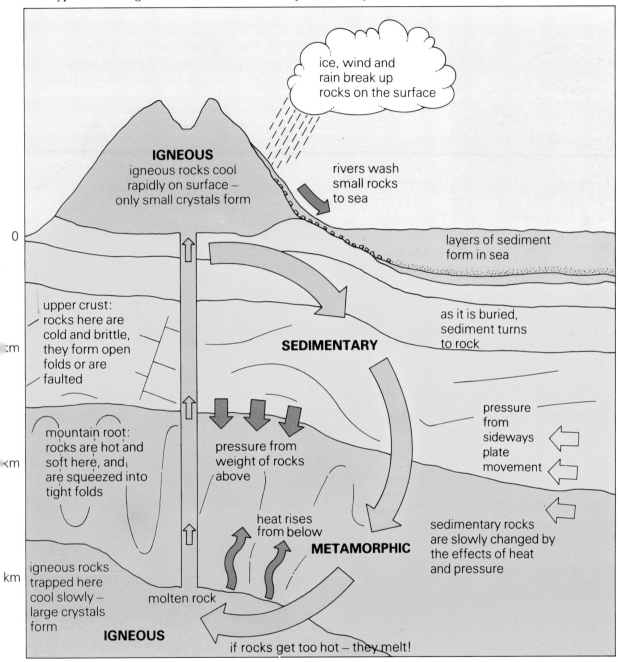

IGNEOUS
igneous rocks cool rapidly on surface – only small crystals form

ice, wind and rain break up rocks on the surface

rivers wash small rocks to sea

0

layers of sediment form in sea

km

upper crust: rocks here are cold and brittle, they form open folds or are faulted

SEDIMENTARY

as it is buried, sediment turns to rock

pressure from sideways plate movement

km

mountain root: rocks are hot and soft here, and are squeezed into tight folds

pressure from weight of rocks above

km

igneous rocks trapped here cool slowly – large crystals form

heat rises from below

METAMORPHIC

sedimentary rocks are slowly changed by the effects of heat and pressure

molten rock

IGNEOUS

if rocks get too hot – they melt!

1 What must have happened to the rocks to cause an earthquake?

2 What evidence is there that some rocks found in the mountains must have formed in the sea?

3 What happens to limestone when it is buried, heated and squashed deep under the mountains?

4 How does shale change as the heat and pressure increases?

5 Granite and schist are made of similar crystalline minerals. How can you tell them apart?

4 Finding out about the past

How many different folds can you see?

The rocks around us

We are lucky in Britain to live in such a stable area – free from volcanoes. Yet looking around our coasts and mountains, we can see much evidence that this was not always so. Layered sediments have been **folded**, and igneous and metamorphic rocks (see pages 100–103) are common in some areas. All of this is *evidence* which helps us to understand what must have happened in the past.

Firstly, we can compare what we see with what we *know* happens today: pebbles collect on beaches; lava comes out of volcanoes and so on.

Secondly, we can get some idea of the *order* of past events from the order of sedimentary rocks. The oldest layers are those at the bottom; older rocks might also be more altered, or might have suffered more folding and so on.

Any old bones?

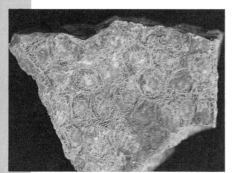

Fossils are often found in sedimentary rocks.

Many sedimentary rocks contain **fossils** – these are the remains of animals or plants which lived millions of years ago. Most fossils consist of an 'imprint' in a rock: the imprint shows the shape of shells, bones or leaves of the animal or plant which formed the fossil. Such fossils can give us a lot of information about the *age* of the rocks and *where* they were formed.

Certain fossils are very much like animals that are alive today. This means we can assume that the animals from which the fossils have come must have lived in a similar way to their modern-day relatives. If the fossils of sea shells are found in rocks at the top of mountains, we can be sure that those rocks must have started off as sediments laid down at the bottom of the sea.

Going back in time

Other fossils are unlike anything we find today, but they can still give us useful clues. In the south and east of England, the rocks are often quite soft, barely changed from the original sediments. Many of these rocks contain the coiled shells of fossil **ammonites**. To the north and west, however, the rocks appear harder and more changed. And here, strange fossil **trilobites** are found. Rocks containing ammonites never lie below those rocks containing trilobites. This means rocks containing ammonites are *younger* than those with trilobite fossils.

Not all the rocks in Britain are of the same age. ▶

Would you 'date' a fossil?!

By careful study of fossils, the idea of dating the Earth has been extended to produce a standard sequence known as the **stratigraphic column**. Any rock containing fossils can be matched up to this to give the *relative age* of the rock. Life on Earth has changed steadily – **evolved** – over millions of years, so the fossils in each layer act as a 'time fingerprint'. The three main levels are shown here, but these have been further split into hundreds of different levels.

How old is this fossil?

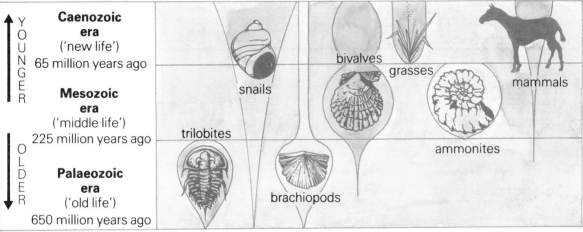

▲ *A stratigraphic column.*

A modern way to measure the past

Look closely at fossils – a simple solution to an age-old problem!

The one thing that fossils cannot do is indicate a precise age in millions of years. But scientists have found a way to do this by studying the **radioactive elements** in the rocks. This study has allowed us to add dates (as shown above) to the stratigraphic column. Radioactive dating also shows that fossils only tell us about part of the Earth's history. The oldest rocks dated in this way have been found to go back to 4000 million years – compare this to the paltry 650 million years age of the oldest rocks with trilobites.

Radioactive dating can give us an age in millions of years, but is very difficult and expensive to do. But a fossil expert could match a fossil to the stratigraphic column in seconds – for nothing! So which is better? It all depends on how accurate you want to be, the period you are seeking to date – and how much money you have got!

1. In a layered sequence of rocks, which is the oldest rock?

2. How is it possible for rocks on hill-tops to contain fossils of sea shells?

3. Give two advantages of radioactive dating.

4. Which era do these rocks come from?
   Rock A contains grass seeds and bones of horse-like mammals.
   Rock B contains trilobites and brachiopods.
   Rock C contains ammonites, bivalves and snails.

5 Useful rocks

Limestone

Limestone is a very important raw material, from which you can make lots of different products. Over 150 million tonnes of limestone are quarried and used in Britain every year.

Some of these products just involve quarrying, cutting or crushing the rock. Carefully cut limestone blocks have been used for centuries; for example, to build important buildings such as cathedrals. It can also be finely carved for statues and ornamentation. More recently, much limestone is simply crushed to make chippings for roads. The chippings are set in bitumen which is made from oil (see page 111).

Canterbury Cathedral was built from blocks of limestone, the road is surfaced with limestone chippings.

Heating limestone

Powdered limestone can also be put onto fields as a simple fertiliser, as it can neutralise acid soils. But to make this more effective, the limestone is usually roasted first, which turns it into a new chemical.

Limestone is made of a chemical called **calcium carbonate**. This breaks down when it is heated strongly, and carbon dioxide gas is given off – that's the same gas that you breathe out! The calcium oxide powder that is left is called **quicklime**. It is very dangerous and corrosive and would burn your skin.

This farmer is putting slaked lime on his fields to improve the soil.

$$\text{calcium carbonate} \rightarrow \text{calcium oxide} + \text{carbon dioxide}$$

If calcium oxide is put into water, it reacts very violently, giving out a lot of heat. It turns into calcium hydroxide (**slaked lime**), which is safer to handle.

$$\text{calcium oxide} + \text{water} \rightarrow \text{calcium hydroxide}$$

Calcium hydroxide has been made by farmers to put on their fields for hundreds of years. Now it is also put into lakes that have become too acid because of pollution. Calcium oxide was also mixed with water to make a paste called **mortar**, which was used to stick bricks together. The paste gradually turns hard when it is exposed to the air.

Cement and concrete

Much of the limestone we quarry nowadays is heated up with clay to make **cement**. Cement is made into a paste with water, like mortar, but it hardens quickly when it dries.

Most cement is mixed with sand and gravel to make **concrete**. This versatile material can be poured into any shape of mould, but quickly sets rock-hard. It is used to make road-pavements, bridge supports, building frameworks and foundations. It is often covered with brick or decorative stone, though some architects think it looks great on its own.

You can mix concrete yourself in a cement mixer – but it is brought in by tanker for larger jobs!

Sand and sandstone

Sand and sandstone are also common rocks. They are mostly made from **silica**, silicon dioxide. We use 160 million tonnes of **sand** (or the coarser **gravel**) every year as **aggregates** – the fillers that are mixed in with the cement in concrete. They may be quarried from ancient sand beds, or dredged from rivers.

Some sands are very pure, consisting of nothing but worn grains of crystalline silica – quartz. These pure sands are heated with limestone to make glass. They have to be pure or the glass will not be clear and **transparent**. The two chemicals react and melt, driving off carbon dioxide.

calcium + silicon → calcium + carbon
carbonate dioxide   silicate   dioxide

Only the purest quartz sand can be used for glass-making.

Clay

Clay is no good to use on its own for building as it turns to mud in the rain. But if it is heated strongly in a kiln it turns to hard **brick**. Over 5 million tonnes of clay are quarried in Britain every year and used for brick making or in cement.

Sometimes granite weathers to give a very pure white form of clay. This can be softened with a little water and moulded into shape. When it is baked it makes **china**.

1 Much of the limestone that is quarried today is simply crushed into small pieces. What are these pieces used for?

2 What chemical reaction happens when limestone is heated?

3 Why do farmers put slaked lime on their fields?

4 What advantage does cement have over old-fashioned mortar?

5 Why is concrete such a useful building material?

6 Why does glassmaking sand have to be so pure?

7 Why might London have so many brick houses?

6 Fossil fuels

Trapping sunshine

Plants make their own food from simple chemicals, using the energy from sunlight. When you eat plants, you tap into this 'sunlight energy' that is stored in the plants. Trees contain large amounts of stored 'sunlight energy' in their wood. You also get this energy back when you burn wood as a **fuel**.

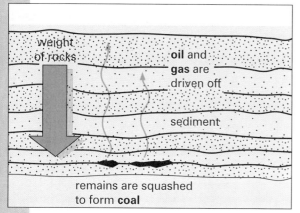

Great heat and pressures deep in the Earth transformed buried plant material into coal.

Fossil fuels - ancient energy stores

This process of 'trapping sunlight' has been going on for millions of years. Most of the plant material formed in this way broke down soon after the plants died. It then released its energy to bacteria and fungi that cause decay.

But some plant material became trapped in sediments. This material was sealed in and protected from total decay. This material has retained its trapped energy – until now, when we dig up this '**fossil**' material and use it as fuel. When we burn fossil fuels – **coal**, **oil** and **gas** – we are releasing the energy store that was built up by plants, using sunlight, millions of years ago.

Millions of years in minutes!

This experiment shows how fossil fuels might have formed when plants (and animals) were buried by sediments, millions of years ago.

Wood is heated in a closed container, away from the oxygen that would make it burn.

As the wood is heated, any liquids and gases in it are driven off and the complex chemicals break down. What is left behind is charcoal – almost pure carbon. Coal must have formed, deep underground, in a similar way.

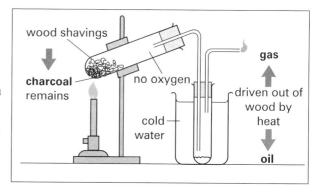

Heating wood without oxygen.

British coal

Britain is very lucky in having large coal reserves. This is because about 300 million years ago, it was largely covered by great swamp forests. Rivers rushing from mountains in the north poured sediment into the area, burying great areas of forest that had sunk beneath the water. This process was repeated many times. Eventually the forests were crushed and the many British coal fields were formed.

From soft plants to hard rocks – powerful cutting machines are needed to remove the coal.

A long time coming

Oil and gas were also produced from the remains of dead plants and animals that collected at the bottom of ancient seas. They were covered by layers of sand and mud, which prevented them from decaying. Instead, great heat and pressure broke the materials down into **crude oil** and **natural gas**. The tiny droplets of oil and bubbles of gas rose through sponge-like **porous rock** like sandstone. In some places, they kept on rising until they reached the surface. The black oil collected there as a black sludge.

Black sludge to black gold

Nobody bothered with it until 1859 in Pennsylvania, USA where it was discovered that the black sludge could be made into a good substitute for the whale oil used in lamps. Soon people began drilling all over for the crude oil. By **purifying** the sludge, different parts could be used for heating, lighting and water-proofing. Soon it was in demand as a fuel for cars. The oil rush had begun! Nowadays, oil is also used to make plastics and other useful chemicals.

Most oil and gas is trapped under dome-shaped rocks. ▶

Oil traps

Once all the oil near the surface had been used up, scientists had to look for it deeper in the ground. Sometimes the dead plant and animal material had been covered up by mud millions of years ago. This mud eventually formed **non-porous shale** which trapped the oil and gas. All the scientists had to do was to find the right rock formation, drill a hole and pump up the oil and gas. Sounds easy, but it costs millions to drill one well – and only 1 in 40 wells turn out to be in the right place!

The many dome shapes on the surface of this area suggest oil may be below – the many small oil wells confirm it! ▶

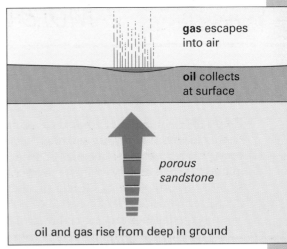

Oil was first found at the surface. ▲

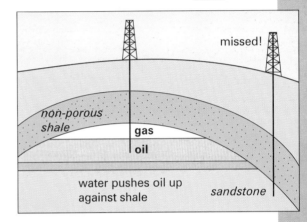

1 Where did the stored energy in fossil fuels originally come from?

2 When dead wood is left to rot on the surface it turns back to simple gases, just like when it is burnt in air. Why didn't this happen to the wood that has now turned into coal?

3 Why has Britain got such a lot of coal?

4 How can oil and gas rise up through rocks such as sandstone?

5 Why do oil and gas collect under domes of shale?

6 a What were the three original uses for crude oil?
   b What are crude oil products used for today?

7 More about crude oil

What is crude oil?

Crude oil is a mixture of compounds called **hydrocarbons**. Hydrocarbons contain particles called **molecules**. These molecules are made up of even smaller particles – **atoms** – of hydrogen and carbon joined together in chains. Each molecule has a backbone of carbon atoms. The number of carbon atoms – the **chain length** – is different for each type of hydrocarbon. Molecules with a long chain length are heavier, and so those hydrocarbons are less runny than those with short chain molecules. Crude oil is a mixture of molecules with different chain lengths.

Figure 1. Crude oil is a mixture of many different parts. Each part of the mixture is made up of hydrocarbons with a particular number of carbon atoms. ▼

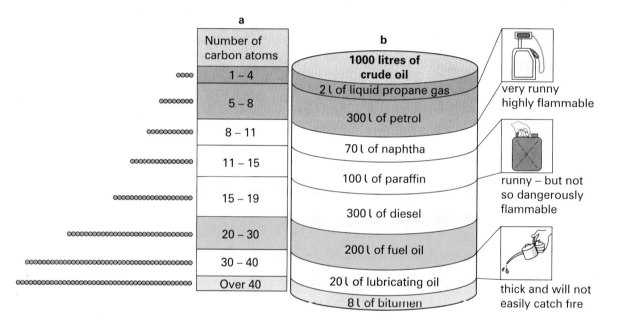

a

Number of carbon atoms
1 – 4
5 – 8
8 – 11
11 – 15
15 – 19
20 – 30
30 – 40
Over 40

b

1000 litres of crude oil
2 l of liquid propane gas
300 l of petrol
70 l of naphtha
100 l of paraffin
300 l of diesel
200 l of fuel oil
20 l of lubricating oil
8 l of bitumen

very runny highly flammable

runny – but not so dangerously flammable

thick and will not easily catch fire

How can you separate them?

The temperature at which a liquid turns to a gas is called its **boiling point**. Some liquids, like petrol, are made up of particles that are very small and light. These particles are free to move about easily, so only a little energy is needed to change them into a gas. Such liquids have low boiling points.

Other liquids, like lubricating oil, are made up of large, heavy molecules that need a lot of energy to make them move fast enough to become a gas. These liquids have high boiling points. Lubricating oil boils at 250 °C.

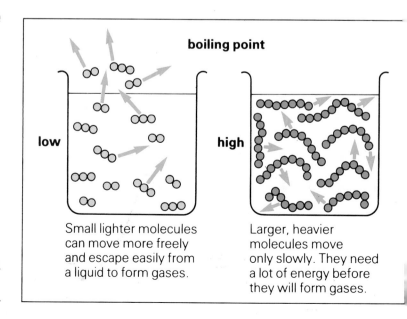

boiling point

low

high

Small lighter molecules can move more freely and escape easily from a liquid to form gases.

Larger, heavier molecules move only slowly. They need a lot of energy before they will form gases.

In the school lab

The different hydrocarbons that are mixed up in crude oil have different boiling points. Some have particles that are small and light and so they boil before the larger and heavier ones.

If you slowly increase the temperature, the light particles boil off first. They can be cooled and turned back to a liquid (**condensed**). After more heating, the heavier particles boil off – these can also be cooled and collected. This process is called **fractional distillation**. You can separate crude oil like this in the school laboratory.

A typical apparatus for the distillation of a mixture of liquids. ▶

light particles
boil off first
at low temperature

cold water out

after cooling, the gas particles condense to form a liquid

heavy particles boil off much later at high temperature

cold water in

a mixture of short and long chain molecules

HEAT

empty beakers to collect different **fractions** of the mixture

In industry

Crude oil is separated into its different parts by fractional distillation in industry, too. But there they use a different method. The oil is heated strongly in a furnace so that it all boils. The gases are then passed up into a **fractionating column**, which is hot at the bottom but cold at the top. The different hydrocarbons condense out at different levels in the tower and can be run off.

This is done on a very large scale in industry. The crude oil is continuously piped in at one end, and the different fractions piped out at the other. This helps to keep the costs down.

Figure 2. You can see how useful crude oil is once it is separated into its various fractions. ▶

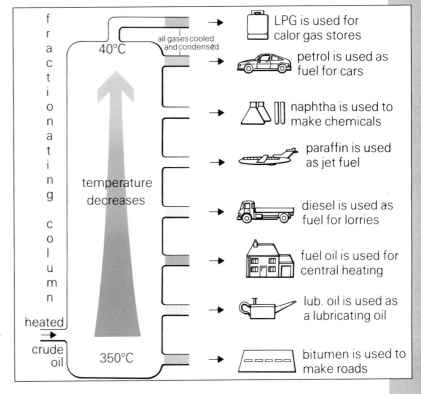

fractionating column

40°C

all gases cooled and condensed

LPG is used for calor gas stores

petrol is used as fuel for cars

naphtha is used to make chemicals

paraffin is used as jet fuel

temperature decreases

diesel is used as fuel for lorries

fuel oil is used for central heating

lub. oil is used as a lubricating oil

heated

crude oil

350°C

bitumen is used to make roads

1 What is crude oil a mixture of?

2 a Look at Figure 1. How does it show you that paraffin is a mixture of hydrocarbons and not a pure compound?
b How does Figure 1. show you that petrol is more runny than bitumen?

3 How does the boiling point of hydro-carbons change with their chain length?

4 Describe how you could separate molecules with different chain lengths from crude oil in the school laboratory.

5 How are the different fractions in crude oil separated in industry?

6 Make a list of all the useful products made from crude oil.

8 New products from crude oil

More uses of oil

Crude oil can be processed even more to produce 'extra helpings' of the parts that are in great demand. This processing also produces chemicals which are used to make **plastics**.

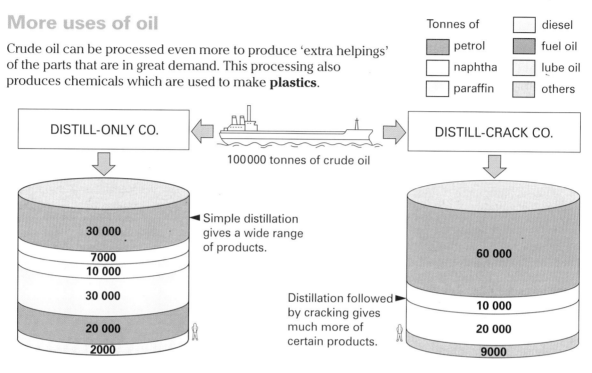

Tonnes of
- petrol
- naphtha
- paraffin
- diesel
- fuel oil
- lube oil
- others

DISTILL-ONLY CO.

100 000 tonnes of crude oil

DISTILL-CRACK CO.

30 000
7000
10 000
30 000
20 000
2000

◄ Simple distillation gives a wide range of products.

60 000
10 000
20 000
9000

Distillation followed ► by cracking gives much more of certain products.

What is cracking?

The biggest demand is for short-chain hydrocarbons like those in petrol, so oil companies have plenty of long-chain hydrocarbons left over. Fortunately these can be 'chopped up' into smaller pieces by **cracking**. This happens if the molecules are heated to very high temperatures.

If petrol, naphtha and paraffin are in great demand, which company will find it easiest to sell its products?

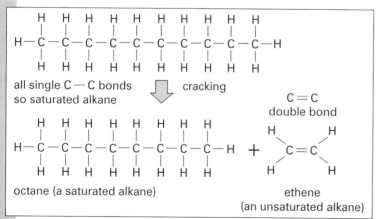

all single C — C bonds so saturated alkane

cracking

C = C double bond

octane (a saturated alkane)

ethene (an unsaturated alkane)

*Strong heating causes long-chain hydrocarbons to split into shorter pieces. This one has split into saturated **octane** and unsaturated **ethene**.*

Alkanes and alkenes ━━ Ⓗ

Crude oil hydrocarbons are called **alkanes**. They have their carbon atoms joined by single chemical bonds. They cannot make any more bonds so they are said to be **saturated**. When they are cracked, there are not enough hydrogen atoms to go on all the bonds, so a double bond forms between two of the carbon atoms. This forms a new hydrocarbon called an **alkene**. More atoms could be added if this double bond opened up again, so alkenes are said to be **unsaturated**. Unsaturated hydrocarbons are very useful...

How are they useful?

The double bonds in alkenes can 'snap open' and join with other molecules in what are called addition reactions. Small alkene molecules, called **monomers**, can join together in this way, to form long-chain molecules called **addition polymers**. For example, ethene can be made to **polymerise** like this, forming chains of between 1000 and 2000 carbon atoms in length. This new substance is called **poly(e)thene**, and is very useful for making bottles and bags!

Substances like this are called **plastics**, as they are so easy to shape. Different monomers can be made into different polymer plastics, with different properties. Propene can be made into polypropene for bowls, crates, ropes and carpets. Styrene can be made into polystyrene, which is used for radio and cassette player cases. It is also made into a foam for packaging or ceiling tiles.

Monomers can be chained together to make an addition polymer.

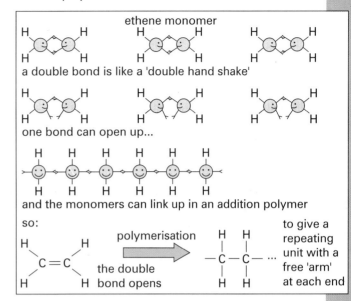

What are plastics used for?

Today we really do live in a 'plastic' world...

Different forms of plastics have different properties – each property gives rise to different uses.

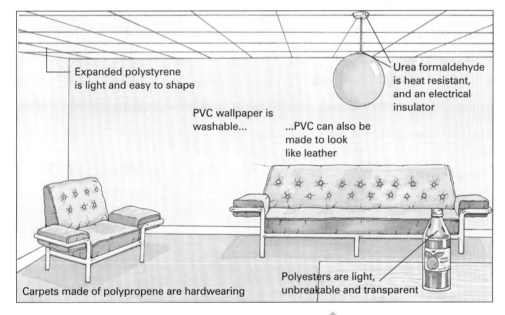

Expanded polystyrene is light and easy to shape

Urea formaldehyde is heat resistant, and an electrical insulator

PVC wallpaper is washable...

...PVC can also be made to look like leather

Carpets made of polypropene are hardwearing

Polyesters are light, unbreakable and transparent

---

1 Look at the figure on the opposite page.
  a Which fractions are cracked after being distilled?
  b Which fraction was produced in the greatest amount by cracking?

2 Why is heat needed for cracking?

3 What is the difference between a saturated and unsaturated hydrocarbon?

4 Draw the shape of the polymer formed by joining 10 ethene monomers. Explain why the polymer can still increase its chain length.

5 Plastic bottles for fizzy drinks are made of polyester. What properties does it have which make it ideal for this use?

6 Why do some people think the use of crude oil as a fuel wastes resources?

9 Burning up

What's in the air?

The air is mostly made of just two gases. Just under four-fifths is an unreactive gas called nitrogen. Just over a fifth is oxygen – the gas you need to breathe.

The air also contains a small amount of other unreactive gases and carbon dioxide. Plants need the carbon dioxide to grow.

Burning up

When things burn in air, they are reacting with the oxygen to make new chemicals called **oxides**. Sometimes these oxides are solids.

When you burn magnesium ribbon, a white powder called magnesium oxide is formed. You also get a lot of heat and light.

magnesium + oxygen → magnesium oxide + energy

Burning simple fuels

When you burn a fuel, the fuel is reacting with oxygen and you get oxide gases formed – but you are usually more interested in the heat and light!

Hydrogen is the simplest fuel. When you burn it you get hydrogen oxide – better known as water! As it is so hot, the water comes off as steam.

hydrogen + oxygen → water + energy

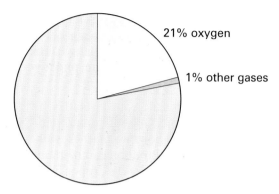

21% oxygen

1% other gases

78% nitrogen

The air is one fifth oxygen. This is the gas you need to breathe – or start a fire!

Magnesium burns to give white magnesium oxide.

The Space Shuttle burns hydrogen in its main engines, so it is steam powered!

Coal is made of carbon. When you burn this you get carbon dioxide – the same gas that you breath out.

carbon + oxygen → carbon dioxide + energy

The space shuttle blasts steam out of its main engines as the hydrogen burns.

Burning other fuels

Other fuels such as oil, gas or wood contain carbon and hydrogen, so you get both carbon dioxide *and* water when you burn them. For example, with gas:

natural + oxygen → carbon + water + energy
gas   dioxide

Wax contains carbon and hydrogen, so you get these gases when you burn a candle, too. You can collect the gases as shown, using a pump.

Water condenses and collects in the cold tube. You can test it with blue cobalt chloride paper: it will turn pink, which proves the liquid is water.

Limewater is used to test for carbon dioxide. As the gas bubbles through the limewater, it turns milky. This shows that carbon dioxide has been produced too.

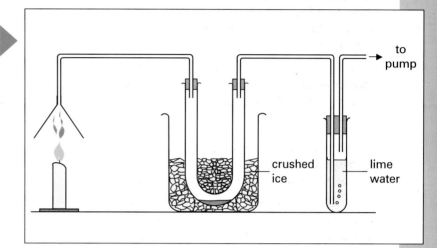

Fires and fighting

We have to burn fuels to get the stored energy from them. That's fine, as long as we have everything under control. But sometimes fires start by accident or spread out of control. Then they are very dangerous. How can they be put out?

Fires need something to burn (a fuel) and oxygen for the fuel to react with. They also need heat! Most fuels need a 'kick-start' of energy to light them – you need a spark to light the gas, for example – but once started they provide enough energy to keep themselves going.

So three things make up the **fire triangle**: fuel, oxygen and heat. If you can get rid of any one of these, the fire will go out.

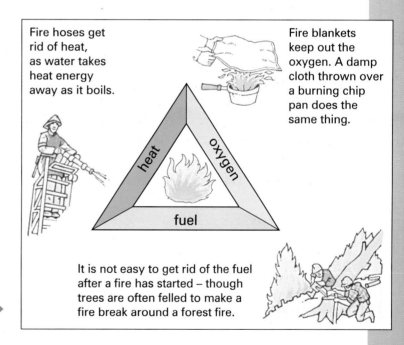

Fire hoses get rid of heat, as water takes heat energy away as it boils.

Fire blankets keep out the oxygen. A damp cloth thrown over a burning chip pan does the same thing.

It is not easy to get rid of the fuel after a fire has started – though trees are often felled to make a fire break around a forest fire.

---

1 Which gas in the air do you need when you breathe? How much of it is there in the air?

2 In what way is the Space Shuttle steam powered?

3 What does your breath have in common with a coal fire?

4 How can you show that the waste gas from a burning candle contains:
  a water?
  b carbon dioxide?

5 What three things are needed for a fire to keep burning?

6 Why does water put out simple wood fires?

10 Polluting the air

Acid rain

If fossils fuels were pure, you would just get carbon dioxide and water when you burn them. Unfortunately, they often contain sulphur as an impurity. When this burns, it makes the choking, poisonous gas, sulphur dioxide.

$$\text{sulphur} + \text{oxygen} \rightarrow \text{sulphur dioxide}$$

When this gas dissolves in water and reacts with more oxygen, it makes sulphuric acid!

In the past, power stations that burnt fossil fuels to get the energy to make electricity just pumped this sulphur dioxide into the air, causing terrible pollution. The gas dissolved in the rain to make **acid rain**, which fell on the surrounding areas.

Sometimes the rain was as acid as the vinegar you put on your chips! Acid rain damages limestone buildings and ruins statues, but it also kills trees and the fish in lakes.

To stop this happening, power stations had tall chimneys built, to carry the sulphur dioxide away in the wind. Unfortunately, this just meant that acid rain fell somewhere else. Much of Britain's acid rain was blown across the North Sea and fell on Norway, killing trees and fish there. The Norwegians were not very happy about this!

One British export that was not welcome!

Today, power stations have to spray water through their waste gases to dissolve the sulphur dioxide before it gets into the air. Lakes that have become too acid can be improved by adding lime, which neutralises the acid.

City smog

If you visit a large city on a still, sunny day, the chances are that your enjoyment will be spoilt by the choking fumes from car and lorry exhausts. When the petrol/air mixture burns in a car engine, some of the nitrogen in the air reacts too, forming nitrogen monoxide. This reacts in the air to make brown nitrogen dioxide. You can often see this as a brown haze in the distance on 'smoggy' days.

But it is not just the appearance that is the problem. Exhaust gases contain other poisonous gases such as carbon monoxide, and diesel engines give out tiny soot particles. When these mix with the air, sunlight sets off reactions that make ozone. The result is a lethal cocktail of gases that makes asthma worse and even kills many people who have severe breathing problems.

Smog over the Thames in London.

The greenhouse effect

These problems come from impurities in fuels. But what about the carbon dioxide that is produced? You breathe that out too, so surely *that* cannot be a problem, can it?

The Earth is in balance between the heat it gets from the sun during the day, and the heat it loses to space at night. Carbon dioxide in the air acts like a greenhouse, trapping some of the day's heat and stopping it from escaping. If there wasn't enough carbon dioxide, the Earth would start to cool down. If there is too much, the Earth will start to warm up.

Over the past hundred years or so, burning fossil fuels has pumped extra carbon dioxide into the atmosphere. Some of this is used up by plants, but so much extra has been produced that all the plants in the world cannot keep up with it. It does not help, of course, that vast areas of rainforest have also been cleared over the same period. The rainforests act as the 'lungs' of the planet, removing carbon dioxide and making more oxygen.

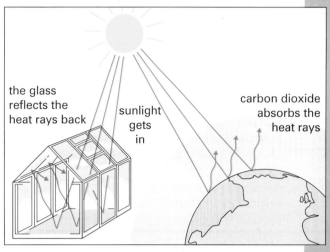

the glass reflects the heat rays back

sunlight gets in

carbon dioxide absorbs the heat rays

The glass in a greenhouse lets sunlight through but stops heat energy escaping. Carbon dioxide in the atmosphere does a similar thing.

Low-lying countries such as Bangladesh will be even more prone to flooding if the greenhouse effect causes the ice caps to melt.

'Global warming'

Scientists now think that this extra carbon dioxide has increased the **greenhouse effect** and so started to warm up the planet. It may only be a degree or so on average, but that could be enough to upset the weather patterns, bring drought to some areas and floods to others. It also makes some of the ice locked up at the poles melt, which will raise the sea level enough for the sea to completely flood some low-lying areas. We need to cut back on our use of fossil fuels before this gets out of control!

---

1 Where does the sulphur dioxide that causes acid rain come from?

2 How did 'British' acid rain end up in Norway?

3 How do power stations help to prevent acid rain today?

4
  a How does 'city smog' form?
  b What does it look like?
  c Why is it so dangerous?

5
  a How does the greenhouse effect work?
  b Why has the effect got greater over the last 100 years?
  c Why does cutting down forests make it worse?

11 The evolving atmosphere

In the beginning

Viewed from space, the Earth seems very beautiful, with the blue of the oceans and the white swirling clouds in the atmosphere. But when the Earth first formed, $4\frac{1}{2}$ billion years ago, things were very different. The Earth was molten at first, and any original atmosphere boiled away into space. Eventually the surface rocks cooled and hardened, forming a thin crust, and water vapour condensed to form the oceans. Volcanic activity continued to blast out gases such as steam, carbon dioxide, ammonia and methane, forming an atmosphere totally unlike the one we have today. So how did it change?

The Earth from space – but it hasn't always looked as beautiful as this.

You can still find some anaerobic bacteria in the mud of stagnant ponds – but oxygen still kills them!

Plants the polluters

Life started to evolve on Earth billions of years ago – simple bacteria that lived in the sea, 'eating' the simple chemicals that formed with the Earth. But one group of bacteria evolved that could make their own food, using the energy from sunlight – they had evolved **photosynthesis**. These were the ancestors of the modern plants, and they changed the world!

These simple plants produced oxygen as a waste product of photosynthesis, just as plants do today. But to the other life-forms of the time, oxygen was a deadly poisonous gas – as poisonous as chlorine gas is to you now! So plants were the first polluters, and their polluting oxygen nearly killed off all the other life-forms on the planet. You can only find the descendants of these other types of bacteria today in oxygen-free (**anaerobic**) environments such as the stinking mud at the bottom of stagnant ponds.

Changing the balance

Since those early times, the atmosphere has changed in various ways. The oxygen levels rose because of photosynthesis, but have been steady now about 200 million years. The carbon dioxide levels dropped as more plants grew, eventually spreading over the land. Plants 'lock up' carbon in their woody tissues. Carbon dioxide also dissolves in the sea, where shellfish lock it up in calcium carbonate in their shells. Nitrogen formed in the atmosphere as ammonia reacted with oxygen. More nitrogen was added by bacteria that release it from rotting plant material as they feed.

The ozone layer...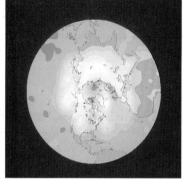

Although the oxygen started off as a poison in the atmosphere, it did help higher life-forms to evolve on the Earth. The surface of the Earth was originally being bombarded by dangerous cosmic rays, but these react with oxygen to make **ozone**. Ozone is a dangerously poisonous gas near to the surface of the Earth, but if it drifts up into the upper atmosphere it makes a protective shield, blocking out the harmful radiation. In this protected environment, animals evolved that could use the oxygen to get energy from plant material – your primitive ancestors!

The thinning ozone layer over Antarctica, shown up on a colour-enhanced satellite image.

... at risk!

Recently, there have been concerns that the protective ozone layer has become thinner in places, letting harmful radiation through. Some **ultraviolet** radiation gets through in any case; it can cause sunburn if you don't have a protective tan. But where the ozone layer is thinner it lets through much more dangerous radiation that increases the chances of sunburn and can also cause skin cancer.

The main culprits for this seem to be **CFC** chemicals, which have been used in fridges and aerosol cans for years. They were used because they were so unreactive, but because they did not react with ordinary oxygen they got up to the ozone layer. Ozone is so reactive that they *did* react there, weakening the protective layer. CFCs are banned now, but it will be a long time before all their effects are removed.

A delicate balance

So the atmosphere has slowly evolved to its present composition, and is in a state of delicate balance. The waste products from our modern technology are in danger of upsetting this balance. There is the ozone layer problem, but also the greenhouse effect and acid rain. How can we help to protect the atmosphere? First, we must do whatever we can to reduce our pollution levels. One way would be to use less fossil fuels. But we could also help the Earth to heal itself. The great forests and the shallow seas help to look after the atmosphere, so we must look after *them*.

If we look after the Earth, perhaps it will look after us!

MAD ABOUT... TROPICAL RAIN FORESTS

THE WORLD'S RAINFORESTS ARE IN DANGER! Every year, an area of rainforest the size of England and Wales is DESTROYED or DAMAGED. This means that EVERY SECOND an area of rainforest the size of a football pitch is destroyed.

FRIENDS *of the* earth

1 What was the original atmosphere of the Earth like?

2 What effect did the evolution of primitive plants have on the other early life-forms?

3 How has carbon dioxide been removed from the atmosphere?

4 How has nitrogen been added?

5 How did oxygen in the atmosphere help animals to evolve?

6 Why is the ozone layer thought to be at risk?

7 What can be done to maintain the delicate balance of our atmosphere?

12 Earth: the inside story

Don't be daft, Use a seismometer.

How can we tell?

The Earth is a planet – a great ball of rock 13 000 km across! How can we hope to find out what it's like inside? Our deepest mines scratch barely 13 km into the surface! There are some clues. For one thing, the density of the Earth is just about twice that of ordinary rock, so it must get denser inside. And meteorites that crash to Earth tell us what else there is in the solar system. Some meteorites are rocky, like dense basalt. But others are made of nickel and iron, and these are much denser. Nickel and iron are magnetic, and the Earth has a magnetic field, so that could be another clue.

What else?

Another line of evidence uses the same trick that builders use to find out what's behind a wall – tap it and listen to the vibrations! Of course, it's not quite that simple. You would need a very loud tap to pass right through the Earth. But nature often does the job for us – with **earthquakes**.

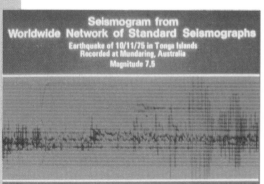

Seismogram from Worldwide Network of Standard Seismographs
Earthquake of 10/11/75 in Tonga Islands
Recorded at Mundaring, Australia
Magnitude 7.5

◀ A seismometer recording.

Measuring earthquakes

We can easily feel earthquakes if we are unfortunate enough to be standing too close. But we need a special instrument to measure the tiny vibrations from distant ones. This instrument is called a **seismometer**, and the world is now dotted with seismometer stations. These are able to detect even the slightest tremor. The results are then put together and analysed by computers.

What they tell us

As soon as an earthquake is detected, seismometer stations compare the information to find out where it occurred. When all the earthquakes are plotted on a map we find that the powerful, destructive ones follow the lines already marked out by volcanoes – around the Pacific and along the young mountain chains, with a weaker set along the undersea volcanic ridges.

Cuba
Puerto Rico
Jamaica
Haiti
Dominican Republic
Martinique
Caribbean Sea
Grenada
Panama
Venezuela
Colombia
Key: ● Volcano   × Earthquake

Earthquake and volcano sites in the Caribbean.

A soft boiled Earth

Shock waves pass down through the Earth too. It is these fainter signals that can give us an 'inside-view' of our planet. The results tell us that we live on a round, rock version of a soft-boiled egg!

The crust This is the hard, brittle outer layer. Compared to the diameter of the Earth, the crust is very thin. You could compare its thickness to that of a piece of 'cling-film' wrapped around a football. It is broken in places, but still holds together – rather like the cracked shell of a soft-boiled egg.

The mantle Beneath the crust is a very large layer of dense, hot, semi-liquid rock – the **mantle**. Over millions of years, the mantle moves around. This gradually changes the shape of the crust above the mantle. In the terms of the 'soft-boiled egg' model, the mantle is like the white of an undercooked boiled egg.

The core The Earth has a liquid centre – the **core** – which consists of molten metal (iron and nickel).

It is the effect of swirling electric currents in this core that gives the Earth its magnetic field. Radioactive decay in the core and mantle is the source of all the heat energy released by the Earth. The core is like the yolk of an egg, but with strong swirling movements that keep the core well-mixed. There is evidence, however, that the very centre of the Earth is a ball of solid metal.

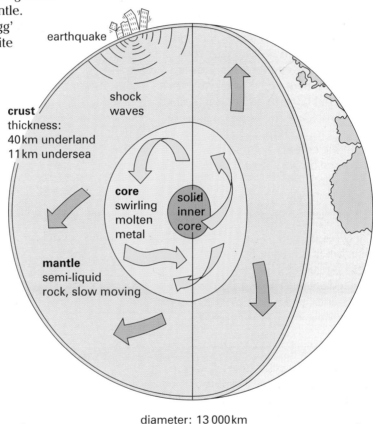

earthquake

shock waves

crust thickness: 40 km underland 11 km undersea

core swirling molten metal

solid inner core

mantle semi-liquid rock, slow moving

diameter: 13 000 km

How did it happen?

5000 million years ago, the Earth was a molten ball of rock and metal. On cooling, the **crust** formed – just like ice forming on the surface of water (or the skin forming on custard). At the same time, the dense iron and nickel sank down to form the **core**. This left behind the molten rock which formed the **mantle**.

1 How can we find out what the inside of the Earth is like?

2 **a** How did the crust of the Earth form?
b What causes part of the crust to change shape?

3 Describe simply the layers of the Earth. Do these layers remind you of anything apart from an egg?

4 Find out how a seismometer works.

13 Tecton the builder

Wear it down – build it up

All around the world, weathering and erosion are steadily wearing away the ancient mountains. It's a slow process – perhaps just 1 mm every few years – but don't forget that the Earth has been around for 4.5 billion years!

The material worn from the mountains is turned into layers of new sediment in the sea, which harden to sedimentary rock. Sometimes those sedimentary rocks are simply lifted up high above sea level again, as in the Grand Canyon, Arizona. There the beds of rock are still horizontal, with the youngest rocks at the top. If you walk down into the Grand Canyon, you are walking down through time, as the rocks get older and older.

More often, however, the sediments have been squeezed from the sides, and forced up into great folds, or broken up into blocks by **faults**. When the rocks break along faults, earthquakes occur, and these processes are often accompanied by volcanic activity and metamorphism. Most sediments end up like this – recycled into mountains. How could this happen?

The horizontal beds in the Grand Canyon have been lifted nearly 2 km above sea level.

The mountains of the Himalayas are built from folded sediments and volcanic rock.

The heat is on

Have you ever noticed how warm air rises above a radiator, while cold air flows out over your toes when you open a fridge? This also happens when you heat water: the hot water rises, and a swirling **convection cell** is set up.

Something very similar seems to be going on in the rocks of the Earth's mantle. These rocks seem fairly solid, yet over millions of years, they can change shape and circulate round just like water! This has caused the Earth's crust (and a slab of mantle) to crack up into a gigantic jigsaw-puzzle of pieces called **plates**. And what is more, these plates are still moving around...by a few centimetres every year! That is enough to cause earthquakes where the plate edges rub against each other. Over millions of years, this process can make major changes to the surface of the Earth. This process of change is called **plate tectonics**, after Tecton, the builder in Greek mythology.

Convection: The purple colour rises with the hot water at the centre. As the water cools, you can see that it moves to the side and then downwards.

Cracking up!

Where hot mantle rock rises, it splits the crust apart! This is even happening today – in Africa. Arabia continues to be torn out of Africa, opening up the Red Sea by a few centimetres every year.

300 million years ago, Europe was joined to America: but a large crack formed. Molten rock rose up from the mantle to fill the gap. This crack has continued to widen ever since. Topped up with water, the result is the Atlantic ocean! Iceland sits across the crack – and is getting wider every year!

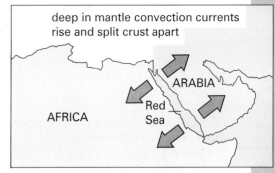

Arabia is splitting away from Africa.

Fold mountains

If some of the jigsaw pieces of the Earth are moving apart, others must be coming together! When this happens the sediments at the edges of the plates are folded and crumpled into new mountains. Explosive volcanoes are common in these areas, such as those in the 'Ring of Fire' around the Pacific.

Where continents collide, great **fold mountains** form between them. The Alps formed as Africa collided with Europe, and the Himalayas rose up as India rammed into Asia.

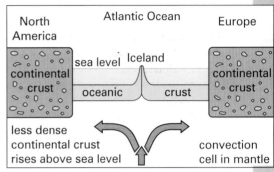

The Atlantic Ocean is getting wider by about 2 cm every year.

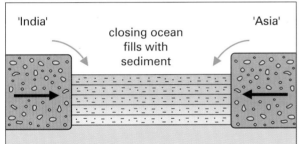

New mountains form when continents collide.

The plate tectonic jigsaw

If you look at the way the plates of the Earth are arranged now, and at the way they are moving, it is easy to explain why some areas are more at risk from earthquakes and volcanoes than others.

Britain is more than 1000 km from the edge of the Eurasian plate. This means there are no active volcanoes and no severe earthquakes.

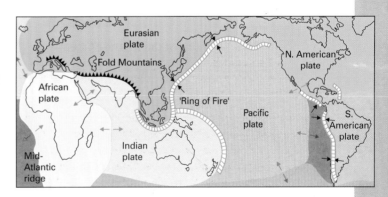

1 How are sediments 'recycled' into mountains?

2 What process makes the plates move?

3 Why is Africa 'cracking up'?

4 How did the Himalayas form?

5 Why is Iceland getting wider?

6 a What is the 'Ring of Fire'?
   b Suggest other areas that might have a lot of volcanoes.

14 More about plate tectonics

The jigsaw fit

A hundred years ago, scientists noticed that South America and Africa seemed to fit together. They thought that perhaps the Earth had got bigger and split a continent apart, forming the Atlantic ocean. But there was no other evidence for this, so no-one took any notice.

In 1912, another scientist called Alfred Wegener looked in detail at the fit between South America and Africa and concluded that they *must* have split apart. He called this **continental drift**, but he couldn't explain how it could work, so nobody believed him either.

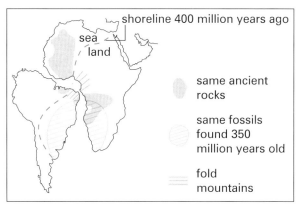

South America and Africa fit together so well – could it just be chance?

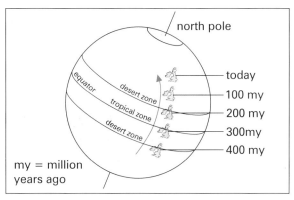

Britain has slowly moved northwards over the last 400 million years.

A drifting pole?

In the 1950s, scientists studying the Earth's magnetic field found that it left a record in the rocks. From this, you could tell where the north pole must have been in the past. To their surprise, they found that the position of the pole seemed to be different in older rocks. One explanation was that the pole was staying still, but the continents were drifting as Wegener had suggested. Over the last 600 million years, Britain seems to have moved from south of the equator to its present position. But still no one knew how this could happen.

The crack in the ocean

Also in the 1950s, the floor of the Atlantic Ocean was surveyed in detail. This survey showed a symmetrical pattern with thin ocean crust and a central volcanic ridge.

In the 1960s, the magnetic pattern of the rocks across the ridge was discovered. The Earth's magnetic field was found to reverse every half million years or so, and this left a fingerprint-like pattern in the rocks. Also, this pattern was repeated symmetrically on either side of the ridge. The oceanic crust was splitting apart and new crust was forming in the gap (picking up the magnetic polarity of the time). This was then split apart in turn, and so on, slowly pushing the continents apart! So, at last, the cause of continental drift was discovered.

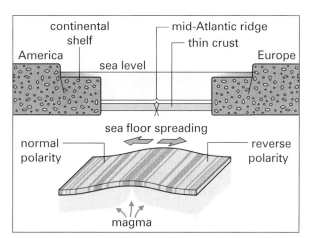

The Atlantic Ocean has a crack down the middle, with a symmetrical magnetic pattern across it.

Closing old oceans...

From these ideas, the theory of **plate tectonics** was born. If continents were moving apart on one side of the globe, they must be being pushed back together on the other. When this happens, the edge of the thin but denser oceanic crust slides beneath its neighbouring continent, dragged down by the sinking current in the mantle. Along the margin, the bed of the ocean is buckled down into a deep trench, up to 11 km below sea level.

As the oceanic crust slides into the **subduction zone** beneath the continent, any sediments that had collected there are either scraped off to form new, marginal fold mountains (like the Andes), or are dragged into the upper mantle. Here some of the rocks melt and vast volumes of molten rock rise up into the crust above, causing metamorphism below and explosive volcanic activity at the surface. Powerful earthquakes are also set off along the sinking plate, as it is slowly absorbed back into the mantle. Eventually old oceans disappear completely, and the continents on either side are welded back together, with a line of new fold mountains for the join! (See page 123.)

A slice through South America and its subduction zone.

Slipping sideways

In a few places, the plates are simply slipping sideways against each other. Perhaps the most famous example of this is the **San Andreas Fault** in California. A narrow coastal strip is sliding northwards at a rate of 7 cm a year, as is clearly shown in the photo of orange groves that were planted in straight lines just a few decades ago.

Unfortunately, San Francisco has been built astride this great fault. In places, the plates glide evenly against one another, but near San Francisco they are locked tight. This is why San Francisco is such a high 'earthquake risk' zone. San francisco was destroyed in 1906 and hit by another powerful earthquake in 1991. How long will it be before the next disaster there?

This orange grove clearly shows up the line of the San Andreas fault.

1 How did scientists try to explain the 'jigsaw' fit of the continents a hundred years ago?

2 The 'jigsaw' fit of South America and Africa is very good when the details are studied. Why did no-one believe Wegener's continental drift idea at first?

3 Magnetic evidence from ancient rocks supports the idea that the continents have drifted. Explain this link.

4 How does the activity above a subduction zone help to explain the rock cycle?

5 How can pieces of continent be 'welded' together by plate tectonic activity?

6 Why is it dangerous to live in San Francisco?

15 For you to do

1 What are the three main types of rock? Describe the rock cycle in your own words and diagrams.

2 From the rock descriptions given, what can you say about the way in which these rocks were formed?

A

B

C

Rock A is hard and dark, but is full of air bubbles. No crystal may be seen with the naked eye but a thin slice viewed under the microscope shows it to be made up of a mass of tiny crystals arranged randomly.

Rock B is quite hard, but can be split into wavy layers with a hammer. The surfaces are very shiny and small, plate-like crystals may be seen lying flat along them.

Rock C is soft and can easily be split into layers with a knife. The exposed flat surfaces show the remains of shellfish including ammonites. When ground up with water the rock becomes mud.

3 Describe how the wearing away of mountains in one place can lead to the formation of new land in another.

4 Granite, with its large interlocking crystals of quartz and feldspar, is now found exposed at the surface of the Earth on Dartmoor. How does granite form? How deep in the crust? How come it is now exposed at the surface?

If this granite formed towards the end of the Palaeozoic era, what has the average rate of erosion been since then? (Round the figures to simplify the maths!)

5 If you want to build from limestone, you have to cut blocks of rock to the correct size and shape and fit them carefully together. Concrete can be made from limestone. Why is it so much easier to build with concrete?

6 Oil forms naturally in sedimentary rocks.
  a Why do scientists often look for dome-shaped folds in the rocks when they are looking for oil?
  b Oil can be trapped in other ways. Copy the diagram and mark in where oil and gas might have collected here.

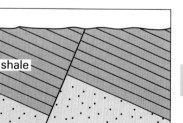
shale · fault · sandstone

7 If crude oil escapes to the surface, all that will be left is a pool of bitumen.
  a What are the physical properties of bitumen?
  b How are these properties explained by the number of carbon atoms chained together in the molecules?
  c What happens to the 'shorter-chain' molecules when they reach the surface?

8 Crude oil is often cracked to break up unwanted long-chain molecules.
  a How is this done?
  b What are the products of cracking?
  c Why are the alkanes produced so useful?

9 If you breathe onto blue cobalt chloride paper it turns pink; if you breathe through limewater it turns milky.
  a What two chemicals are there in your breath to cause these reactions?
  b The food you eat contains carbon and hydrogen. What is your food reacting with to give the chemicals from **a**?
  c What chemicals would you get if you burnt your food instead of eating it?

10 The gunpowder in fireworks contains sulphur. Why would pH paper turn red if held in the mist on the 5th November?

11 a Explain what is meant by the phrase 'carbon dioxide is a greenhouse gas'.
  b Methane (natural gas) is 30 times as bad a greenhouse gas as carbon dioxide. Some oilfields burn off unwanted methane from the oil wells, forming carbon dioxide. Others just release the methane into the air. Which of these two options is the worse for the Earth?
  c Trees take in carbon dioxide from the air. Cows each produce about 24 litres of methane a day from their digestive systems. Give two reasons why cutting down forests to graze cattle is harmful to the Earth.

12 Describe the internal structure of the Earth and explain the evidence that has allowed us to find out about it.

13 How old is the South Atlantic Ocean? To work it out, assume that it is 4000 km wide and that the central rift is splitting apart at a rate of 2 cm per year.

14 Propene is an unsaturated hydrocarbon with three carbon atoms in its chain.
  a Draw a diagram to show how the propane monomer can be combined to give an addition polymer. Show three monomer molecules combining.

$$
\begin{array}{ccc}
H & & CH_3 \\
| & & | \\
C & = & C \\
| & & | \\
H & & H
\end{array}
$$

  b What would be the name of this polymer?
  c This polymer is used for making crates, bowls, ropes and carpets. How do its properties compare to those of polythene, which is used for 'plastic' bags and bottles?

15 The first atmosphere of the Earth contained carbon dioxide and ammonia, with no 'free' oxygen or nitrogen.
  a Where has the oxygen in the air come from?
  b Make a list of the ways in which carbon dioxide can be removed from the air.
  c Suggest *two* ways in which 'free' nitrogen has got into the air.
  d Carbon trapped in the rocks is naturally recycled into the air by volcanoes as the rock cycle progresses over hundreds of millions of years. Why is it a problem if we simply 'short-circuit' this natural process by burning the fossil fuels?
  e Too much carbon dioxide will cause flooding as the ice caps melt. What might happen if there was *not enough* carbon dioxide in the air?

16 The rocks that formed in Britain 400 million years ago are red desert sandstones. About 300 million years ago, coal deposits were formed in tropical swamps. And 200 million years ago, red desert sands were again formed. How does the evidence in the rocks tie in with the palaeomagnetic evidence for continental drift?

17 a How did the 'magnetic anomalies' found in the Atlantic help to explain how continental drift worked?
  b If the Atlantic Ocean is getting wider, what must be happening to the Pacific Ocean?

18 If no new mountains were ever formed, the surface of the Earth would be worn flat by now.
  a Explain how the processes of plate tectonics 'recycle' sediments into new mountains.
  b What drives this plate tectonic activity, and where does the energy to do this come from?

Index

NEW MODULAR SCIENCE
for GCSE

MODULE *Maintenance of life*

Spread

Cover photograph *A paintbrush –* Castilleja miniata *– flourishes in a hostile environment*

1 Maintaining life

Clear signs of life

You can usually see an animal move – movement is one of the clearest signs of life. As well as being able to move from place to place, there are also movements taking place inside your body, such as your heart beating, your lungs expanding and contracting – clear signs that you are alive! Movements in plants are less obvious. Most of their movements are so slow that you cannot see them happening.

Movements often take place as a result of changes in the surroundings of a living organism – like running away from a predator. By responding to change an organism increases its chance of survival.

A snake responds quickly to change using its tongue; plants respond too, but too slowly for your eye to see.

Responding to change

Like any living organism your body is always responding to changes in your surroundings. You will start to sweat if you are too hot; shiver if you are cold. Any change in the surroundings that affects an organism is called a stimulus. For example, a snake will flick out its tongue as it moves around to taste chemicals in the air. The chemicals released into the air (from other animals and plants) are stimuli that snakes can detect. The snake's tongue picks up chemicals, and carries them to receptors in its mouth which can detect even the slightest trace of chemicals. The ability to respond to stimuli in this way is called sensitivity. The snake's mouth is sensitive to chemicals produced by plants and animals. It uses this to find food, and to avoid being attacked by predators – a 'whiff' of life and death for the snake!

All living organisms release energy by **respiration**.

All living organisms **excrete**.

All living organisms **move**.

All living organisms respond to changes in their surroundings ...the sight of food! This is called **sensitivity**.

All living organisms need nutrients. Animals feed for **nutrition**; plants make their own food.

All living organisms **reproduce**... and **grow**.

Organs to do the job

Different parts of plants and animals carry out different jobs. Your body is made up from a number of different **organs**, such as your eyes, stomach, brain and heart. Each organ looks different from the rest because it is specialised to carry out its job. For example, your heart is an extremely effective pumping organ which transports blood to all parts of your body. It can even change how hard it works to suit your requirements! Each organ works as part of an organ system with other organs. Your heart works with arteries, veins and capillaries to form your circulatory system.

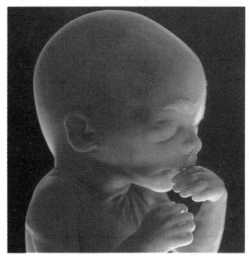

The organs which keep you alive were formed before you were born.

Energy for life

All living organisms need a supply of energy to stay alive. Animals take in the energy they need in the food they eat. Their food contains a store of trapped energy. Green plants obtain energy in a very different way. They can use energy from sunlight to make their own food. This process is called **photosynthesis**. When plants *and* animals need to use energy, the energy trapped in their food is released during respiration. Plants and animals use the released energy for the various processes which are essential for their *maintenance of life*. You can read more about photosynthesis on pages 134 and 135.

Some plant organs make food – other organs store food which you can eat too!

1. Make a copy and then complete this table which shows some human organ systems.

System	Examples of organs
circulatory system	heart, arteries, veins, capillaries
	brain, eyes, ears
reproductive system	

2. The table below shows the organs which plants use to carry out various processes. Make a copy and then complete the table.

Organ	Function
	Anchors the plant down and takes in water
leaf	
	Produces pollen and egg cells for reproduction

2 Plant design

Plant organs

You will know that plants make their own food. To do this they must have **organs** and **systems** designed for that purpose. Although you may not think of plants as having organs, this is exactly what leaves, roots and stems are. The leaves are where the food is made. The roots take in water and minerals from the soil and anchor the plant. Stems hold the plant upright and transport substances between the different organs.

A plant's organs are above and below ground. What are they?

Plant cells

Under the microscope we can see that all living things are made of **cells**. Animal cells consist of a nucleus, cytoplasm and a cell membrane. A plant cell is also made up of these parts. The nucleus controls the cell's activities, including the chemical reactions that take place in the **cytoplasm**. The **cell membrane** controls the passage of substances in and out of the cell. Unlike animal cells, a plant cell also has a **cell wall** which strengthens it, and often a permanent **vacuole** filled with cell sap. The cell walls and vacuole form the skeleton of the plant. Some plant cells also contain **chloroplasts**, which give plants their green colour. They are needed by the plant to make its food.

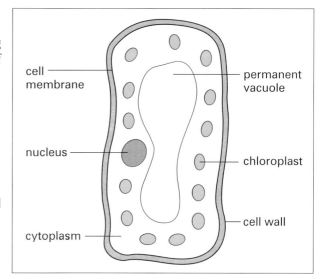

A leaf cell.

Plant tissue

To make their own food plants need light. Chloroplasts absorb energy from light. Leaves need to be made from cells that contain lots of chloroplasts. **Palisade cells** have a lot of chloroplasts and in a leaf they are packed together so that as much light energy as possible is absorbed. So part of the leaf organ is made up of palisade cells arranged in a layer of palisade **tissue**.

Epidermal cells form a transparent, protective outer layer of tissue (**the epidermis**) which is also part of the leaf organ. **Spongy layer cells** are much less closely packed and have air spaces between them.

● cells → tissue → organ

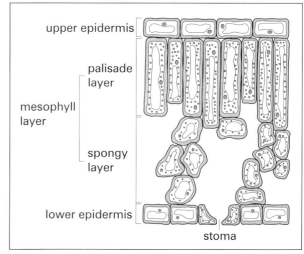

Section through a leaf, showing cells. Like animal organs, plant organs are made up of tissues which are made up from cells.

Making food

To make their own food plants need carbon dioxide. To respire they need oxygen. How do these gases get through the leaf surface? In the layer below the palisade layer, air spaces separate the cells. Gases move by diffusion from the air around the leaf through the stomata and into the spaces between the mesophyll cells spreading from high to low concentrations.

By having lots of air spaces between cells, the surface area in contact with air is greatly increased. This helps to make exchange of gases highly efficient.

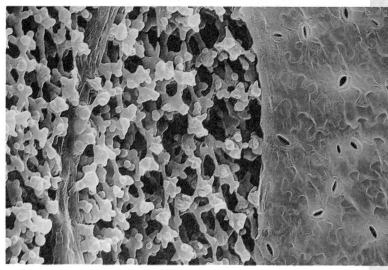

This microscopic picture shows the spongy layer of mesophyll cells underneath the epidermis of a leaf. The air spaces around the cells provide plenty of space for oxygen and carbon dioxide to diffuse into.

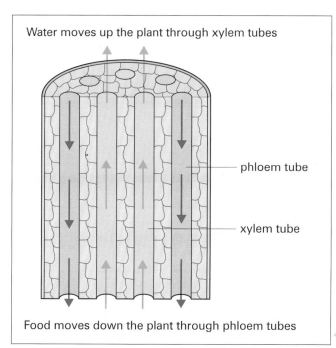

Water moves up the plant through xylem tubes

phloem tube

xylem tube

Food moves down the plant through phloem tubes

Transport systems

You have seen that in a leaf a group of cells of a similar structure and a particular function form a tissue. You also find this in plant stems.

Food from the leaves needs to be moved around the plant to the growing regions and the storage organs. This is done by the **phloem** tissue. Phloem is made up of living cells which are able to exercise some control on the movement of the food. Water is moved by a separate transport system. This is made up of **xylem** tissue. Xylem cells are mainly dead and form tubes which transport water from roots to the stems and leaves.

Plants have two separate transport systems. Can you think why?

1   Name the parts of a plant cell that are also found in animal cells.

2   Carbon dioxide is needed by the plant to make food. Describe how this gas gets into a palisade cell from the outside.

3   a   Describe the structure of the following mesophyll:
       i) palisade
       ii) spongy
    b   Explain how the structure of each tissue helps it to do its job.

4   Describe the difference in structure and function between phloem and xylem tissue.

3 The energy factory

Plants make food...

Plants produce their own food. This is why they are called producers. All animals, including you, depend on plants for food. The method plants use to produce food is called **photosynthesis**. This picture shows you what happens.

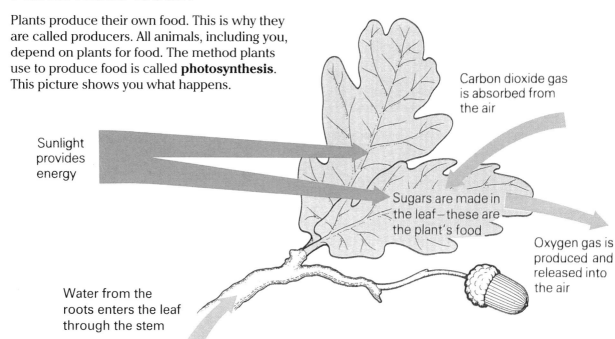

Sunlight provides energy

Carbon dioxide gas is absorbed from the air

Sugars are made in the leaf – these are the plant's food

Oxygen gas is produced and released into the air

Water from the roots enters the leaf through the stem

This can be summarised by an equation.

Carbon dioxide + water + light energy ➡ glucose + oxygen

... from simple chemicals

Plants use a green chemical called **chlorophyll** to absorb the energy from sunlight. The chlorophyll is found in the small disc-shaped bodies called **chloroplasts** in the plant's cells. Other parts of the plant specialise in *collecting* the raw materials. The roots draw in water and minerals from the soil. Carbon dioxide is taken in through the leaves, which also pass out oxygen as a waste product. Some water vapour evaporates through the stomata.

Leaves are specially adapted to get light, water and carbon dioxide directly to the chloroplasts – to produce sugars and oxygen.

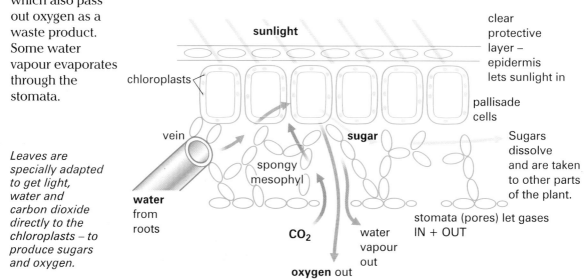

sunlight

chloroplasts

vein

water from roots

spongy mesophyl

sugar

CO_2

oxygen out

water vapour out

clear protective layer – epidermis lets sunlight in

pallisade cells

Sugars dissolve and are taken to other parts of the plant.

stomata (pores) let gases IN + OUT

What happens to the sugars?

Since most of the chlorophyll is found in the leaves, most of the food is made there. But the food is needed by every part of the plant, so the sugars dissolve in water and are carried round to all parts of the plant. Once there, the sugars provide the starting point for making the larger molecules, such as **cellulose** and **proteins**, which are used in plant growth. If the sugars are not used straightaway, they are turned into **starch** which is an insoluble form of carbohydrate.

The starch is stored by the plant as a reserve food supply. It can be turned back into sugar again later on and used for **respiration**. Cellulose forms cell walls and makes them stiff and strong. It cannot be turned back into sugar.

Stems hold plants upright but also transport sugars to cells. Roots anchor the plant but can be used to store sugars as starch.

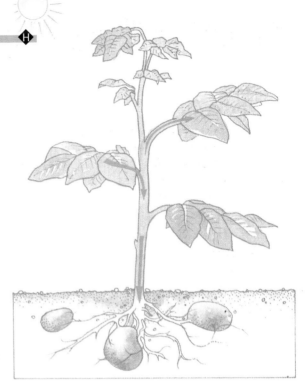

Plants make proteins by combining nitrogen with sugars. The nitrogen comes from nitrates in the soil. These are soluble and plants take them in through their roots dissolved in soil water. Proteins are used in making the new cells needed for plant growth.

Releasing the stored energy

Plants need energy just like you do. They use it to make the materials they need to grow. They use energy to help take in nutrients from the soil and to transport chemicals around the plant. They use the process called respiration to release energy locked up in sugars. Respiration releases energy stored during photosynthesis. This diagram shows you more.

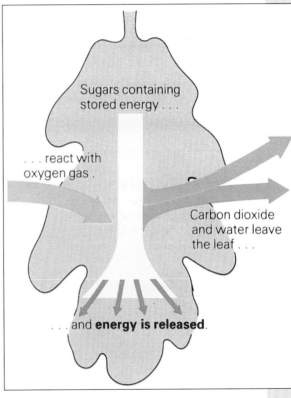

Sugars containing stored energy . . .

. . . react with oxygen gas .

Carbon dioxide and water leave the leaf . . .

. . . and **energy is released**.

1   Study the first picture on page 134 carefully. Pick out the materials the plant needs for photosynthesis. Which materials are *produced* by the process?

2   What do plants use the green chemical chlorophyll for?

3   Look at the diagram of the structure of a leaf on page 134.
   a   Why is the epidermis on top of the leaf clear?
   b   Why are more chloroplasts found near the top of the palisade cells?

4   Make up a table to show what is used up and what is produced during respiration and photosynthesis.

5   Describe the route a carbon atom takes from the atmosphere to ending up in the wall of a root cell.

4 Bigger and better crops

Investigating the rate of photosynthesis . . .

A group of students carried out an investigation to find out how photosynthesis is affected by changing certain conditions. They measured the rate of photosynthesis by counting the number of bubbles produced each minute by an aquatic plant called *Elodea*. They each used a 4 cm length of *Elodea*.

Leroy carried out his investigation near the window. Peter worked in the middle of the room using a lamp as light.

Lisa placed aluminium foil around the tube containing the plant.

The students measured the rate at which photosynthesis takes place by counting the number of bubbles produced each minute. The results of their investigation are shown in the table.

	Number of bubbles given off each minute
Leroy	34
Peter	25
Lisa	2

1
  a Why is the number of bubbles produced different for each student?
  b Name the gas in the bubbles.
  c Why did the students use the same length of *Elodea*?

. . . and its conditions

Peter noticed that the tube he was using became warm during the investigation. The group decided to change the design of their apparatus and to repeat the investigation at two different temperatures. They also decided to control the amount of light by changing the distance from the lamp to the beaker. Their results are shown in the table.

Distance of lamp from beaker	Number of bubbles given off each minute	
	15°C	25°C
10cm	34	62
20cm	18	22

2
  a Why did the students place the tube containing *Elodea* in a beaker of water?
  b The students concluded that the rate of photosynthesis is increased by increasing the amount of light and by increasing temperature. Do you agree with their conclusion? Explain your answer.

Does changing the conditions affect the rate of photosynthesis?

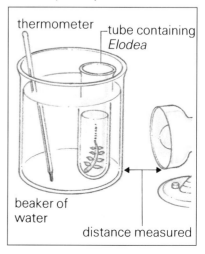

thermometer
tube containing *Elodea*
beaker of water
distance measured

Making the most of sunshine

Plant growers try to improve crop **yields** by providing ideal growing conditions. A very common way of doing this is by using a greenhouse. The conditions inside a greenhouse allow plants to be grown earlier in the year and in regions where they would not normally grow. The temperature in a greenhouse is usually much higher than the outside temperature because it keeps in the heat from the sun's rays.

Improving conditions

Many commercial growers use greenhouses which are heated during cold weather. Some use electricity to provide heat while others burn fuels such as paraffin. When fuels burn the following reaction takes place:

fuel + oxygen ➡ carbon dioxide + water + heat energy

The diagram shows the same type of tomatoes grown in an unheated greenhouse and in a greenhouse heated by burning paraffin. Both greenhouses received the same amount of sunlight.

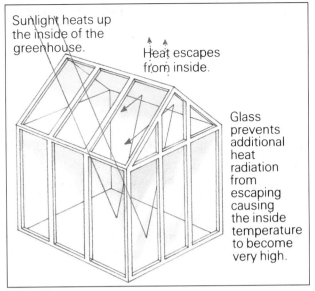

Sunlight heats up the inside of the greenhouse.

Heat escapes from inside.

Glass prevents additional heat radiation from escaping causing the inside temperature to become very high.

 3
  a Which greenhouse produced the highest yield?
  b Give two reasons why the yield was different.

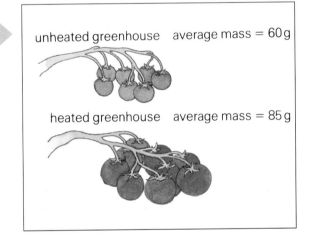

unheated greenhouse   average mass = 60 g

heated greenhouse   average mass = 85 g

Better lighting

Artificial lighting can be used to grow plants when the amount of sunlight falls too low. However, very few growers use artificial lighting – it's expensive. They mostly rely on sunlight as the only source of energy. The bar chart opposite shows the amount of sunlight entering greenhouses in southern and northern England throughout the year. The chart also shows the minimum amount of light needed to grow chrysanthemums.

 4
  a During which months would you advise chrysanthemum growers in the south of England to use artificial lighting?
  b Why do chrysanthemums not grow well in January even when the greenhouse is heated?

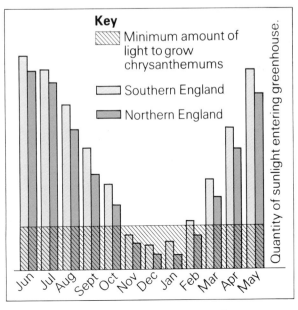

Key

▨ Minimum amount of light to grow chrysanthemums

▢ Southern England

▨ Northern England

Quantity of sunlight entering greenhouse.

Jun Jul Aug Sept Oct Nov Dec Jan Feb Mar Apr May

5 How does your garden grow?

Healthy plants

The plants in the photograph opposite are very healthy and will produce a good crop of fruit and vegetables. Plants need to be grown in the right conditions to produce good crops. Temperature, humidity, light and nutrient content can all affect the growth of plants. This is why farmers and gardeners grow plants at the right time of the year and treat the soil to make sure it contains the right amount of nutrients and moisture. The water inside plant cells gives support to young plants. The plants will wilt if they are short of water. With these methods, fields and gardens have become controlled environments which are very different from natural **habitats**.

To provide crops like this plants need good growing conditions.

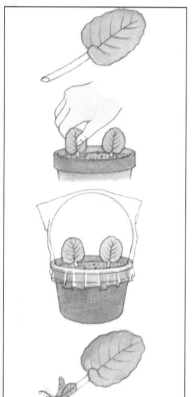

Good homes for young plants

Gardeners keep cuttings healthy by enclosing them in polythene bags or by using specially designed **propagators**. This provides the cuttings with a warm and **humid** environment with plenty of sunlight – ideal conditions for successful growth. A humid environment is essential because the cuttings will soon die if they begin to dry out.

Plants lose water from the surface of their leaves. This is called **transpiration**. Most plants have a waxy layer on their leaves which stops them losing too much water.

How do leaves lose water?

A group of students carried out an investigation to find out how water was lost from leaves. They treated three fresh sycamore leaves as shown in the diagram.

The leaves were then left hanging from string in the laboratory. Each one was weighed at 30 minute intervals. The table gives the results the students obtained.

Time (minutes)	Loss of mass (in mg)		
	Leaf 1	Leaf 2	Leaf 3
30	10	11	3
60	19	18	11
90	26	27	19
120	44	41	25

Leaf 1 — No treatment

Leaf 2 — Vaseline smeared over the upper surface.

Leaf 3 — Vaseline smeared over the lower surface.

The students made the conclusion that most water is lost from the lower surface of leaves. Do you agree with their conclusion?

The Good Food Guide for Plants

For healthy growth plants also need special nutrients called **mineral ions**. Information on fertiliser bags usually carries a code of three numbers such as 10:10:27. These numbers show the amount of the three main nutrients which plants need to survive and to grow well. The first number shows the amount of **nitrogen** in the fertiliser. Nitrogen is needed to make proteins. The second number shows the amount of **phosphorus**, and the third the amount of **potassium**. Phosphorus and potassium are needed for reactions involved in photosynthesis and respiration to work properly. These three nutrients are known as the **NPK** content. As well as these main nutrients or **macronutrients** there are others called **micronutrients** which are needed in smaller amounts.

Nutrient	Part played	Effects of shortage
nitrate (N)	For leaf and shoot production. Provides proteins – the building blocks of all life.	Stunted growth, small, pale leaves and weak stems.
phosphate (P)	Helps in the reactions of photosynthesis and respiration.	Stunted roots and shoots, purplish leaves and low crop yield.
potassium (K)	Good for flowers, fruit and disease resistance.	Leaf edges yellow or brown. Poor flowers and fruit.

These nutrients are essential for healthy plant growth.

Choosing the best fertiliser

The table opposite shows the result of a soil test carried out to find the concentration of nitrogen, phosphorus and potassium in the soil in a vegetable garden. The gardener wants to add fertiliser to the plot so that there is a high concentration of each of these nutrients.

Nitrogen level	Phosphorus	Potassium
low	medium	low

The second table gives information about 5 different types of fertiliser. The figures show how much of each fertiliser needs to be added to each square metre. Study the tables carefully.

Name of fertiliser	Type of nutrient in fertiliser	Amount of fertiliser to be added(g/m²)		
		If test result high	If test result medium	If test result low
1 Hoof and Horn	Nitrogen	17	43	85
2 Sulphate of Ammonia	Nitrogen	9	26	51
3 Bone Meal	Phosphorus	17	43	85
4 Superphosphate	Phosphorus	17	43	85
5 Sulphate of Potash	Potassium	9	17	34

1 a Which leaf in the students' investigation shows the greatest loss in mass?
   b Use what you know about leaf structure to explain why most water is lost from the lower surface.
   c Suggest two improvements that you could make to improve the design of their investigation.

2 Suggest why some desert plants have a thicker layer of wax on their leaves.

3 a Which fertilisers would you add to the vegetable plot? How much of each would you add to each square metre?
   b How much nitrogen fertiliser would be needed if the plot was 10 metres by 15 metres?
   c What nutrients would be missing from the soil if the cabbages grown in the garden had stunted growth and yellowing leaves?

6 Watering holes

Losing water

Water inside plant cells provides the plant with **support**. You have seen that leaves have a waterproof layer but also that there are pores in this layer. Through these pores water is lost by **evaporation**. If the rate of evaporation is higher than the rate of water uptake the plant will lose water overall. This can be fatal for the plant.

 Under what conditions will a plant wilt quickly?

How is water lost from the leaf surface?

The xylem tissue brings the water to the leaves. The leaf, with its flattened shape and internal air spaces, has a large surface area. This allows efficient exchange of gases and absorption of light. Water loss by evaporation is called **transpiration** and assists the movement of water and dissolved nutrient ions through the plant but creates the risk of the plant drying out. Transpiration is more rapid in hot, dry and windy conditions.

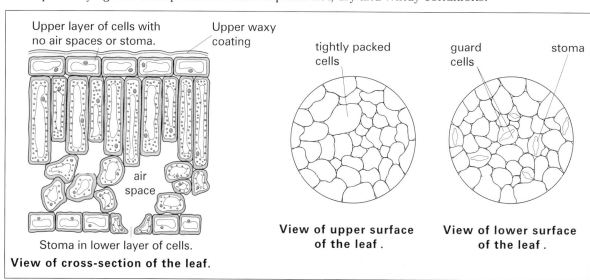

Upper layer of cells with no air spaces or stoma.

Upper waxy coating

air space

Stoma in lower layer of cells.

View of cross-section of the leaf.

tightly packed cells

View of upper surface of the leaf .

guard cells

stoma

View of lower surface of the leaf .

Controlling water loss

The stomata in leaves can be opened and closed by guard cells. During the day the stomata are usually open to allow large amounts of carbon dioxide to enter the leaf for photosynthesis. During the night they are closed. Some plants can close their stomata when water loss is high to prevent water being lost faster than it is absorbed by roots. Plants have developed many different features in their leaves to prevent too much water being lost.

Conifer trees have thin, needle-like leaves which lose less water. Some plants which live in dry conditions have a thick waxy layer on their leaves.

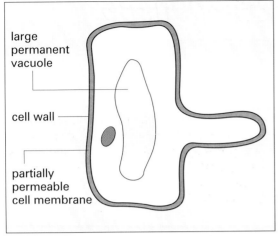

large permanent vacuole

cell wall

partially permeable cell membrane

▲ *A root hair cell. The shape of the cell increases the surface area. But why no chloroplasts?*

Water for support

Water enters a plant through its roots. Most of the water that enters a root is absorbed by **root hair cells**. This is another example of a cell being adapted in its structure to match its function. Look at the picture.

Substances moving in and out of the cell can easily pass through the permeable cell wall. The cell wall strengthens the cell. When water enters the cell it increases the pressure inside. The cell walls are strong enough to withstand this pressure. It is this pressure of **turgor** which keeps cells rigid and provides support.

Osmosis or special diffusion

There are more water molecules outside the cells than inside. The vacuole and cytoplasm inside cells contain fewer water molecules, but have a high concentration of solute molecules. Because of these differences water will tend to diffuse into the cells and solute molecules would tend to diffuse out of the cells. However, the **partially permeable** cell membrane allows only water to diffuse through it and not the solute molecules. The diffusion of water from a dilute to a more concentrated solution through a partially permeable cell membrane is called **osmosis**.

The plant needs to be able to control the concentration of dissolved substances in the cell sap, so that water can enter and move to where it is needed. This is why it must store excess carbohydrates as an *insoluble* storage compound (starch).

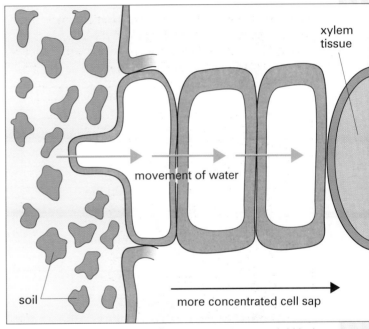

xylem tissue

movement of water

soil

more concentrated cell sap

▲ *Osmosis is a special kind of diffusion.*

Roots can also absorb some mineral ions against a concentration gradient: the ions move from a dilute solution to a more concentrated one. This is called **active uptake** and requires energy from respiration.

1 A student made drawings of a section of a leaf under the microscope. The drawing is shown on page 140. How is the leaf adapted to balance the need for gas exchange, transpiration and protection against the risk of drying out?

2 Describe how a root hair cell is adapted to perform its function.

3 Cobalt chloride paper is blue when it is dry and pink when wet. A student attached a strip of cobalt chloride paper to two leaves using Sellotape. She attached one to the upper surface and the other to the lower surface. The student observed the leaves every 30 minutes. How do you think the paper on each leaf will change? Will the result be the same for both leaves? Explain your answer.

7 Plant growth responses

Slow to respond

If you look into bright sunlight you will immediately screw up your eyes. Like other animals you respond quickly to **stimuli**. Plants, on the other hand, do *not* usually respond to stimuli by sudden movements. Their responses normally involve very slow growth movements. Shoots will grow towards light and against gravity. Roots grow towards moisture and in the direction of gravity. This type of growth is controlled by special chemicals called **plant hormones**.

What stimulus could cause the plant to respond in the way the chart shows?

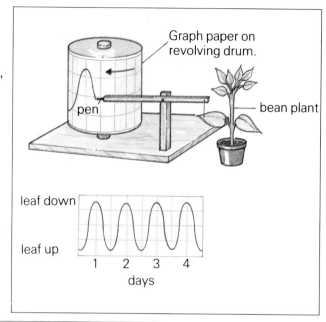

Testing for chemical control

The following experiment was carried out to test the chemical control hypothesis. Three groups of grass seedlings were treated. Each group of 20 seedlings was placed in a box with bright light shining on them from one side only. The appearance of the seedlings after two days is shown on the right. The lengths of the seedlings were measured at the start and at the end of the experiment. The average measurements are shown in the table below.

	Group 1	Group 2	Group 3
Average initial length (mm)	20.2	19.9	19.1
Average final length (mm)	24.3	23.2	19.2

Control by hormones

This experiment supports the idea that a chemical produced in the shoot controls the growth response. This chemical is called auxin. The responses of plant roots and shoots to light, gravity and moisture are the result of unequal growth rates. When a shoot is lit from one side, more auxin collects on the far side. The cells grow more there causing the shoot to bend towards the light.

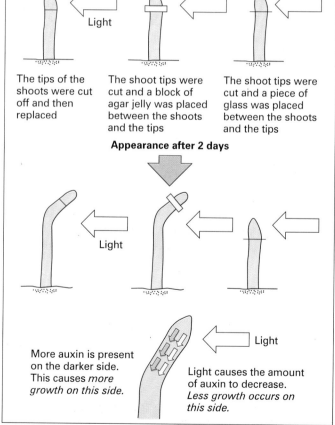

The direction of light affects the distribution of auxin in the shoot tip. The agar will allow a chemical through, the glass will not.

Using control

Plant hormones are now manufactured and used by gardeners and commercial growers to control the development of plants. Large numbers of plants can be produced quickly by taking cuttings. Rooting powder containing hormones is added to stimulate the growth of roots. Hormones which control reproduction can be used to ripen fruit on the plant to order, or even delay ripening during transport to the shops and the consumer.

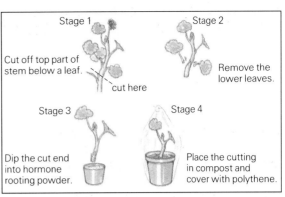

Stage 1 — Cut off top part of stem below a leaf. cut here

Stage 2 — Remove the lower leaves.

Stage 3 — Dip the cut end into hormone rooting powder.

Stage 4 — Place the cutting in compost and cover with polythene.

These are the stages in taking a stem cutting from a geranium plant. You can grow a new plant this way.

The poppies and other weeds only grow where the weedkiller has not been used. Selectively killing weeds in this way improves the crop yields.

Selective killing

As well as promoting growth plant hormones are used to kill plants. The broad-leaved weeds that are a nuisance in fields of cereal crops and in garden lawns can be killed by applying plant hormones. The hormones selectively destroy the weeds without harming the cereal crop or the lawn grass. This is why the hormones used are called **selective weedkillers**. Millions of acres of cereal crops are sprayed each year to achieve selective weed control. **Competition** for space, water and nutrients is removed by destroying weeds. This increases the yield of crops making them cheaper for you to buy. However, the problem with using weedkillers is that the spray drifts onto the plants in the natural habitats surrounding the fields which causes rare species to disappear.

1
  a Calculate the average change in length of each group seedlings shown on page 142.
  b Why was there hardly any growth in group 3?
  c Explain how these results support the hypothesis that growth responses are controlled by a chemical.
  d Why were there 20 seedlings in each group instead of just one?
  e Describe how you would accurately measure the lengths of the curved shoots at the end of the experiment. (Straightening them may cause them to break.)

2 You blink when dust enters your eye. How does this response differ from the way a plant shoot bends towards light?

3 Another experiment was carried out on some seedling shoots – the cut tip being pushed to one side.

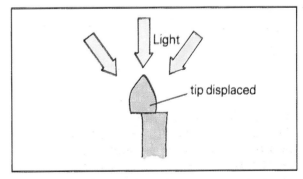

Light — tip displaced

Predict what the shoots will look like in two days. Explain your answer.

8 Responding to change

Detecting change

Like many animals, you have a **nervous system** that enables your body to detect and to respond quickly to stimuli. Your **senses** make you aware of changes taking place inside your body and around you. Special sense organs contain **receptors** that detect different kinds of stimuli.

You have receptors in the sense organs of your body which detect different stimuli.

Stimulus	Receptor	Sense
Light energy	Light sensitive cells, called rods + cones in the retina of the eye	Vision
Sound energy	Cells in the cochlea of the ear	Hearing
Gravity e.g. falling (Movement energy)	Gravity receptors in the ear	Balance
Change in temperature (Heat energy)	Temperature receptors in the skin	Temperature detection
Pressure, pain and touch	Pressure, pain and touch receptors in the skin	Touch and p
Chemicals in the air, drink and food (Chemical energy)	Chemical receptors in the nose and tongue	Smell and ta

Linking all parts of the body ◈

The main parts of the nervous system are shown here. The **brain** and **spinal cord** form the **central nervous system** (**CNS**) which is linked to all parts of the body by a network of thousands of branching nerves. The CNS and nerves are made up of nerve cells or **neurones**. Each neurone has a cell body with long fibres spreading from it. The long nerve fibres carry impulses from one part of the body to another. Hundreds of tiny nerve fibres are bundled together to form a single nerve.

Organising the best response ◈

When the receptors in your sense organs are stimulated, impulses are carried along **sensory neurones** to the central nervous system. Your brain or spinal cord coordinates your body's response to the stimulus by sending impulses along **motor neurones** to the part of your body that needs to react.

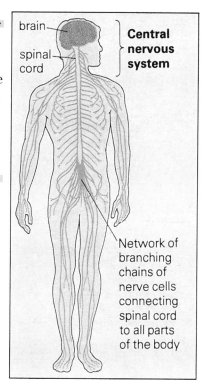

brain
spinal cord

Central nervous system

Network of branching chains of nerve cells connecting spinal cord to all parts of the body

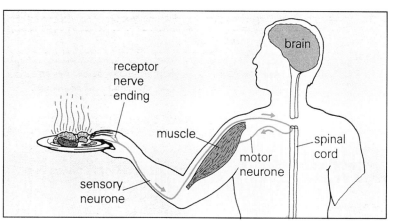

receptor nerve ending

brain

muscle

motor neurone

spinal cord

sensory neurone

When you touch a hot plate impulses are sent from your fingertips to your central nervous system. This can be summarised as follows.

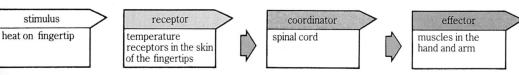

stimulus	receptor	coordinator	effector	response
heat on fingertip	temperature receptors in the skin of the fingertips	spinal cord	muscles in the hand and arm	rapid withdrawal of hand and arm

sensory nerves   *motor nerves*

Protecting the body from damage ▬▬◆

Pulling your hand away from a hot plate is a **reflex action**. *Blinking*, when dust gets into your eye; *narrowing the pupil* of your eye in bright light; *coughing* when food goes down the 'wrong way' and touches the windpipe – these are all instant reflexes. In each case you cannot help yourself from reacting – stimulation of particular receptors has caused an *involuntary response* to take place.

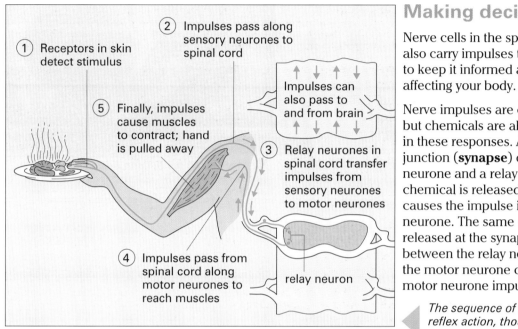

① Receptors in skin detect stimulus

② Impulses pass along sensory neurones to spinal cord

Impulses can also pass to and from brain

⑤ Finally, impulses cause muscles to contract; hand is pulled away

③ Relay neurones in spinal cord transfer impulses from sensory neurones to motor neurones

④ Impulses pass from spinal cord along motor neurones to reach muscles

relay neuron

Making decisions ◆

Nerve cells in the spinal cord also carry impulses to your brain to keep it informed about events affecting your body.

Nerve impulses are electrical but chemicals are also involved in these responses. At the junction (**synapse**) of a sensory neurone and a relay neurone, a chemical is released which causes the impulse in the relay neurone. The same chemical released at the synapse between the relay neurone and the motor neurone causes the motor neurone impulse.

◀ *The sequence of events in a reflex action, though complex, takes place in an instant.*

1 Copy and complete the following table.

Reflex	Stimulus	Receptor	Response	Purpose
Blinking	?	Touch receptors in eyelid	Eyelid muscles contract	?
Narrowing pupil	Bright light	?	Iris closes	To reduce light entering eye, improves vision
?	Dim light	?	Iris opens	?
Withdrawal of foot	Standing on a sharp nail	?	?	?

2 Use the sequence –

stimulus → receptor → coordinator → effector → response

to explain what happens when:
a you prick your finger with a needle.
b you smell tasty food.
c you accidentally pick up a hot plate and realise it is very expensive!

3 Explain why a reflex is not just electrical energy.

9 The way of seeing

The eyes have it!

It is easy to take good eyesight for granted. If you can read this unaided you are lucky. You have learned to read, of course, but you have also learned to see and your eyes are working as they should.

When you were very young your eye reflexes were not well developed. A baby cannot judge distance very well or adjust to changes in the amount of light. Any sudden movement or bright light will simply cause blinking or a closing of the eyes. As a baby grows it learns to control the amount of light entering the eye and to focus on near or distant objects.

Look at the diagram below. Can you decide which effector is involved when the eye responds to the stimulus of bright light?

He won't catch the balloon because he can't control his eye reflexes – his eyes close when anything is near his face.

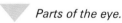

Parts of the eye.

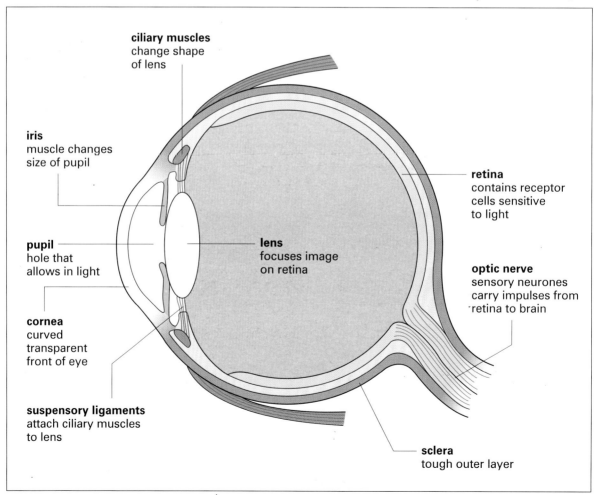

ciliary muscles
change shape
of lens

iris
muscle changes
size of pupil

retina
contains receptor
cells sensitive
to light

pupil
hole that
allows in light

lens
focuses image
on retina

optic nerve
sensory neurones
carry impulses from
retina to brain

cornea
curved
transparent
front of eye

suspensory ligaments
attach ciliary muscles
to lens

sclera
tough outer layer

Light work

Light enters the eye through the **cornea**. This, like the **lens** is curved. They both bend light rays towards the **retina**. The retina of the eye contains cells that are sensitive to light. These cells are attached to sensory neurones in the **optic nerve**, which leads directly to the brain.

Bright light can damage the cells in the retina. As light intensity increases, these receptors detect this stimulus and send impulses to the brain. The brain sends an impulse to the effector: the circular muscle in the iris. This muscle contracts and makes the pupil smaller. So the amount of light entering the eye is reduced. The work done by these muscles protects the eye and allows you to see in bright light.

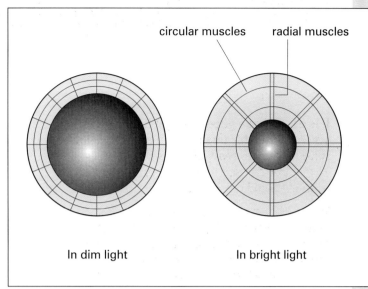

In dim light   In bright light

▲ *The size of the black pupil is controlled by the coloured iris.*

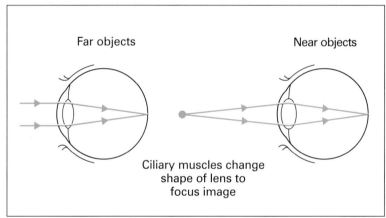

▲ *A camera lens can be moved to cope with a moving object – but your eye lens is fixed in position. How close up to your eye can you still see an object clearly?*

Near and far ━━━━ ◆H

Muscles also enable you to see objects at different distances. When the ciliary muscles are contracted the shape of the lens allows light from near objects to produce an image on the retina. When the ciliary muscles relax, changing the shape of the lens, the light rays from the distant object can now be bent to produce an image on the retina.

1 Describe in stages how the eye changes in dim light.

2 Explain how the eye responds to light from a distant object by describing the stimulus, receptor, coordinator, effector and response involved.

3 Explain in detail why, even if you did not notice something thrown at your eye until very late, the muscles in your eyelid could still close your eye in time. You may need to refer to page 145.

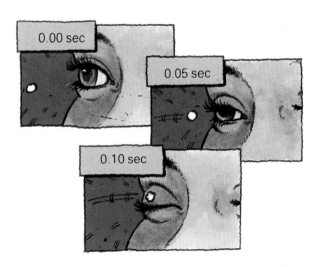

10 Staying in control

Changes inside the body can be caused by a change in the enviroment.

Chemical control

A hormone is a chemical which when released into the blood causes a change. The effect of some hormones lasts a lifetime. Others cause short term change. For example, mammals control the amount of sugar in their blood by using the two hormones **insulin** and **glucagon**. These are made by the pancreas.

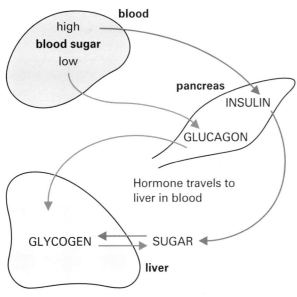

Sugar or glycogen? Hormones from the pancreas tell the liver what to do.

Controlling the inside

We try to provide the best conditions in the environment for ourselves and other animals to live healthily. But an animal cannot survive unless the conditions for health *inside* its body are also controlled, such as body temperature and removal of waste products. This process of control inside the body is called **homeostasis**. The brain checks the temperature and levels of substances in the blood. If levels need to be altered nerve messages are sent to the organs concerned – or the brain causes the release of a substance called a **hormone**, from the appropriate gland.

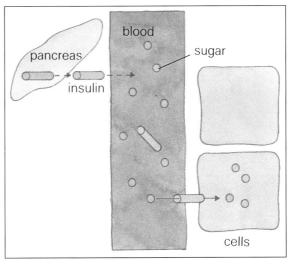

Insulin from the pancreas helps sugar to enter the body's cells.

Too sweet?

After you eat a meal more sugar is absorbed into your blood – more than you may need. The pancreas then makes more insulin. This causes cells in the liver to take more sugar from the blood than they need. Liver cells can change sugar into an insoluble substance called glycogen. The sugar can now be stored until it is needed. Then if your blood sugar level falls the pancreas makes glucagon. This causes the liver to change glycogen back into sugar which is then released into the blood – so your blood sugar level rises again. Simple isn't it?

This man is taking in insulin artificially – by injecting it – because his body does not make enough naturally.

2 in every 100

You may know someone who is a **diabetic**. This means their pancreas cannot make enough insulin. Diabetes can be treated with daily injections of insulin. Insulin used to be taken from the pancreas of pigs and cattle. Now it is possible to produce large amounts of human insulin by **genetic engineering**.

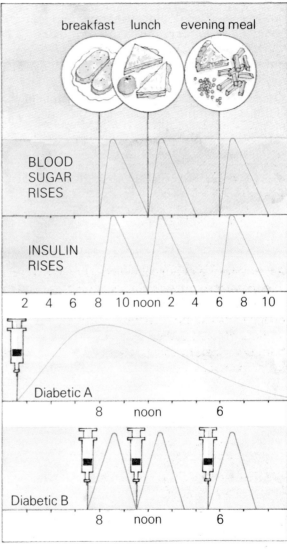

Different types of control

A non-diabetic produces more insulin *after* an increase in the level of blood sugar – in other words after eating. The body can respond quickly to this change.

Diabetic A who uses a slow but long-acting insulin must only take food in amounts which match the level of insulin. When could she eat her largest meal?

Diabetic B uses quicker but short-acting insulin which provides more control. How long before a meal must Diabetic B take insulin?

1 What is a hormone?

2 Some hormones, such as insulin, are proteins. Why do you think insulin cannot be taken in tablet form?

3 Explain why diabetics must be careful when they exercise.

4 Explain what causes the liver to change glucose into glycogen.

11 Cleaning the bloodstream

Removing the body's waste

Like any other organism, you need to get rid of waste which is produced from the necessary chemical reactions that take place to keep you alive. Your main organs for this process of waste removal, called **excretion**, are your lungs and kidneys. Your *lungs* remove **carbon dioxide** which is produced in respiration. Your *kidneys* remove **urea** which is formed when amino acids are broken down in the liver. Your kidneys also remove any excess water and salts taken in in your diet, and remove any foreign substances in the blood such as drugs and alcohol.

Within each of your kidneys there are thousands of tiny tubes. These filter out waste substances from the blood in groups of capillaries called glomeruli.

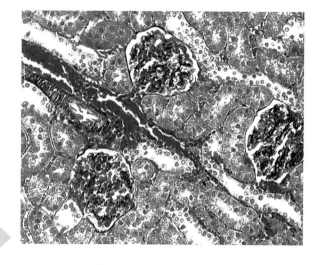

Saving and removing ⊞

Each of your kidneys contains between one and two million tiny tubes call **nephrons**. At the end of each nephron is a small cup-shaped capsule, called **Bowman's capsule**, which contains a knot of capillaries called a **glomerulus**. This detailed network of blood capilliaries and tubes acts both to *filter* off waste substances, and to *reabsorb* important substances back into your blood. Your kidneys perform some very important functions in your body.

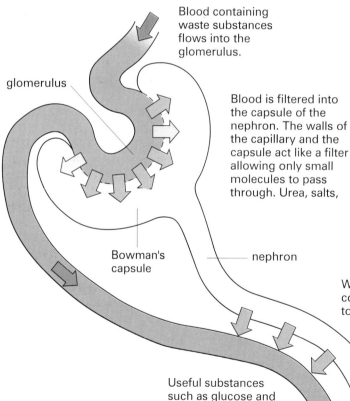

Blood containing waste substances flows into the glomerulus.

glomerulus

Blood is filtered into the capsule of the nephron. The walls of the capillary and the capsule act like a filter allowing only small molecules to pass through. Urea, salts,

Bowman's capsule

nephron

Water moves from a concentrated solution to a more dilute one.

Useful substances such as glucose and some dissolved ions are reabsorbed into the blood. This requires energy.

Urine containing unwanted substances flows on to the ureter and bladder.

Cleaned blood flows back to the rest of the body.

Kidneys as regulators ◈

As well as removing waste substances, your kidneys also regulate the amount of water in your blood. When you drink large quantities of fluids, your blood becomes diluted – *less* concentrated. Your kidneys remove this excess water by producing *large* quantities of urine to restore water balance. On the other hand, when you are short of water your blood becomes *more* concentrated, so the kidneys produce *less* urine to conserve body water.

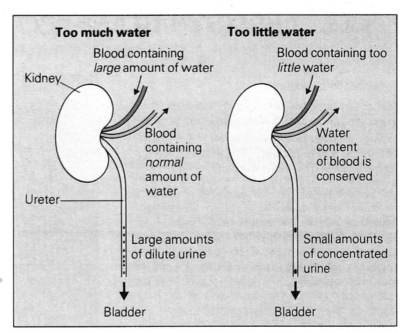

Too much water

Blood containing *large* amount of water

Kidney

Blood containing *normal* amount of water

Ureter

Large amounts of dilute urine

Bladder

Too little water

Blood containing too *little* water

Water content of blood is conserved

Small amounts of concentrated urine

Bladder

BRAIN

ADH

Concentrated blood

ADH in bloodstream

Most water is absorbed back into blood

Concentrated urine
(*small* amount)

BRAIN

Dilute blood

No ADH in bloodstream

Little water is absorbed back into blood

Dilute urine
(*large* amount)

Chemical control ◈

The amount of water you lose in your urine is controlled by a hormone called the **antidiuretic hormone** (**ADH** for short). ADH is made by the pituitary gland in your brain and it is released when your body becomes short of water and your blood becomes concentrated. The hormone makes the wall of the kidney nephron *more porous* – so water can be reabsorbed back into your blood. *Less* water then passes in urine to your bladder. If you drink a lot of fluid, however, ADH will not be released because your blood will be quite dilute. In the *absence* of ADH, less water is reabsorbed and *more* water is present in the urine passing to your bladder – hence all those trips to the toilet!

◀ *ADH is one of the many hormones your body produces to maintain its steady state. ADH controls the amount of water removed from the body.*

1
  a State two waste products and where they are lost from the body.
  b Describe the function of the kidney.

2 Explain the effect that you think each of the following will have on the amount of urine produced:
  a drinking a large amount of fruit juice.
  b cold weather.
  c long periods of vigorous exercise.
  d damage to the gland that produces ADH.

Cold comfort

Maintaining a constant body temperature is another example of how your body can respond to stimuli. Your **core body temperature** needs to be kept at 37°C. This is the ideal or optimum temperature for enzymes to work at their best. These enzymes are involved in all the vital reactions in your body, including respiration. This is the reaction that makes the heat energy which warms your body.

Core body temperature		
38	–	Fever
37.2	–	Normal body temp
36		
35	–	Shivering
34	–	Tiredness
33	–	Sleepiness
32	–	Loss of feeling
31		
30	–	COMA
29		
28	–	Breathing stops
27		
26		
25	–	CERTAIN DEATH!

H Y P O T H E R M I A

Old people and young children are particularly vulnerable to a condition called **hypothermia**. *Can you think why?*

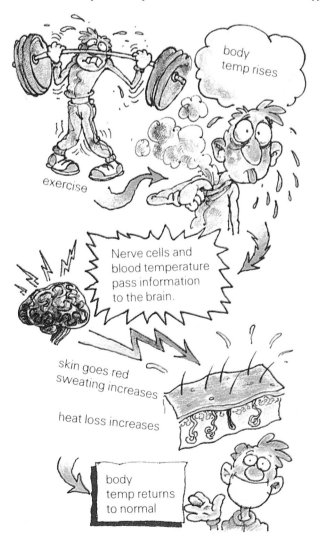

body temp rises

exercise

Nerve cells and blood temperature pass information to the brain.

skin goes red
sweating increases

heat loss increases

body temp returns to normal

Controlling body temperature

Your temperature can change because of changes inside or around you. Body temperature is monitored by a collection of cells in the brain called the **thermo-regulatory centre**. This has receptors which are sensitive to the temperature of the blood flowing through the brain. It also receives impulses about skin temperature from receptors in the skin. It then coordinates the correct response to maintain body temperature at 37°C.

You know that when you are too cold you begin to shiver. Shivering is simply the muscles beneath the skin contracting. This requires more energy so respiration increases. This in turn gives off more heat energy which warms you up. Shivering will not make enough heat if the body is exposed to cold conditions for a length of time.

If core body temperature is too high the response is to cause sweating to increase and the skin to go red. But how does this allow more heat to be lost from the body? What do you think?

Nerve cells are vital in maintaining a steady body temperature acting as messengers of information to the brain.

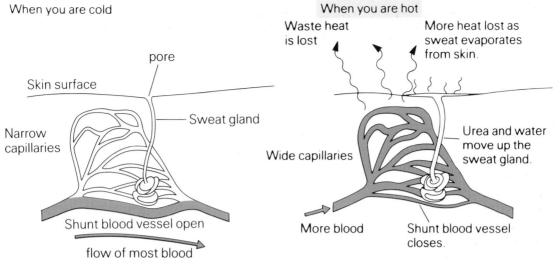

When you are cold

pore

Skin surface

Sweat gland

Narrow capillaries

Shunt blood vessel open

flow of most blood

When you are hot

Waste heat is lost

More heat lost as sweat evaporates from skin.

Urea and water move up the sweat gland.

Wide capillaries

More blood

Shunt blood vessel closes.

It's in the blood

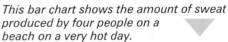

Heat is carried around the body in the blood. When blood flows near the surface of the skin some heat is lost from the body by radiation and convection. The amount of blood flowing near the surface of the skin can be controlled.

If core body temperature is too low, the response is to lessen the amount of blood near the surface of the skin. This reduces the heat loss. The effectors in this case are muscles surrounding the blood vessels which supply the skin capillaries. These blood vessels become narrow or 'constrict', thus reducing the flow of blood to the skin surface.

The opposite effect occurs when core body temperature is too high. The blood vessels supplying the skin capillaries are made to widen or 'dilate'. More blood now reaches the surface of the skin. This accounts for a red face after exercise. Now more heat is lost from the body by radiation and convection.

Heat is also lost as sweat evaporates off the skin. The effectors in this case are the sweat glands in the skin. The amount of sweat they produce varies in response to impulses from the thermoregulatory centre. The hotter the blood the more sweat they produce. This is why on hot days it is important to balance this loss by taking in water as drink or in food.

This bar chart shows the amount of sweat produced by four people on a beach on a very hot day.

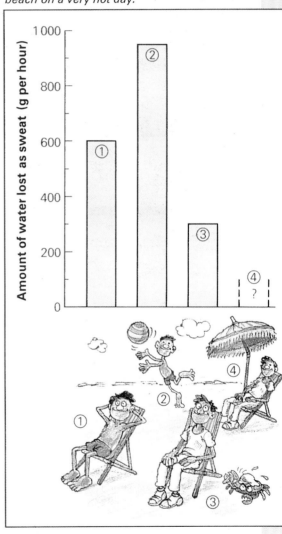

1
a Why is a constant body temperature needed?
b The temperature of your body will increase during exercise. Describe how your body detects and then makes adjustments to keep body temperature at 37°C.

2 Use the information on the bar chart to answer the following:
a Why is more sweat produced when playing compared to sitting in the sun?
b Why is less sweat produced if you wear white clothes in the sun?
c Predict how much sweat will be lost per hour by the person sitting in the shade. Explain your answer.

13 Bad maintenance

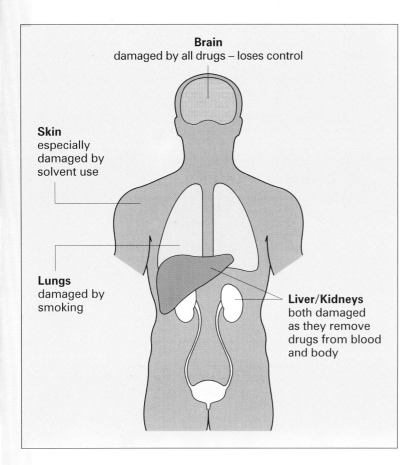

Brain
damaged by all drugs – loses control

Skin
especially damaged by solvent use

Lungs
damaged by smoking

Liver/Kidneys
both damaged as they remove drugs from blood and body

It's up to you

Do you recognise these symptoms: headache, high temperature, cold sweats, bad breath, pain in your kidneys and even passing blood in your urine? They could mean you are ill. If you had such an illness you would want to be cured and to know how to avoid having it again. But some or all of these symptoms could also be self-inflicted. They could be the result of taking drugs. Even common, legal, drugs such as alcohol and tobacco harm our bodies. If used to excess over a long period of time they can kill.

The systems that help our bodies stay in control are all affected by drugs. That is why drugs create the effect they do. The nervous system is directly affected. Then the liver and kidneys, which try to remove the poisons, are damaged as they try to cope. Good or bad maintenance; it is up to you. The diagram shows where the damage is done.

Smoking

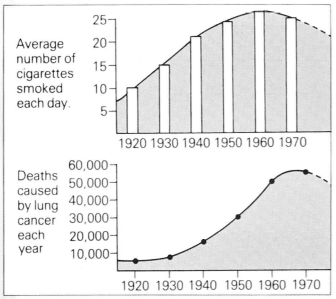

Average number of cigarettes smoked each day.

Deaths caused by lung cancer each year

Increases in cigarette smoking and increases in lung cancer over the same period.

When someone smokes a cigarette, their heart rate gets faster. Their blood vessels get narrower and this makes the flow of blood more difficult. The increase in heart rate and the poor blood flow means that their heart has to work much harder to pump blood around the body. Also carbon monoxide gas in the smoke poisons your blood and stops it carrying oxygen.

The cigarette contains tar and large smoke particles. These get stuck in the small air sacs in your lungs. This makes it difficult to breathe easily. Smoking weakens your heart and blocks up your lungs – so if you want to be fit, don't smoke!

As well as affecting your fitness, smoking is a major cause of several lung diseases. These diseases, such as lung cancer and emphysema, will eventually kill you.

Alcohol

Alcohol is a drug which affects your brain and your reactions and may lead to lack of self control, unconsciousness and even coma. This is why people who are drunk slur their words and become clumsy. The capillaries below the skin become larger and make the skin look more red. In large or frequent doses, alcohol is a poison which can seriously damage your liver and nerves. But small doses make people feel relaxed and this is why it is a widely used drug.

A bad decision now may mean you cannot make future decisions. Leah Betts was killed by ecstasy. She had used it before.

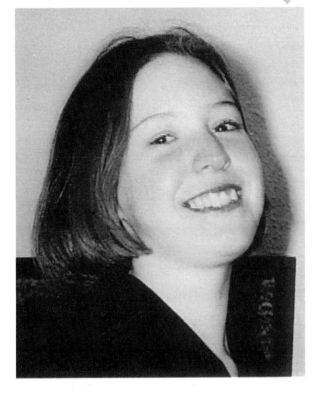

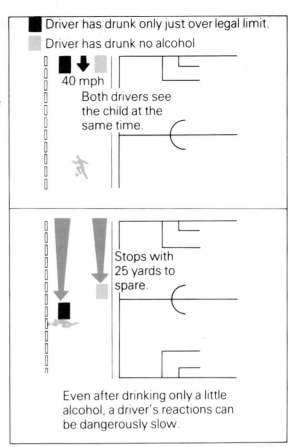

Driver has drunk only just over legal limit.

Driver has drunk no alcohol

40 mph

Both drivers see the child at the same time.

Stops with 25 yards to spare.

Even after drinking only a little alcohol, a driver's reactions can be dangerously slow.

Alcohol slows the reflexes and drivers cannot stop quickly enough in an emergency.

Drugs

Illegal drugs can also make people feel relaxed. However, they change chemical processes in the body and people can easily become dependent upon them. Without them, addicts will suffer withdrawal symptoms. Solvents affect behaviour and are particularly dangerous. They can cause instant death on first use. They affect the lungs, liver and brain.

1 Write down four ways in which smoking makes your heart do extra work.

2 **a** What has happened to
   i) the amount of tobacco smoked each year since 1920?
   ii) The number of deaths due to lung cancer over the same time?
   b Do the graphs suggest any link between smoking and lung cancer? Explain your answer.

3 **a** Why is alcohol a popular drug?
   b Why is it dangerous?

4 Look at the braking diagram above. What does it tell you about the risks of 'drinking and driving'?

5 Explain why some drugs kill the body although the body may 'need' them.

14 What a life you lead!

Decisions, decisions

You make decisions about your life all the time. A simple example like whether to eat your dinner may mean you go hungry for the rest of the day. Some decisions, of course, affect the rest of your life. These are the decisions about how you live your life and how you treat your body. They are not easy ones to make. Decisions about drink and drugs are difficult. It is hard to judge how you will feel later, if what you would like to do now might make you feel good. But! what does feeling good really mean? Remember you now know that the nervous system, the liver and the kidneys are all vital if your body is to survive and they are all affected by use of drink and drugs.

Decisions and consequences

You may be fortunate enough to be able to make decisions about your life. You may also be unfortunate to suffer the consequences. The case studies show how three people live their lives. They have to make decisions about their lives all the time...just like you.

Young children often cannot make decisions about the food they eat.

Case studies

The following descriptions about Jamie, Meta and Simon are from people who know them well. Read the descriptions carefully and pick out as much information as possible.

Jamie is 14 and plays football for the school and the Town team. He trains about 4 times a week and usually plays twice a week.

His parents make sure he eats the right foods and even give him a special packed lunch. Although he plays a lot of football, he doesn't ever seem to get tired out.

He is friendly with some older boys and has started drinking cider and smoking cigarettes on his way home from training and matches.

Meta is 16 and is usually top of the class. She does not join in the sports activities because she is often too tired.

She hardly eats at all during the day and her best friend says that after meals at home she is sick.

Her skin is not as good as it used to be and she has become very moody.

Her old friends can tell that her skin and moods are not just part of growing up. They also know that her new friends use drugs. They say, 'Meta is always short of money yet her parents give her loads'.

Simon is nearly 40 and wishes he was younger. He is overweight and knows he drinks too much but he tells his children he 'hasn't the time to look after himself because he is too busy with work'.

Simon likes to watch sports he used to play. Now he watches his children play for their school. He never misses the match on TV and he watches it in the pub and then drives home.

He eats a lot of junk food but drinks 'diet' drinks because he is worried about 'getting diabetes'.

1 What would you advise Jamie, Meta and Simon to do so as to live a healthier life? Make a life plan for one or more of the people. In each life plan:

   a list the things they do that **may do them harm;**

   b list the things that are **good for them;**

   c plan what they should do to have a **life they will enjoy**.

You may find some useful ideas by looking back through this module.

15 For you to do

1 This diagram shows a seedling.

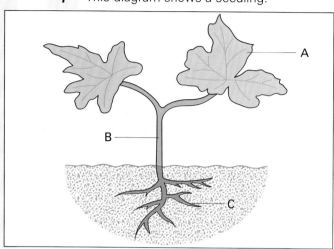

a Write down the names of A, B and C.
b Which parts of the plant do cell x and cell y come from?

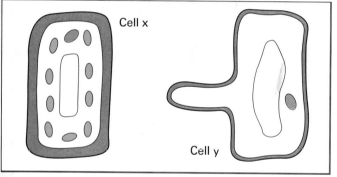

c Describe how cell x is adapted to do its job.
d How would an animal cell be different to cell x?

Substance	Concentration in parts of kidney (g/100 cm³)		
	blood in	nephron	urine
glucose	0.2	0.2	0.00
protein	8.00	0.00	0.00
salts	0.75	0.75	1.50
urea	0.05	0.05	2.00

2 a Explain why protein does not appear in the nephron.
b Where is urea made in the body and what is it made from?
c Calculate the concentration increase from nephron to urine for   i) salts
                                                ii) urea
d Suggest a reason for the difference in these values.
e Draw a flow diagram to explain how ADH controls the amount of water in your body.

3 A group of students carried out this investigation to find out why pruning affects the growth of plants. Study the diagrams below which show the effects of pruning.
a State a hypothesis to explain how hormones affect the growth of side shoots.
b Use the results of the pruning investigation to explain why removing the terminal bud makes the plant become branched.

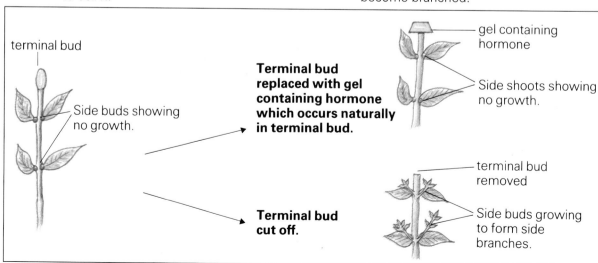

4 An investigation was carried out to find out how the amount of glucose in the blood is controlled. At the start of the investigation the people being tested were asked to drink 50g of glucose dissolved in a cup of water.

The graph shows the changes in the levels of glucose and insulin in the blood of the people being tested during the investigation.

a i) What happens to the amount of blood glucose in the *first 15 min* of the investigation?

ii) Explain what causes the amount of glucose to change during this time.

b Explain the changes in blood glucose concentration that take place between 20 min and 50 min.

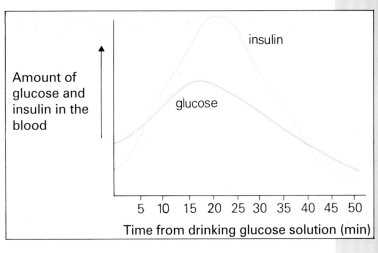

5 **a** Which *three* of the following are needed for photosynthesis?

carbon dioxide   nitrogen   oxygen
light   water   soil

A plant with leaves containing two colours was put into a dark cupboard for two days and then placed on a well lit windowsill for several hours. A leaf was then removed and tested for the presence of starch. The diagram below shows the results of the test.

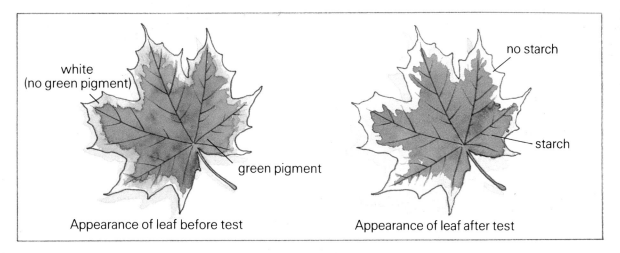

white (no green pigment)   green pigment   no starch   starch

Appearance of leaf before test   Appearance of leaf after test

b What is the green pigment found in the leaf?

c Why was no starch found in the outer part of the leaf?

Index

NEW MODULAR SCIENCE
for GCSE

MODULE | *Metals*

Spread

Cover photograph *Highway sculpture, Lanzarote, Canary Islands*

1 Metals

Metals

Metals are a very important class of materials. In this module you will find the answers to the following questions as well as information on many other aspects of metals *and* their compounds.

Why are metals useful?

There are metals all around you. This is because they have so many uses. Although many metals are being replaced by other materials such as plastics, you will find out that they still have many properties that make them very useful.

Metals have many properties that make them useful.

What do metals combine with?

Some metals combine in chemical reactions with other substances such as air and water. If a metal reacts with another substance it is changed into a new material. Chemists observe the reactions of metals. These observations help chemists to place metals into a league table of reactivity.

The rusting of iron shows that not all metal reactions are a good thing.

How are metals obtained?

Most metals are found on the Earth combined with other elements as **ores**. In order to obtain the pure metal, the other elements have to be removed. The method used to obtain the metal depends on how reactive the metal is. Chemists use their knowledge of a metal's reactivity to decide which method to use.

The iron and aluminium used in some bicycles are obtained by different methods.

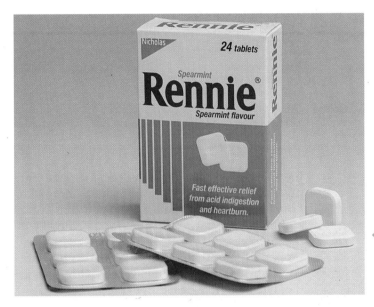

Why are metal compounds useful?

Some metal compounds react with **acids**. When they react, they cancel out the effect of acids. Metal compounds that react with acids are called **bases**. One example of using this reaction is to relieve acid indigestion.

Some metal compounds are used to relieve acid indigestion.

What are salts?

When an acid reacts with a base, the product formed is called a **salt**. The salt formed depends on the acid being used. The salt formed also depends on the base being used. There are many different types of acids and bases, so there are many different salts.

Sodium chloride, or table salt, is just one example of a salt.

1 Look at the first picture.
Name as many uses of metals in the picture as you can.

2 Which metal rusts and why do we try to prevent rusting?

3 Name two metals that are extracted from their ores.

4 State one use of a base.

5 What is formed when an acid reacts with a base?

2 Metals and non-metals

Sorting things out

The world you live in is made of simple building blocks called **elements**. About 150 years ago, scientists knew of the existence of about 60 elements. Today we know that there are 92 elements found naturally on the Earth and about 20 elements that have been made in the laboratory. Scientists wanted to sort out the elements into different types. This would help them to make predictions about what the elements could be used for and perhaps lead them to the discovery of other elements.

Just as CDs are sorted out into different types, scientists wanted to sort out elements.

People have characteristic features. Elements have their own properties.

Name of element	Appearance	Melting point (°C)
copper	shiny solid	1083
sulphur	dull solid	113
oxygen	colourless gas	-218
aluminium	shiny solid	660

Metals and non-metals have different properties.

Using properties

If you are describing someone's appearance you might talk about the colour of their hair or eyes or how tall they are. These are characteristic features or **properties** that help you to identify that person. In a similar way, scientists use properties to describe elements; for example, the way they look, feel and behave. Just like you and me, each element has its own properties that enable you to tell it apart from other elements.

Looking different

Most elements are solids at room temperature. Most of the elements are shiny in appearance when freshly cut or scratched but a few remain dull. Shiny solid elements are called **metals**. Dull solids are called **non-metals**. Only two elements, mercury and bromine, are liquids at room temperature. (Mercury is the shiny liquid metal used in thermometers and bromine is a reddish brown non-metal used in the production of flame retardants.)

The majority of non-metals, however, have low melting and boiling points. This means they occur as gases at room temperature. Two non-metals, nitrogen and oxygen, are colourless gases and are the major elements in the air you breathe.

So, metals are shiny solids with high melting points (except mercury) and non-metals are dull solids with low melting and boiling points.

Under the hammer

Metals are tough and strong so that they can be easily hammered or bent into shape. A tough, strong material is one that is difficult to break when you apply a force, like a crushing blow from a hammer. The tough material is able to absorb the energy from the force by changing its shape slightly so that it will not break. Materials that usually crack or crumble when you crush them are said to be **brittle**. The few solid non-metals are brittle and crumble when they are hit with a hammer.

Conductors and insulators

If heat and electricity are able to pass through a material it is called a **conductor**. Materials that allow heat and electricity to pass through them easily are called good conductors. Materials that do not allow heat and electricity to pass through them easily are called poor conductors or **insulators**. A group of students decided to investigate some metals and non-metals to find out if they were good or poor conductors of electricity. They passed electricity through the elements and observed if a small light-bulb came on. Look at their table of results. They discovered that metals are good conductors of electricity and non-metals are poor conductors.

Metals can easily be hammered into shape.

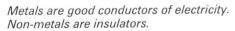

Metals are good conductors of electricity. Non-metals are insulators.

Name of element	Does the bulb light up?
copper	✓
aluminium	✓
sulphur	✗

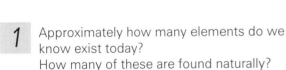

1 Approximately how many elements do we know exist today?
How many of these are found naturally?

2 Name the two elements that are liquids at room temperature and give a use for each element.

3 Look at the table on page 164.
  a Which element is a gas at room temperature?
  b Which element has the highest melting point?
  c Identify each element as either a metal or a non-metal.

4 State three properties of aluminium mentioned on these two pages which clearly indicate that it is a metal.

5 Make a list of properties that the non-metal solids sulphur and phosphorus would have in common.

6 State three properties the metal copper would have that are different to the non-metal, sulphur.

3 Useful metals

Useful properties

Metals have many properties in common. Many metals, for example, can be bent or hammered into shape. Properties like these make metals useful. The soft drinks industry makes use of this property to make metal cans for soft drinks. Some metals have other properties too that can also be very useful. Iron, for example, is one of the few metals that can be attracted by a **magnet.** Recycling plants make use of this property to separate the **aluminium** cans from those made of **iron.**

Metals are shiny and can be used for jewellery.

Good conductors

Metals are good **conductors** of **heat** and **electricity** (see page 165). This means that heat energy and electrical energy can pass along them easily. Metals can therefore be used to control the movement of these two types of energy. Electrical energy is carried along thin metal wires in your home or thick metal cables such as those supported by electricity pylons. Many items used for cooking food are made from metals such as copper and aluminium. The heat from the cooker is transferred through the metal of the saucepan to the food.

Metals are used in electrical wiring and in cooking.

Spoilt for choice

All metals are conductors, but some are better conductors than others. Look at the picture. The **silver** is a better conductor of heat than either **iron** or **copper**. However, it is very expensive so it is not a good choice for everyday use.

The choice of which conductor to use depends on how quickly it can transfer energy – and its cost.

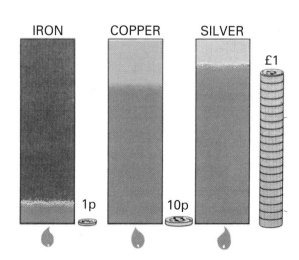

IRON   COPPER   SILVER

£1

1p   10p

Mixing metals to produce new uses

There are about 80 metals found on the Earth and they all have their own properties. These properties don't change. They are like a fingerprint that identifies the metal and stays with it for life but you can produce new properties by mixing liquid metals together. When the liquid mixture cools, the solid mixture of metals formed is called an **alloy**. Alloys can have completely different properties to those of the metals they were formed from. You can vary the amounts of metals in the mixture to produce different alloys. Each alloy will have different properties and so can be put to different uses. The table below shows you some alloys which contain the metal, copper.

Copper has many different alloys with different uses. ▼

Amount of copper	Other metal(s)	Name	Property	Use
100%	–	copper	soft, good conductor	plumbing pipes, electrical wiring
97%	tin	bronze	easily shaped	ornaments, complex shapes, e.g. taps
75%	nickel	cupro-nickel	hard wearing	coins
4%	aluminium	Duralumin	low density	aircraft bodies

The right steel for the job

Iron is a cheap metal but it has very few uses because it rusts too easily. One alloy of iron is called steel which is most commonly alloyed with carbon. The properties of the steel can be changed by altering the amount of carbon. Iron containing 4% carbon is very brittle so it breaks easily but steel with 1% carbon is strong and hard wearing. Other elements such as chromium can also be added to the iron to change its properties. The addition of between 12% and 25% chromium produces steels which do not rust. These steels are called stainless steels and are used in cutlery. They are, however, too expensive to be widely used as a solution to rusting.

Carbon steel is an alloy of iron and carbon. It is much stronger than iron. ▲

1 When iron cans are recycled, how are they separated from unwanted paper and food?

2 Give two examples of metals being used as good conductors of heat or electricity in a kitchen.

3 Look at the metal rods at the bottom of page 166. If you held each metal at the top end, which metal would feel warm first?

4 Look at the table.
a What is pure copper used for?
b What elements are used in coins?
c What property of Duralumin makes it useful in building aircraft bodies?

5 What is the difference in property between iron containing 1% carbon and 4% carbon?

6 How does chromium improve the properties of iron?

4 Chemical properties

Chemical changes taking place

Thousands of years ago the Egyptians were very good at doing experiments. The Egyptians used these experiments to make many things, such as the blue dye indigo and also glass. The word 'Chemistry' comes from an old Greek name for Egypt since this was the place where the people did experiments to make things. Chemists still make things today. They change materials into different or new materials. The change is called a **reaction** – or chemical reaction. One substance is said to react with another to produce a change.

Chemical changes take place all around you. Some, such as the burning of petrol in a car's engine and the rusting of a bicycle, you may already be aware of but others are not so obvious. Chemical changes take place inside you. Your body changes the food that you eat into many useful materials. One of these is called protein and you need it for growth. Chemists call the materials at the beginning of a chemical reaction the **starting materials** or raw materials. The materials at the end are called the **products** of the reaction. This means your body uses food as the starting material to make protein as the product.

You can see some chemical changes very easily.

Exploring the change

The simplest type of chemical reaction is that between metallic and non-metallic **elements**. Elements are made up of very tiny particles called **atoms**. All the atoms of one element are the same but are different to the atoms of another element. This means all atoms of sodium are identical but they are different to atoms of oxygen. When a chemical reaction takes place by mixing the elements the atoms of different elements collide and join together. The new substance formed is called a **compound** – a compound has two or more elements joined together. The use of a flame to light gas for cooking and to set off fireworks reminds you that many chemical reactions need heating before a chemical change will take place. The heat energy provided makes sure that when the atoms collide some have sufficient energy to join together. A compound has completely different properties to the elements it was formed or made from.

Element or compound	Appearance	Does solid conduct electricity?	Does gas relight a glowing spill?
element sodium	shiny solid	✓	✗
element oxygen	colourless gas	✗	✓
compound of sodium and oxygen	white solid	✗	✗

Compounds have different properties to the elements they were made from.

In a different way

Mixing substances and, if necessary, heating them, is not the only way to make a chemical reaction take place. Energy can also be supplied to substances in the form of electricity. Substances that can be chemically changed by electricity are made up of charged atoms called **ions**. The type of charge on the atom depends on the nature of the element – metals form positive ions and non-metals form negative ions. The type of chemical change brought about by electricity is called **electrolysis**. You can find out more about this on pages 180–183.

Uncombined element	Element in compound
oxygen	oxide
sulphur	sulphide
fluorine	fluoride
chlorine	chloride
bromine	bromide
iodine	iodide

Some non-metallic elements change their name when joined to metals.

Changing the name

When a metal reacts with a non-metal the name of the metal in the compound that is formed remains unchanged. However, the names of some non-metals do change. Look at the table. It lists those non-metallic elements that change their names. Chemists might call a material iron oxide. The material is a compound made from two elements. The first is iron but the second is not oxide since this element doesn't exist. The table shows you that the other element is oxygen. The iron is chemically joined to the oxygen so that there is no free oxygen or uncombined iron. Note also that by tradition the name of the metal always comes first, so that you would not refer to the compound as oxide iron.

Writing the change

On any day the weather might change every few hours but it may be described on the weather forecast as 'sunny with showers'. In other words the overall weather is described in as few words as possible. Chemists use the same idea to describe chemical reactions. Chemists describe the overall changes in a chemical reaction only in terms of the starting materials and the products. They also put an arrow between the starting materials and the products. It is then called a **word equation**. Look below at how a chemist would describe as briefly as possible the reaction between iron and oxygen.

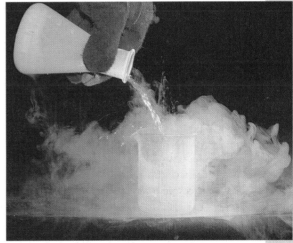

To describe reactions like this, chemists use a word equation.

Iron   +   Oxygen   ➡   Iron oxide
(metal)   (non-metal)   (compound)

1 Give an example of chemical change taking place:
  a in a car engine
  b on a bicycle
  c in your body.

2 State two chemical reactions that need heat to get them started.

3 What is the name of the chemical change brought about by electricity?

4 Name the compound formed in each case when the metal magnesium combines with:
  a oxygen
  b chlorine
  c bromine.

5 Write word equations for all the reactions taking place in question **4**.

5 Metals, air and water

A dull finish

Some people wear **copper** bracelets either as an ornament or to relieve the symptoms of arthritis. Copper tarnishes after a couple of days and turns your wrist green. **Gold** bracelets, however, might lose their lustre but won't go dull, even after a few years. **Sodium** is a rather different metal. It has a dull outer coating, but you can cut through it as easily as cutting through a piece of cheese. This reveals a shiny inside which tarnishes almost immediately. Different metals behave very differently when they are exposed to air. Some are clearly more **reactive** than others. Why do you think sodium is more reactive than copper or gold?

The gold handle and iron blade of the Viking sword have reacted differently.

Metals such as iron react with oxygen when they are heated.

Metal oxidation

If the surface of a metal is being altered by being left in contact with the air, it is because it is reacting with a gas in the air. The active gas in the air is called **oxygen**. When a metal reacts with oxygen, it combines with the oxygen to form a compound called a metal oxide. The metal oxide is much duller in appearance than the metal and this results in the surface of the metal appearing to be tarnished. This reaction can be represented by a word equation.

Metal + Oxygen ➡ Metal oxide

The addition of oxygen to an element or compound is called **oxidation**.

Reactions with water

Metals also react with other naturally occurring substances such as **water**. The photo shows you how **potassium** metal reacts with cold water. When metals react they release bubbles of **hydrogen** gas. Potassium is so reactive that the energy released makes the hydrogen gas catch fire. In general, the more bubbles of hydrogen gas released, the more reactive the metal.

Magnesium reacts slowly with cold water but reacts far better with hot water or steam.

Different metals react differently with cold water.

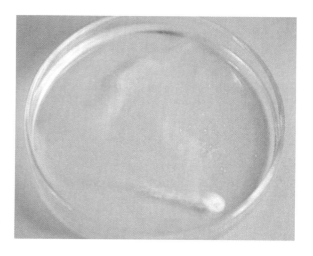

Stealing the oxygen

Another name for water is hydrogen oxide (H_2O). This means it is a compound containing 2 atoms of hydrogen to 1 atom of oxygen. If a metal reacts with water it 'steals' the oxygen from the water, leaving hydrogen. The metal with the oxygen now joined to it becomes a metal oxide. This can be represented by a word equation.

Metal + Hydrogen oxide (water) ➡ Metal oxide + Hydrogen

Some metal oxides then react with water to form metal hydroxides.

Metal oxide + Water ➡ Metal hydroxide

When calcium, for example, reacts with water it forms a calcium oxide and hydrogen. The calcium oxide then reacts with more water to produce calcium hydroxide.

Copper is used to make tanks for heating water. Copper doesn't react with water.

REACTIONS WITH AIR	REACTIONS WITH WATER
Sodium	Potassium
Iron	Calcium
Copper	Magnesium
Gold	Copper

A league table of reactivity can be produced for metals.

A league table of reactivity

Chemists use the information from the reactions of metals with air and water to produce a league table of reactivity. The more reactive metals appear at the top of the league table. The table shows you two league tables for the reactions of metals that have been used as examples in these pages; reactions with air and with water. With more information about how other metals react with air and water as well as many other substances, chemists can produce an overall league table of reactivity. This overall league table of reactivity is called the **reactivity series**.

1 Write a word equation for the reaction of iron with oxygen.

2 Why is copper used to make tanks for heating hot water?

3 Write a word equation for the reaction of potassium with water (potassium oxide reacts with water).

4 Zinc reacts with steam but its oxide does not react with water. Write a word equation for this reaction.

5 Predict what you think will happen when a piece of potassium is cut with a knife and also when gold is added to water.

6 • Sodium does not catch fire when it is added to cold water.
• Calcium tarnishes in air more slowly than sodium.
Use this information to produce an overall league table of reactivity for the reactions of the metals mentioned on these two pages with air and water.

6 Displacement reactions

Competitions

Many teenagers take part in sports such as football, netball and running. Some young people enjoy just taking part and being in a team. However, most sporting events are competitions. People do compete against each other so that in any competition there are winners and losers. Just as there are many sporting events that are competitions, many chemical reactions could be described as competition reactions. This is because in these reactions two elements are competing against each other. Chemists observe these reactions very closely to see which element turns out to be the winner.

When people compete against each other, there is usually a winner.

A new coating

If you dip the blade of a penknife that contains **iron** into a blue solution of **copper** sulphate and then take it out after a few minutes, you will notice that the blade has turned brown. Closer examination of the blade will reveal a thin brown coating on its surface. This brown coating is copper and the only place it could have come from is the solution. The copper has been removed from the copper sulphate solution. Chemists prefer to use the word '**displaced**' rather than 'removed' and they call this type of reaction a **displacement reaction**.

It is easy to coat some metals with copper using displacement reactions, but electroplating like this gives longer lasting coatings.

Displacement – a type of competition

The main features of a displacement reaction are a solid metal and a different metal compound dissolved in water – an **aqueous solution** of a metal compound. These features were present when the penknife was dipped into the copper sulphate solution – can you explain why? If the solid metal is more reactive than the metal in solution, it displaces it or pushes it out of solution. It is a particular type of competition reaction between two metallic elements. The winner of the competition is the metal that is in solution at the end. This means that the less reactive metal, copper, will now appear as the solid and the more reactive metal, iron, will be dissolved in water as the metal compound.

The reaction between the iron in the penknife and copper sulphate solution can be represented by a word equation.

Iron + Copper sulphate ➡ Iron sulphate + Copper

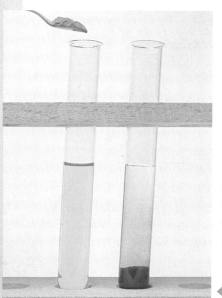

If zinc is added to copper sulphate solution copper is displaced.

Investigating displacement reactions

A group of students decided to use displacement reactions to investigate the reactivity of the four metals shown in Table 1. They did this by adding solid metal to a solution of a metal sulphate. As an example, they added solid **magnesium** metal to **iron** sulphate solution. They left the reaction for a while to observe if a reaction had taken place. Magnesium did displace the iron from solution so a ✓ was placed in the table. If no displacement occurred a ✗ was placed in the table.

metal ↓ metal compound ➡	Magnesium sulphate	Iron sulphate	Copper sulphate	Zinc sulphate
Magnesium		✓	✓	✓
Iron	?		✓	✗
Copper	?	✗		✗
Zinc	✗	✓	✓	

Table 1 A table of results for some displacement reactions.

Making predictions

If you look at Table 1 you will notice that there are gaps in the table. This is because the students didn't have time to complete all their experiments. All is not lost, however, because they can use what they have learnt from the investigations they did do to make predictions about the other reactions – can you see how? They didn't have time to add **copper** to magnesium sulphate solution but they did manage to add magnesium to copper sulphate. If you look at the table you will see that a ✓ was placed in the square. This means that magnesium must be more reactive than copper. What do you now think will happen if you add copper to magnesium sulphate?

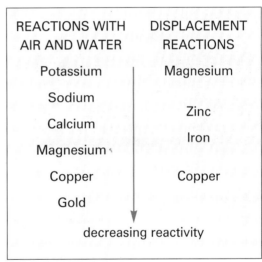

REACTIONS WITH AIR AND WATER	DISPLACEMENT REACTIONS
Potassium	Magnesium
Sodium	
Calcium	Zinc
Magnesium	Iron
Copper	
Gold	Copper

decreasing reactivity

Table 2 Displacement reactions give us another league table of reactivity.

1   Name another object that is plated by a metal.

2   Write a word equation for the reaction between zinc and copper sulphate solution.

3   What do the students have to do to make sure that their investigation is a fair test?

4   Why did the students not add magnesium to magnesium sulphate solution?

5   Look at Table 1. What would you put in the gaps, ✓ or ✗? Give a reason for your answers.

6   Zinc and iron do not react vigorously with cold water. Write one overall reactivity table for all the metals in Table 2.

7 Principles of metal extraction

Metals have many uses, ranging from jewellery to transport and in the home. Before you can use them, however, most have to go through certain stages of extraction.

Mining

Metals or metal compounds (**minerals**) are found in the Earth's crust mixed with other substances. The amount of metals and their minerals varies in different parts of the world. In some parts of the world there are very rich deposits of the metal or mineral. These deposits are usually obtained by underground or opencast mining. If there is enough metal or mineral found in the rock to make it profitable to mine then the rock is called an **ore**. For example, deposits of **tin** ore are found in Cornwall and Bolivia.

Concentrating the ore

Although the ore might be rich in the mineral, it still has to be separated from the worthless material. The first stage is always to crush the rock into a fine powder. This sets free the individual grains of mineral from the rest of the material. The most common method now used to separate the ore is called **froth flotation**. Water containing detergent is poured onto the powdered rock. Air is blown into this mixture causing it to produce a froth of air bubbles. The mineral grains stick to the air bubbles which float to the surface of the water. The froth of air bubbles can then be scooped off, leaving behind a muddy mixture of waste material.

Prospectors were attracted to rich deposits of gold. They separated the metal from other materials by panning.

Smelting – roasting the material

Unreactive metals such as gold, which are found in the ore as the metal itself, do not need any more separation. Most metals, however, are found joined to other elements as minerals or metal compounds. The metals have to be chemically separated from the other elements. One way of doing this is called **smelting**. Some minerals called sulphides contain the metal joined to the element sulphur. To extract the metal from sulphides, the mineral has to be changed to an oxide. This is done by heating the sulphide mineral in air, which is called **roasting**. Oxygen from the air adds onto each of the elements in the mineral so that a word equation for the roasting of the mineral **copper** sulphide would be:

Copper sulphide + Oxygen ➡ Copper oxide + Sulphur oxide

Copper mineral is roasted in a smelter.

Reducing the mineral

Metals can be obtained from metal oxides by removing the oxygen. Chemists use the principles of a competition reaction based on a league table of **reactivity** (see page 173). They use another element to remove the oxygen from the metal oxide. The other element has to be more reactive than the metal in the metal oxide. The removal of oxygen from a substance is called **reduction**. Chemists say that a metal oxide can be **reduced** to its metal. Look at the table. It shows you that carbon is more reactive than tin so carbon could be used to release tin from tin oxide.

A LEAGUE TABLE OF REACTIVITY	
Sodium	Na
Aluminium	Al
Carbon	C
Zinc	Zn
Tin	Sn
Lead	Pb

This league table is used to decide which element will reduce a metal oxide.

Releasing a problem

The roasting of sulphide ores produces large quantities of a sulphur oxide called **sulphur dioxide** which can be released into the atmosphere. The breathing of air containing sulphur dioxide can cause lung diseases such as bronchitis. Sulphur dioxide can also dissolve in rainwater to produce **acid rain**. When acid rain falls it collects in lakes, making the water acidic. This causes serious damage to the animal life in the lakes. Trees and other vegetation also suffer from the effects of acid rain. In Europe large areas of forest are dead or dying as a result of acid rain. The amount of suphur dioxide released into the air, therefore, has to be strictly controlled.

This truck is spraying lime powder onto a field to reduce the acidity of the soil caused by acid rain.

1 Name a metal used in
   a jewellery
   b the home
   c transport.

2 State an environmental problem that could be caused by froth flotation.

3 Write a word equation for the roasting of zinc sulphide in air.

4 Write a word equation for the reduction of lead oxide by carbon.

5 Why can't carbon be used to remove the oxygen from aluminium oxide?

6 Name another reason why the amount of sulphur dioxide in the atmosphere is increasing. How and why should it be controlled?

8 The blast furnace

Iron ore – a raw material for making iron – is dug out of the ground.

A useful metal

More **iron** is produced by industry every year than any other metal. This is because iron is a very useful metal, particularly in the form of its alloys which are called '**steels**'. They have a wide range of uses from car body construction to cutlery. Compounds of iron are very common, making up to 4% of the Earth's crust. However, iron ores (rocks that contain rich deposits of iron) are only found in certain places such as Australia and Canada. Some rocks may contain as much as 70% iron ore and only 30% waste.

Releasing the metal...

The most common mineral found in iron ore is a type of iron oxide called haematite. Oxygen has to be removed from the iron oxide in order to release the metal. The removal of oxygen from a substance is called **reduction** (see page 175) and requires a reducing agent. Carbon is one element that is more reactive than iron. Almost pure **carbon** is available cheaply and in large quantities as **coke** and this can be used to remove the oxygen from the iron oxide.

A stockpile of coke, a raw material for making iron.

... in a blast of hot air

The reduction of iron oxide by the carbon in the form of coke needs very high temperatures. The high temperatures needed are produced in a furnace by burning the coke in a continuous blast of hot air. The carbon combines with the oxygen from the blast of hot air to form carbon monoxide (carbon with one oxygen). It is this reaction which provides much of the energy needed to keep the furnace very hot.

> Carbon + Oxygen ➡ Carbon monoxide

Carbon monoxide is also a reducing agent and it is mainly this gas, not the solid coke, which reduces the iron oxide to iron. The temperatures produced in the furnace are so high that the iron melts and becomes a liquid.

Removing the waste

The main impurity in the **iron** ore is sand (silicon dioxide). Even at the very high temperatures produced in the blast furnace, the sand cannot be melted so it would be very difficult to remove it if it mixed with the molten iron. **Limestone** is added to the raw materials to remove the sand. Inside the furnace the limestone is broken down or **decomposed** by the heat energy into calcium oxide and carbon dioxide.

Molten iron is tapped off from the blast furnace at regular intervals.

Calcium carbonate ➡ Calcium oxide + Carbon dioxide

The calcium oxide then reacts with the sand (silicon dioxide) to form calcium silicate or **slag**. The slag has a much lower melting point than the sand and like the iron becomes molten.

Calcium oxide + Silicon dioxide ➡ Calcium silicate

The molten iron and molten slag sink to the bottom of the furnace and the slag, being lighter, floats on top of the iron. The diagram on the right shows you that they can be tapped off separately. The iron produced in the blast furnace is about 95% pure. It is called **pig iron** but it is too brittle to have many uses of its own.

Iron is made in a blast furnace by passing hot air through a mixture of iron ore, coke and limestone.

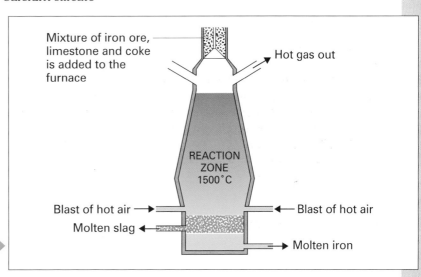

Mixture of iron ore, limestone and coke is added to the furnace

Hot gas out

REACTION ZONE 1500°C

Blast of hot air ➡ ⬅ Blast of hot air

Molten slag ⬅

Molten iron ➡

---

1   Name four raw materials used in the blast furnace.

2   Why is the furnace called a **blast** furnace?

3   Coke has two separate functions in the production of iron. What are they?

4   Oxidation is the addition of oxygen to a substance. Give an example from these two pages of a substance that has been oxidised.

5   What could the hot gases escaping from the top of the furnace be used for?

6   Why do you think blast furnaces work continuously all the year round?

7   Draw a flow diagram for the production of iron. Start with the raw materials and show how by a series of stages they help to convert iron ore into iron.

9 Principles of electrolysis

Electrical conductors

The electrical energy that your TV or video uses is carried by an electric current or **electricity**. Electricity is a flow of negatively charged particles called **electrons**. Electricity flows through metals very easily. Such materials are called good **electrical conductors**. The glowing red bar of an electric fire shows you that electrical conductors can become very hot when they carry electricity. Electrical conductors are, however, unchanged by carrying electricity. When an electric fire is switched off, the metal bars remain the same.

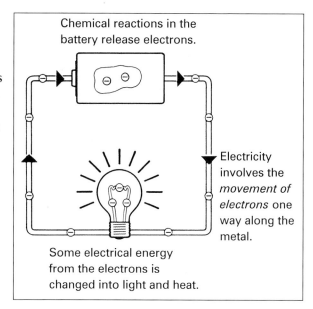

Chemical reactions in the battery release electrons.

Electricity involves the *movement of electrons* one way along the metal.

Some electrical energy from the electrons is changed into light and heat.

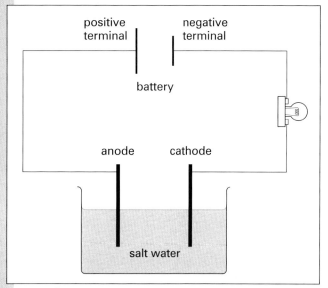

The bulb lights up because salt water is an electrolyte.

Electrolytes and electrodes

Metals are not the only materials that will conduct electricity. Electricity supplied by a battery will pass through some substances that have been dissolved in water (solutions). These solutions are called **electrolytes**. Electricity makes contact with the solution through rods which are made of metals or other materials such as carbon that will conduct electricity. These rods are called **electrodes**. The electrode connected to the positive terminal of a battery is called the positive electrode or the **anode**. The electrode connected to the negative terminal of the battery is called the negative electrode or the **cathode**.

Electrolysis

As we have seen before, when an electric current is passed through a metal it might become hot but it is still the same metal. However, when an electric current is passed through an electrolyte, the electrolyte is broken down or decomposed into simpler substances. This chemical change brought about by an electric current is called **electrolysis**. The change in the substance takes place on the surface of the electrodes. The simpler substances are often gases which appear as bubbles on the surface of the electrode.

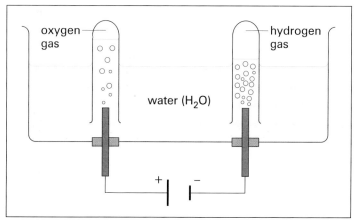

The electrolysis of (acidified) water shows that water is made up of twice as much hydrogen as oxygen – hence its formula H_2O.

Ionic substances

All substances are made up of very tiny particles called **atoms**. The type of substances that are broken down by electricity are called **ionic substances**. These substances still contain atoms but a special type of atom called an **ion**. Ions are the name given to atoms which have an electrical charge. Some ions have a positive charge. These are usually metal ions such as sodium ions and copper ions. Other ions have a negative charge. These are non-metal ions such as oxide ions which are produced from oxygen atoms.

Atom	Symbol of atom	Symbol of ion
copper	Cu	Cu^{2+}
sodium	Na	Na^+
oxygen	O	O^{2-}

Ions are charged atoms.

Electrolytic refining

Electrolytes have many applications in chemistry, ranging from making useful substances such as chlorine from sea water to purifying metals. **Copper** metal can be obtained by reducing copper oxide (see page 175) but it isn't pure enough to be used for conducting electricity. Very pure copper can be obtained by a process known as **electrolytic refining**. Pure copper is deposited at the negative electrode (or cathode). The electrolysis takes about two weeks and during this time the cathode can increase its mass from as little as 5 kg to 105 kg.

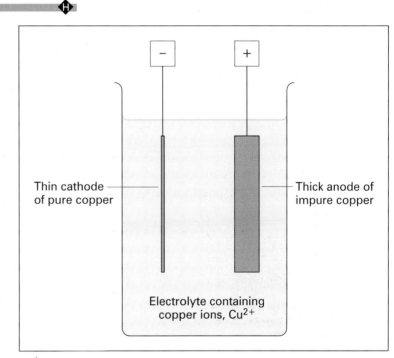

Thin cathode of pure copper

Thick anode of impure copper

Electrolyte containing copper ions, Cu^{2+}

When copper is refined, pure copper passes from the anode to the cathode.

1 Explain what is meant by the following terms: electricity, electrolysis, electrolyte, electrode.

2 How is the conduction of electricity in metals different from that in electrolytes?

3 Name all the electrolytes mentioned in these two pages.

4 Which atom does the sodium ion come from?

5 What is the difference between the charges on metal and non-metal ions?

6 In the refining of copper, what would be the increase in the mass of the cathode after one week?

10 Extracting aluminium

A very useful metal

You may be familiar with **aluminium** being used for chocolate wrapping paper and milk bottle tops. However, it is a very useful metal for all sorts of things. Compared to iron and steel, it is a very light metal. Weight for weight it is a much better conductor than copper and it also conducts heat well. Unlike iron, aluminium doesn't rust. It reacts with oxygen from the air to form a thin layer of aluminium oxide and this oxide layer protects it from corrosion.

Aluminium is used in aeroplanes.

An awkward extraction...

Aluminium is the most abundant metal on the Earth. It makes up about 8% of the Earth's crust. Rich deposits of aluminium are found in an ore of aluminium known as **bauxite**. A white powder is left after bauxite has been mined and purified. Chemically this is pure **aluminium oxide**. A look at the reactivity series shows that aluminium is higher in the table than carbon. This means it is more reactive than carbon, so aluminium cannot be obtained by using carbon to remove the oxygen from the aluminium oxide (or *reduce* the aluminium oxide).

REACTIVITY SERIES	
Potassium	K
Sodium	Na
Calcium	Ca
Magnesium	Mg
Aluminium	Al
Carbon	C
Zinc	Zn
Iron	Fe
Tin	Sn
Lead	Pb

... carried out by electrolysis

Reactive metals such as aluminium are extracted by **electrolysis** (see pages 178 and 179). Aluminium is obtained by passing an electric current through aluminium oxide. The electrolyte – in this case the aluminium oxide – needs to be molten for the electrolysis to take place. The melting point of aluminium oxide is very high – over 2000 °C. This means large amounts of energy would be needed to melt it, and this costs money! If aluminium oxide is dissolved in molten **cryolite** (a less common aluminium ore) the melting point is reduced to just below 1000 °C but it is still high. Aluminium is formed at the negative electrode or cathode. Oxygen gas is produced at the positive electrode or anode, which is made of carbon. At the high temperature used in the electrolysis, the carbon electrodes burn away and have to be continually replaced and this costs money also! They burn away because the carbon reacts with the oxygen to form carbon dioxide gas.

Only metals below carbon in the reactivity series can be obtained by using carbon to remove the oxygen from the metal oxide.

In an aluminium smelter there are a large number of cells connected together.

Reactions at the electrodes

Aluminium oxide is an ionic substance (see page 179). The ions in aluminium are not free to move when it is a solid. When the aluminium oxide has been melted it contains free moving aluminium ions and oxide ions.

At the cathode

The positive aluminium **ions** are attracted to the negative cathode. Each aluminium ion, Al^{3+}, *gains* 3 negative electrons from the surface of the cathode. This is represented as:

$$Al^{3+} + 3e^- \rightarrow Al$$

The gain of electrons is called **reduction**. The aluminium ion has been reduced to an aluminium atom. This means that aluminium metal atoms are formed at the surface of the cathode.

At the anode

The negative oxide ions are attracted to the positive anode. Each oxide ion, O^{2-}, *loses* 2 negative electrons to the surface of the anode. This is represented as:

$$O^{2-} - 2e^- \rightarrow O$$

The loss of electrons is called **oxidation**. The oxide ion has been oxidised to an oxygen atom. Atoms of oxygen then join together to form oxygen molecules at the surface of the anode.

$$O + O \rightarrow O_2$$

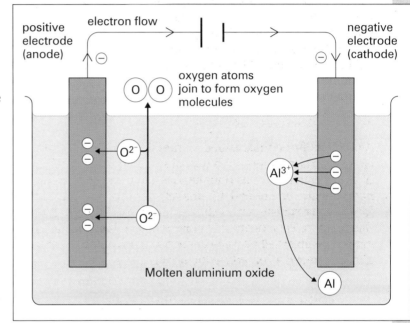

Each O^{2-} ion loses 2 electrons to the surface of the anode to form an oxygen atom.

Each Al^{3+} ion gains 3 electrons from the surface of the cathode to form an aluminium atom.

---

1 Name two properties of aluminium that make it a better metal than iron for aircraft construction.

2 Look at the table on the page 180. Which metals are more reactive than carbon? What method must be used to extract these metals from their ores?

3 Name two parts of the electrolysis of aluminium that cost money.

4 Write a word equation for the burning away of the carbon electrodes by oxygen.

5 Explain reduction by describing:
  a what happens to oxygen if a substance is reduced
  b what happens to electrons if a substance is reduced.

6 At which electrode is the aluminium produced? Write a symbol equation for its production and state whether it is oxidation or reduction. Why do you think reactions involving reduction and oxidation are sometimes called **redox** reactions?

11 Acids and alkalis

The same but different

Common table salt and citric acid crystals extracted from lemon juice are used to flavour food. Caustic soda is often used to clear drains blocked by grease or greasy food. The three substances look very similar. All are white crystalline solids. All dissolve in water to form colourless solutions which look exactly the same. Lemon juice, however, forms an **acidic** solution and caustic soda produces an **alkaline** solution. The salt solution is neither acidic nor alkaline. Chemists refer to it as a **neutral** solution.

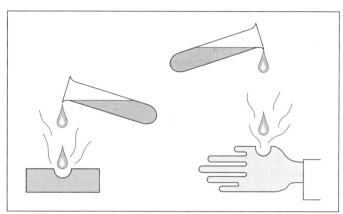

Acids and alkalis have to be handled carefully because they are corrosive to materials and your skin.

Showing the way

Acids and alkalis often look the same so how can chemists tell the difference? Some substances change colour depending on whether they have been added to an acidic or alkaline solution. These substances which change colour are called **indicators** because they indicate or show us whether a solution is acidic or alkaline. The indicators are sometimes used in the form of a solution. A few drops of this indicator solution can be added to another solution and it will change colour. The colour change tells a chemist whether the solution being tested is acidic or alkaline. The table shows you the colour of two different indicators **litmus** and **phenolphthalein** in acidic and alkaline solutions.

Indicators turn different colours in acid and alkali.

Indicator	Colour in acid	Colour in alkali
litmus	red	blue
phenolphthalein	colourless	pink

Measuring the strength

The acid found in lemon juice is safe enough to put on your tongue even though it has a bitter taste. Some acids, however, such as car battery acid, are far too harmful to be swallowed. This is because different acids – and alkalis – have different strengths. Lemon juice is a weak acid but the acid used in car batteries is strong. The strengths of different acids and alkalis can be compared using a scale called the **pH scale**. Lemon juice solution has a pH value of about 3.5. Distilled water and all neutral solutions have a pH of 7.

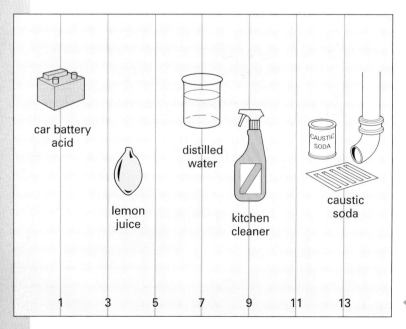

car battery acid

lemon juice

distilled water

kitchen cleaner

caustic soda

1   3   5   7   9   11   13

The lower the pH number, the stronger the acid. The higher the pH number, the stronger the alkali.

Acidic substances

Lemon juice is not the only naturally occurring soft drink that is acidic. The acid responsible for the acidity in the juice is called citric acid. It is also found in a number of other fruits such as limes and grapefruit, which are called citrus fruits. Carbonated water, which is used to make soft drinks fizzy or sparkling, is also an acidic solution, and is produced by dissolving carbon dioxide in water. Other acids found naturally are caused by the burning of fossil fuels such as coal and oil. When these fuels are burnt, oxides of non-metals such as sulphur dioxide, nitrogen dioxide and carbon dioxide are produced and released into the atmosphere. If these gases dissolve in rainwater, acid rain is formed (see page 175).

Alkaline substances

Oxides of non-metals dissolve in water. In contrast, most metal oxides such as **iron oxide** and **copper oxide** are insoluble in water. A few metal oxides, however, notably potassium oxide and sodium oxide and to a lesser extent calcium oxide, are soluble in water. Addition of a few drops of indicator to a solution of a metal oxide shows it to be alkaline. The metal oxide reacts with the water to form a metal hydroxide (see page 171). This means that sodium oxide, for example, reacts with water to form **sodium hydroxide** or, as it is sometimes called, caustic soda. It is the solution of sodium hydroxide that is responsible for the alkalinity.

The burning of petrol releases gases into the atmosphere, some of which dissolve in rainwater to form acid rain.

Metal hydroxide solutions are alkaline.

Metal hydroxide solution	Colour of litmus indicator
sodium hydroxide	blue
potassium hydroxide	blue

1 Make a list of all the substances mentioned in the text under the headings: **acidic**, **alkaline**, **neutral**.

2 What colour would phenolphthalein be if it was added to
  a lemon juice?
  b caustic soda?

3 What is the pH of
  a car battery acid?
  b caustic soda?

4 Name
  a a weak alkali
  b a strong acid.

5 Name three oxides of non-metals responsible for acid rain.

6 What is the chemical name for caustic soda? What colour will it turn litmus indicator?

12 Metals and acids

The disappearing metal

For safety reasons, acids used in the laboratory have water added to them. They still have to be treated with care but they are called **dilute acids**. Before dilution they were called **concentrated acids**. Some metals react with dilute acids, others do not. If a metal reacts with an acid, bubbles of gas are observed on the surface of the metal. The bubbles are soon released from the metal surface and the gas escapes into the air. Over a period of time, the metal becomes smaller as it appears to be 'eaten away' by the acid. This is because when the metal reacts with the acid it dissolves in it.

Tanks have to be made of materials that do not react with acids.

Magnesium   Iron   Copper

You can obtain an order of reactivity by reacting metals with acids.

Tell-tale bubbles

If a metal reacts with an acid, hydrogen gas is produced. The hydrogen gas comes from the acid. The amount of hydrogen gas produced from a particular acid depends on the metal. The more reactive the metal, the greater the amount of hydrogen gas released. This means you will observe more bubbles on the surface of the metal. The photos show you the amount of bubbles observed when **magnesium**, **iron** and **copper** react with dilute acid.

● magnesium is the most reactive metal

● copper is the least reactive metal

Using the table

The three metals magnesium, iron and copper form part of a league table or **reactivity series**. Magnesium is higher in the table than either iron or copper. This is because the more reactive the metal is, the higher its position in the reactivity series. This means calcium will react even more vigorously than magnesium. **Gold**, on the other hand, is even less reactive than copper and, like copper, does not react with dilute acids at all.

REACTIVITY SERIES	
Calcium	Ca
Magnesium	Mg
Zinc	Zn
Iron	Fe
Copper	Cu
Gold	Au

The reactivity series applies to the reactions of metals with dilute acids as well as with water.

Changing the acid

A group of students decided to investigate the effect of changing the type of acid on the reactivity of metals. They used dilute **sulphuric acid** (car battery acid) and **ethanoic acid** (vinegar acid). The observations they made are shown in the sketch below.

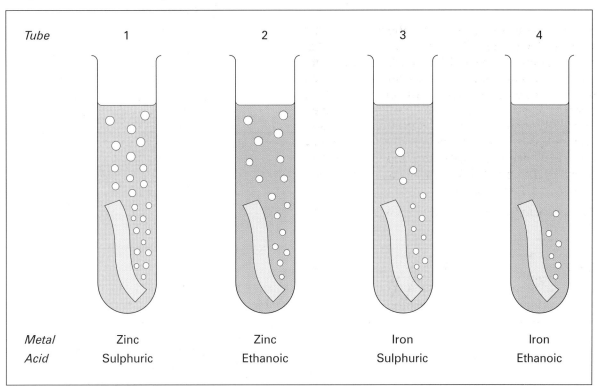

Tube	1	2	3	4
Metal	Zinc	Zinc	Iron	Iron
Acid	Sulphuric	Ethanoic	Sulphuric	Ethanoic

In order to make the test fair, they used the same amount and shape of metal as well as the same volume and concentration of acid. They reached the following conclusions:

● by comparing tubes 1 and 3 *or* tubes 2 and 4, you can tell that **zinc** is more reactive than **iron**;

● by comparing tubes 1 and 2 *or* tubes 3 and 4, you can tell that battery acid (sulphuric acid) is stronger than vinegar (ethanoic acid).

When you use different acids, the amount of hydrogen produced is different.

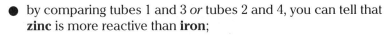

1 How can you tell if a metal reacts with an acid?

2 Place the three metals iron, copper and magnesium in order of reactivity, starting with the most reactive first.

3 Name two metals that do not react with dilute acids.

4 Predict what you would see if zinc metal was added to a dilute acid in a test-tube.

5 State four things the students did during their investigation to make sure the test was fair.

6 Explain why the students can say that zinc is more reactive than iron and car battery acid is a stronger acid than vinegar.

13 Salt formation

Common acids...

Acids are an important class of compound (see pages 182 and 183). **Sulphuric acid**, for example, is the acid used in car batteries and **nitric acid** is used to make fertilisers which help crops to grow better. You need hydrochloric acid in your stomach to help you to digest your food. However, you can sometimes feel the effect of too much acid in your stomach because it can cause indigestion and heartburn. The effects of acids can be cancelled out by other substances.

... and bases

Substances that cancel out acids are called **bases**. If a base is soluble in water it is called an **alkali**. Bases are usually metal compounds. The compounds are often metal oxides and metal hydroxides but they can also be metal carbonates and metal hydrogencarbonates. The table below shows you the bases which are compounds containing the metal sodium. All the bases in the table are soluble in water, so they are also alkalis.

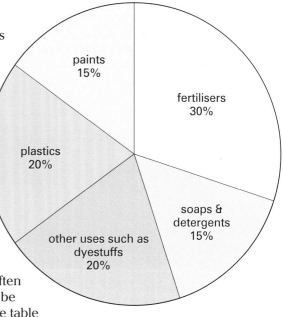

paints 15%
fertilisers 30%
plastics 20%
soaps & detergents 15%
other uses such as dyestuffs 20%

Sulphuric acid is used to make many useful chemicals. The numbers show how the sulphuric acid produced is divided between these different uses.

Common bases	Example
metal oxide	sodium oxide
metal hydroxide	sodium hydroxide
metal carbonate	sodium carbonate
metal hydrogencarbonate	sodium hydrogencarbonate

Sodium can form all four types of bases.

Fast relief

When a base reacts with an acid it cancels out the effect of the acid. Bases such as magnesium oxide are used to give fast relief from the effects of acid **indigestion**. Acid indigestion is caused by too much hydrochloric acid in your stomach. The bases in the medicine cancel out the effect of the extra or excess acid in your stomach. The reaction between an acid and a base is called **neutralisation**. The hydrochloric acid is said to have been neutralised by the magnesium oxide base.

Medicines that give relief from acid indigestion contain bases.

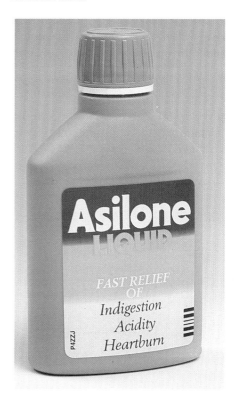

Asilone
LIQUID
FAST RELIEF OF
Indigestion
Acidity
Heartburn
PAZZI

Salt formation...

When an acid reacts with a base it produces a metal compound and other products. The metal compound produced in the reaction between an acid and a base is called a **salt**. The metal part of the salt is the same as the metal part of the base. This means that the base zinc oxide will produce a salt starting with the name 'zinc'. The type of salt formed depends on the acid used.

● Neutralising **hydrochloric** acid produces salts called **chlorides.**

● Neutralising **sulphuric** acid produces salts called **sulphates**.

● Neutralising **nitric** acid produces salts called **nitrates**.

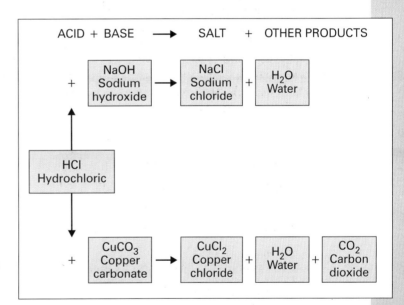

BASE	+	ACID	→	SALT
	+	HCl Hydrochloric	→	ZnCl$_2$ Zinc chloride
ZnO Zinc oxide	+	H$_2$SO$_4$ Sulphuric	→	ZnSO$_4$ Zinc sulphate
	+	HNO$_3$ Nitric	→	Zn(NO$_3$)$_2$ Zinc nitrate

The acid determines the type of salt formed.

... and other products

As well as the formation of a salt, the other products formed in the reaction between an acid and a base depend on the type of base used. One of the other products formed is always water. If the base is a metal oxide or metal hydroxide water is the *only* other product. This means that sodium hydroxide and hydrochloric acid react to produce a salt and water. If the base is a metal carbonate or metal hydrogencarbonate the other products are water *and* carbon dioxide. This means that copper carbonate and hydrochloric acid produce a salt, water and carbon dioxide. You will observe a fizz (effervescence) caused by the release of carbon dioxide gas.

ACID + BASE → SALT + OTHER PRODUCTS

+ NaOH Sodium hydroxide → NaCl Sodium chloride + H$_2$O Water

HCl Hydrochloric

+ CuCO$_3$ Copper carbonate → CuCl$_2$ Copper chloride + H$_2$O Water + CO$_2$ Carbon dioxide

The base determines the other products.

1 Name three acids mentioned in these two pages and give a use for each acid.

2 Name four bases containing the metal potassium.

3 What is the name of the salt formed if the base magnesium oxide reacts with
  a hydrochloric acid?
  b sulphuric acid?
  c nitric acid?

4 Name a base used to give relief from the effects of acid indigestion.

5 What other products will be formed if
  a sodium hydroxide
  b copper carbonate
react with sulphuric acid?

6 Write a word equation for the reaction between nitric acid and potassium hydrogencarbonate.

14 A model for neutralisation

The reaction of an acid and a metal carbonate or metal hydrocarbonate will produce a fizz.

A lot in common....

Chemists use the same name to group substances with similar properties together. They group elements, for example, as either metals or non-metals. Another group of substances with similar properties are called acids. Acids are substances which turn indicators such as litmus certain colours. All acids turn blue litmus solution red. Acids have a lot more in common with each other than their reaction to indicators. The addition of a reactive metal such as magnesium to an acidic solution will cause bubbles of hydrogen gas to be produced. The photo shows you another reaction common to all acid solutions.

... not by accident

The similarity in the properties of acids is not an accident or coincidence. The similarity in chemical properties arises from having similarities in their chemical formula. All acids contain hydrogen, H, atoms. Hydrochloric acid, HCl, and nitric acid, HNO_3, contain one hydrogen atom each. However, sulphuric acid, H_2SO_4, contains two hydrogen atoms.

These acids dissolve in water. When they dissolve they break up into positively and negatively charged particles called **ions** (see page 179). The hydrogen atoms in the acid separate from the rest of the acid and become positive hydrogen ions, H^+. It is these positive hydrogen ions, H^+, which is responsible for the characteristic properties of an acid.

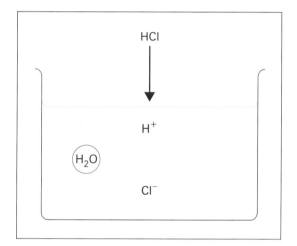

Acids dissolve in water to produce H^+ ions.

What's common in alkalis?

Alkalis also have similarities in their formula. They contain oxygen (O) and hydrogen (H) atoms joined together as an OH. This combination of atoms in a base is called a hydroxide group. Alkalis such as sodium hydroxide and potassium hydroxide contain this group.

● Sodium hydroxide has the formula NaOH.

● Potassium hydroxide has the formula KOH.

Alkalis also dissolve in water and break up into positive and negative ions. When an alkali dissolves in water, the resulting solution contains the negatively charged hydroxide ion, OH^-. It is the OH^- ion that makes the solution alkaline.

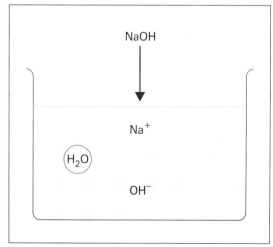

Alkalis dissolve in water to produce OH^- ions.

What happens in neutralisation?

Acids react with alkalis and the reaction is called **neutralisation** (see page 186). The active ingredient of all acids is the hydrogen ion, H^+. The active ingredient of all alkalis is the hydroxide ion, OH^-. Chemists use the shorthand (aq) after these ions to show that they are dissolved in water. On neutralisation, the hydrogen and hydroxide ions react together to produce water molecules. The neutralisation reaction can be represented by the following equation:

$$H^+_{(aq)} + OH^-_{(aq)} \rightarrow H_2O$$

This equation is called an ionic equation. The diagrams show you what happens.

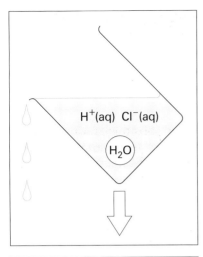

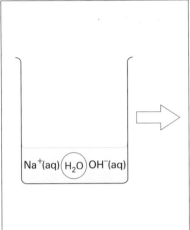

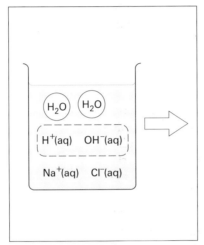

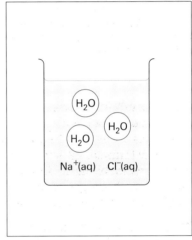

When hydrochloric acid is added to sodium hydroxide solution...

... H^+(aq) ions react with OH^-(aq) ions...

... to form H_2O.

1 Name three typical properties of an acid.

2 Write the name and formula of the ion responsible for acidic properties.

3 Write the name and the formula of the ion responsible for alkaline properties.

4 Look at the model for neutralisation above. Why are the sodium ions, Na^+, and the chloride ions, Cl^-, sometimes called spectator ions?

5 Write an ionic equation for a neutralisation reaction.

6 Draw a model, similar to the one above, for the neutralisation reaction between potassium hydroxide (K^+OH^-) and nitric acid ($H^+NO_3^-$).

15 For you to do

1 The following is a list of some properties of metals:
- good conductors of heat
- good conductors of electricity
- high melting points
- strong
- bendable.

Which of the above properties are useful when making:

a a bicycle frame?
b a guitar string ?
c the element of an electric fire?

2 The following is a list of metals in order of reactivity, starting with the most reactive first:

calcium
magnesium
zinc
iron
copper

The reactions of the metals iron, magnesium and zinc with a dilute acid are shown below.

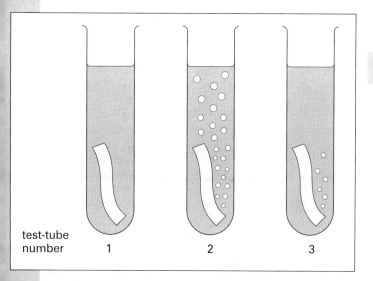

test-tube number   1   2   3

a Use the reactivity series to identify which metal is in which test-tube. Give a reason for your choice.
b Name the gas producing the bubbles.
c What would you observe if calcium were added to the same acid in a test-tube?

3 A diagram for the production of iron ore in a blast furnace is shown below.

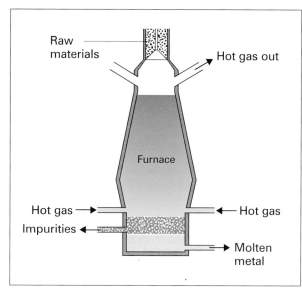

a Name the three raw materials.
b Identify the gas, the impurity and the molten metal.
c Name the gas that reduces the iron oxide.
d State two uses of the coke.

4 Very reactive metals are extracted from their ores by passing an electric current through the molten ore.
a What is the name given to this method of obtaining metals?
b Which of these metals is usually obtained by this method: iron, gold, aluminium?
c State two factors that add significantly to the cost of obtaining this metal.
d Explain how the addition of cryolite helps to reduce the cost of extracting the metal.
e The method can also be used to purify metals such as copper. The half-equation for the purification of copper is given below.

$$Cu^{2+} + 2e^- \rightarrow Cu$$

Has the copper been oxidised or reduced? Give a reason for your answer. At which electrode, the anode or the cathode, is the copper formed?

5

a State whether the following solutions have a pH greater than, less than or equal to 7.
  • pure water
  • potassium hydroxide solution
  • carbon dioxide dissolved in water.

b What is the name given to the reaction between an acid and an alkali?

c Name the salt formed when zinc oxide reacts with nitric acid.

d State a suitable acid and base that could be used to make copper sulphate.

e Write a word equation for the reaction between:
  • sodium hydroxide and hydrochloric acid
  • potassium carbonate and sulphuric acid.

6

a What is the name and formula of the ion contained in all acidic solutions?

d What is the name and formula of the ion contained in alkaline solutions?

c Write an ionic equation for the reaction between sodium hydroxide and hydrochloric acid.

7 What is meant by

a an alloy?

b an alkali?

c electrolysis?

d a redox reaction?

e neutralisation?

8 Use the order of reactivity from question **2** to help you to answer this question.
If grey magnesium powder is added to a beaker of blue copper sulphate solution, a solid brown powder is formed at the bottom of the beaker and a colourless solution is formed.

a Identify the brown powder and the colourless solution.

b What do chemists call this type of reaction?

c Write a word equation and a symbol equation for the reaction.

d What do you predict will happen if copper powder was added to magnesium sulphate?

e Which other metals (if any) would produce a similar reaction to magnesium if they were added to copper sulphate solution?

9 Sodium chloride, NaCl, is an ionic substance.

a What is an ion?

b Write down the formula of the positive sodium ion and the negative chloride ion.

c How does the movement of ions in solid sodium chloride differ from when it is dissolved in water?

d During the electrolysis of sodium chloride solution which ion goes to the positive electrode?

e Name the gas formed at the positive electrode.

f What other method could be used to electrolyse sodium chloride besides dissolving it in water?

g The solution remaining after electrolysis is alkaline. Name a suitable sodium compound that could be responsible for this alkalinity.

10 Blue crystals of a copper salt were made by the following method:
Green copper carbonate powder was added in excess to dilute sulphuric acid in a beaker until there was no more fizzing. The mixture was filtered and the blue filtrate was partly evaporated by heating and then allowed to cool when blue crystals formed.

a What gas was responsible for the fizzing?

b Why was *excess* copper carbonate used?

c What was the residue on the filter paper?

d Name the blue crystals.

e Write a word equation for the reaction.

f Name another copper compound that can be used besides copper carbonate.

g What acid needs to be used to produce copper nitrate crystals?

Index